Experiential Learning Around the World

Higher Education Policy Series

Edited by Maurice Kogan

Higher education is now the subject of far reaching and rapid policy change. This series will be of value to those who have to manage that change, as well as to consumers and evaluators of higher education in the UK and elsewhere. It offers information and analysis of new developments in a concise and usable form. It also provides reflective accounts of the impacts of higher education policy. Higher education administrators, governors and policy makers will use it, as well as students and specialists in education policy.

Maurice Kogan is Professor of Government and Social Administration at Brunel University and Joint Director of the Centre for the Evaluation of Public Policy and Practice.

Transforming Universities
Changing Patterns of Governance, Structure
and Learning in Swedish Higher Education
Marianne Bauer, Susan Marton, Berit Askling and Ference Marton
Higher Education Policy 48
ISBN 1 85302 675 1

Changing Relationships between Higher Education
and the State
Edited by Mary Henkel and Brenda Little
Higher Education Policy 45
ISBN 1 85302 645 X pb
ISBN 1 85302 644 1 hb

University and Society
Essays on the Social Role of Research and Higher Education
Edited by Martin A. Trow and Thorsten Nybom
Higher Education Policy 12
ISBN 1 85302 525 9

Public Expenditure on Higher Education
A Comparative Study in the Member States of
the European Community
Frans Kaiser, Raymond J. G. M. Florax, Jos B. J. Koelman and Frans A. Van Vught
Higher Education Policy 18
ISBN 1 85302 533 X

Higher Education Policy Series 52

Experiential Learning Around the World

Employability and the Global Economy

Edited by Norman Evans

Jessica Kingsley Publishers
London and Philadelphia

42027450   2-12-02

First published in the United Kingdom in 2000 by
Jessica Kingsley Publishers Ltd,
116 Pentonville Road, London
N1 9JB, England
and
325 Chestnut Street,
Philadelphia, PA 19106,
USA.

www.jkp.com

© Copyright 2000 Jessica Kingsley Publishers

Library of Congress Cataloging in Publication Data
Experiential learning around the world : employability and the global economy / edited by Norman Evans
    p.   cm. -- (Higher education policy : 52)
    Includes bibliographical references and index.
    ISBN 1 85302 736 7 (alk. paper)
    1. Experiential learning Cross-cultural studies. 2. Education, Higher--Economic aspects Cross-cultural studies. 3. Educational change Cross-cultural studies. 4. Higher education and state-Economic aspects Cross-cultural studies. I. Evans, Norman, 1923–.
II. Series: Higher education policy series : 52.
LB2324.E95   1999   99--41641
374--dc21   CIP

British Library Cataloguing in Publication Data
Experiential learning around the world : employability and
the global economy. - (Higher education policy : 52)
1. Experiential learning 2. Experiential learning - case
studies 3. Adult learning 4. Adult learning - case studies
I. Evans, Norman, 1923–
374
ISBN 1853027367

ISBN 1 85302 736 7

Printed and Bound in Great Britain by
Athenaeum Press, Gateshead, Tyne and Wear

Contents

Acknowledgements

The publication of this book coincides with celebrations for the first 25 years of life of the Council for Adult Experiential Learning (CAEL) in the USA. An important theme of the book is CAEL's role in the way the theory and practice of the assessment of prior experiential learning has travelled from the USA in the late 1970s around the world, as the various chapters testify.

Hence there are multiple dedications to attribute. First, to my dear friend and precious colleague Morris Keeton, and at many levels. The lucky people are those who can say: 'I was privileged to know and be known by X.' I am one such, knowing and being known by Morris. Professionally he has been an inspiring mentor. I always say: 'Throw him an idea and you'll have three thrown back at you.' But also I appreciate him as a colleague as we have worked together on various projects, not least as he has reviewed my own efforts in this book. Then he is the man whose wise counsel and far-sighted vision as Founding President paved the way for all the subsequent outstanding achievements of CAEL under the leadership of Pamela Tate as President and her colleagues. More than that, as these chapters imply and sometimes make explicit, his influence is worldwide. It would take a different book to document that in detail. Meantime, this one will have to do.

Second, then, the book is dedicated to CAEL – to acknowledge my own huge indebtedness to countless CAEL members over the years; for the joy of meeting with communities of academics whose view of the world is based on the 'respect of persons'; and for being able to combine all this with the excitements of exploring so many of the attributes and areas of America.

But there is more. Without CAEL the study tour programmes which exerted such a powerful influence on developments in the UK, as told later, could never have taken place. They were possible because of the generosity of time and facilities offered by the galaxy of names which follow with the positions they then held, and by their colleagues too numerous to list.

John Strange, Founding Dean of the College of Public and Community Service, University of Massachusetts, and sometimes

Vice-President of CAEL; Barbara Buchanan, Director of Field Services of the College of Public and Community Service, University of Massachusetts; Bill Craft, Vice-President of Bunker Hill Community College; Tom Clarke, President, and Barbara Viniar, Vice-President, of Rockland Community College; Bessie Blake, Dean of the College of New Resources, College of New Rochelle; Steve Brooks, Director of the Philadelphia Center; Lois Lamdin, Director of the Business Development Center, Great Valley; Diana Bamford Rees, Regional Director of CAEL Philadelphia; Richard DeCosmo, President, and RossAnn Craig, Vice-President, of Delaware Community College; Richard Roughton, Director, Continuing Education, American University; Terry Hoffman, Director of Prior Learning Assessment at University College, University of Maryland; and Morris Keeton himself, of course, as President of CAEL and later Director of the Institute for Research on Adults in Higher Education, University College, University of Maryland.

Foreword

A book like this can only be produced if busy people at the front end of developments are willing to give of their own valuable thinking and doing time to a project which, in the event, may well feel more like an unwelcome chore than a welcome opportunity. So whatever their private feelings may have been, I am grateful for the forbearance and willing co-operation of all those who have contributed the various chapters.

Then there is something which touches me directly. The English story is far longer than any of the others, by accident rather than intention. I have asked friendly readers, and indeed Morris Keeton himself, for suggestions where that chapter can be cut, but embarrassingly, back comes the response that to cut it will weaken it and remove important parts of the story. I am left, therefore, with the problem of justifying the length to myself.

Since 1979 I have been in an atypical position, quite different from that of any of the other contributors. Relatively senior in the higher education system, yet without any institutional responsibility, I was free to follow an idea to wherever it took me, without worrying too much about the financial or career development costs. That enabled me to go where in other circumstances I would probably not have been able to go, carrying a message which I did not care whether people disliked but which I was determined they should hear. This allowed me to watch at close hand the powerful impact that people in key positions can have when they get serious about institutional and curriculum change. And not only watch them, but work with them, feel supported by them and in large measure become their agents in a larger enterprise. For the last 20 years that is where I have been – fairly close to the centre of the assessment of prior and experiential learning (AP(E)L) story. And it is all a fluke of timing. Timing was everything. If AP(E)L had appeared earlier, the story would have been utterly different; and, like as not, I would have had no part in it. As it is, I find it difficult to stand outside the story and strip it down to bare essentials.

Well aware that this lack of pruning may be seen as a serious failing, I try to convince myself that I can offer the English story as something of a case book example of what can happen when people with their hands on the levers for change, and the power to pull them, have a vision which both corresponds mysteriously with some felt need in society, and combines with sources of energy to get things done because the timing is right. Sir Charles Carter, Edwin Kerr, Jack Mansell, with Morris as a backroom boy – what would there have been to tell about AP(E)L in England in the last 20 years without them? Between them, perhaps, they constitute the nearest thing here to the movement described by Morris Keeton as the main engine for development in the USA. It is my privilege now to tell the story for which they wrote the structure of the outline draft.

Norman Evans

List of Abbreviations

AAHE	American Association for Higher Education
ACE	American Council on Education
AIT	Auckland Institute of Technology
ANC	African National Congress
AP(E)L	assessment of prior (and) experiential learning
APL	assessment of prior learning
APQC	American Productivity & Quality Center
BITB	Building Industries Training Board (South Africa)
C2T2	Centre for Curriculum, Transfer and Technology (Canada)
CAEL	Cooperative Assessment of Experiential Learning/Council for the Advancement of Experiential Learning/Council for Adult and Experiential Learning (USA)
CAPLA	Canadian Association for Prior Learning Assessment
CATS	credit accumulation and transfer
CAUCE	Canadian Association for University Continuing Education
CEEB	College Entrance Examination Board (USA)
CEEQ	Centre for the Evaluation of Educational Qualifications (South Africa)
CEGEP	collège d'enseignement général et professionel
CLEP	College Level Examinations Program (USA)
CLFDB	Canadian Labour Force Development Board
CNAA	Council for National Academic Awards (UK)
CNTS	Commission on Non-Traditional Study (USA)
COSATU	Congress of South African Trade Unions
COSHEP	Committee of Scottish Higher Education Principals
CPL	credit for prior learning
CSTEC	Canadian Steel Trade and Employment Congress
CTHRB	Canadian Technology Human Resources Board
CUOP	College and University Options Program (USA)
DANTES	Defense Activity for Non-Traditional Education Support (USA)
DEAL	Development of Employment-Based Access to Learning (Project) (Scotland)
EGDP	Employee Growth and Development Program (USA)
ETS	Educational Testing Service (USA)
FÁS	Foras Áiseanna Saothair (Training & Employment Authority) (Ireland)

FEFC	Further Education Funding Council (England & Wales)
FEU	Further Education Unit (UK)
FIPSE	Fund for Improvement of Postsecondary Education (USA)
FNTI	First Nations Technical Institute (Canada)
GCE	General Certificate of Education (England & Wales)
GCSE	General Certificate of Secondary Education (England & Wales)
GED	General Educational Development (tests) (USA)
HEA	Higher Education Authority (Ireland)
HEI	higher education institution
HEQC	Higher Education Quality Council (UK)
HRD	Human Resource Development (Canada)
HRDC	Human Resources Development Canada
HSRC	Human Sciences Research Council (South Africa)
ILEA	Inner London Education Authority
ILTHE	Institute for Learning and Teaching in Higher Education (UK)
IPD	Institutional and Professional Development (programme) (USA)
IPET	Implementation Plan for Education and Training (South Africa)
ITO	industrial training organization (New Zealand)
JET	Joint Education Trust (South Africa)
LET	Learning from Experience Trust (UK)
MEDEF	Mouvement des Entreprises de France
MITAC	Mining Industry Training and Adjustment Council (Canada)
MSC	Manpower Services Commission (UK)
NAGCELL	National Advisory Council on Continuing Education and Lifelong Learning (UK)
NALL	New Approaches to Lifelong Learning (research network) (Canada)
NCEA	National Council for Educational Awards (Ireland)
NCIHE	National Committee of Inquiry into Higher Education (UK)
NCVQ	National Council for Vocational Qualifications (England & Wales)
NEEAN	New England Educational Assessment Network
NGO	non-governmental organization
NIHE	National Institute for Higher Education (Ireland)

NQF	National Qualifications Framework (New Zealand, South Africa)
NSIEE	National Society for Internships and Experiential Education (USA)
NTB	National Training Board (South Africa)
NTSI	National Training Strategy Initiative (South Africa)
NUMSA	National Union of Metalworkers of South Africa
NVQ	National Vocational Qualification (UK)
NZCER	New Zealand Council for Educational Research
NZQA	New Zealand Qualifications Authority
OECD	Organization for Economic Cooperation and Development
OISE	Ontario Institute for Studies in Education
PLA	prior learning assessment
PLAR	prior learning assessment and recognition
PONSI	Program of Non-Sponsored Instruction (USA)
PSI	Policy Studies Institute (UK)
QAA	Quality Assurance Agency (UK)
RCC	recognition of current competence
RPL	recognition of prior learning
RTC	Regional Technical College (Ireland)
SAQA	South African Qualifications Authority
SCOTCAT	Scottish Credit Accumulation and Transfer (network)
SCOTVEC	Scottish Vocational Education Council
SHEEC	Scottish Higher Education and Employers Collaborative (project) (Scotland)
SHEFC	Scottish Higher Education Funding Council
SHSG	SCOTCAT Health Studies Group
SIGI	System of Interactive Guidance and Information (USA)
SITP	Steel Industry Training Program (Canada)
SWAP	Scottish Wider Access Programme
TEC	Training and Enterprise Council (England & Wales)
UAW	United Auto Workers (USA)
UCT	University of Cape Town
UDACE	Unit for the Development of Adult and Continuing Education (UK)
UMUC	University of Maryland University College (USA)
USWA	United Steel Workers of America
VAP	validation des acquis professionnels (France)
VEETAC	Vocational Education, Employment and Training Advisory Committee (Australia)
VET	vocational education and training

WBL   work-based learning
WHEP   Workers Higher Education Project (South Africa)

CHAPTER 1

AP(E)L: Why? Where? How?
Setting the International Scene

Norman Evans

From the late 1970s, governments, employers and trade unions became ever more preoccupied with policies concerned with productivity, the viability of companies large and small, employability for those in work and their job security, and employability and how best to develop it for the unemployed. In different countries at different chronological points, these preoccupations led to two strategic policy developments. They resulted directly in all manner of education and training programmes intended to enhance the knowledge and skill of the workforce generally and to strengthen the position of firms, and hence of national economies, in the fast-growing competitiveness in the global economy. At the same time, pubic policies attempted to reach the same goal by widening access to post-secondary education and increasing participation levels.

It turned out that the assessment of prior and experiential learning (AP(E)L) has a vital twofold contribution to make to both these policy commitments. It can identify what workers and would-be students know and can do already as the foundation for further training and learning. It avoids wasting time and money for all concerned, because it cuts out the risk of people following courses which merely repeat what has been learned already.

Nevertheless, the potential of experiential learning can easily sound a rather boring topic, or even off-putting as a touchy-feely business next door to the 'getting in touch with myself' merchants. Hardly the serious stuff of academic learning for public recognition. But it is just that. 'Prior learning assessment' (PLA) in the USA[1] is

---

1   Or variously: the 'assessment of prior and experiential learning' (AP(E)L) in Great
     Britain; the 'recognition of prior learning' (RPL) in Australia, New Zealand, Ireland
     and South Africa; 'prior learning assessment and recognition' (PLAR) in Canada;
     and the 'validation of professional learning' (VAP) in France.

15

very serious indeed. It refers to ways of making visible and assessable learning which has been acquired and is stored up inside people, when there is no external evidence of its existence. It brings uncertificated learning into the realm of certificated learning which merits recognition for publicly validated qualifications. When connected with questions about the economy, all of that becomes anything but boring. In the longer run, AP(E)L raises questions about the well-being of individuals and so of societies, both national and international. That is what this book is about.

However, there is a possible confusion to be cleared up at the outset. Prior learning may get bracketed with experiential learning. This is very clear when Americans talk about PLA. There, as well as experiential learning, PLA can include examination results from the College Level Examinations Program (CLEP), a national open-access system of external examinations. It can include the Defense Activity for Non-Traditional Education Support (DANTES), available through the Education Testing Service at Princeton or through the Program of Non-Sponsored Instruction (PONSI), education and training courses offered by the military or industrial and commercial companies whose programmes have been scrutinized, approved and given recommended academic credit ratings by qualified academics. All refer to knowledge which has been certificated, but not necessarily for the purpose for which it is being submitted for consideration. The same is true in Great Britain when a qualification awarded by the Business and Technology Council may be submitted as prior learning for credit towards a degree programme offered by a university. So in some of the countries which feature in this book, prior learning includes experiential learning even though the origins of the two are different.

There is another point to clarify. Work-based learning (WBL) refers to learning acquired through the worksite from whatever tasks people undertake. Though that is obviously experiential learning (learning through experience), calling it WBL makes it sound as if it is something else. But experiential learning is inclusive, whether it comes from experience at work, from living, leisure, reading, hobbies or looking at the sky, it makes no matter.

Right at the beginning, there is a very important caveat to enter. Assessment is not the only part of the story about experiential learning. While there has been great emphasis throughout on assessment leading to the formal recognition of experiential learning, which in turn can provide access routes to courses for publicly recognized qualifications and, where appropriate, credit towards those qualifications, there are other ways of thinking about experiential learning. In every country, experience shows that some people find personally transforming the experience of trying to articulate for themselves what they have actually learned although they did not know they had learned it. Confidence can be boosted. Aspirations can expand. Motivation for learning more is often strengthened. And as the sense of self strengthens, so the world can become a different place. Often this is referred to as the empowerment of individuals.

In Britain, it was clear at the outset that while some people were interested in using assessments of their experiential learning to advance along a formal qualification route, some were using their documented experiential learning for career advancement or personal satisfaction. For some educators, this is now seen as a paradox. Some employers are learning to value the uncertificated learning of their employees without being much interested in its formal assessment. Thus, it can be claimed that documented but unassessed experiential learning may actually undercut the value of the very credentials experiential learning assessment originally sought to make accessible to people who had somehow missed out earlier. This argument takes little account of the value that, for a variety of reasons, individuals put on securing additional qualifications. It assumes that career advancement is all they are interested in. It also seems to run counter to one of the strongest reasons for promoting AP(E)L: removing obstacles from large numbers of people who otherwise have fewer opportunities for choosing what they want to do with their lives. For the future, though, this issue is bound to be raised in some of the countries whose stories are told in this book.

In Britain, when the Learning from Experience Trust (LET) began in 1986, it produced a brochure trying to outline what it was established to do. To catch the essence of the simple idea, it proclaimed: 'Most people know more than they think they know, if only they knew that they know it.' And that is it. For some people, coming to realize that they are better at learning than they thought they were is sufficient. And the sad thing is that so many have been convinced by what their schools told them or led them to believe was correct – that they were not much good at learning. But it is also glorious. The assessment of experiential learning can tell them something different. Tails go up, eyes shine. Maybe credit does not matter at all compared with the secure knowledge that they can learn, do learn and have learned effectively. In those ways, experiential learning and its assessment connects with the human condition. In turn, for many, that connects with the social concept of equity, an aspect of AP(E)L which is highlighted in many of the chapters that follow.

Furthermore, this connects experiential learning with the significance of voluntary bodies and volunteering in society as a whole. As well as non-governmental organizations (NGOs), which cover almost every aspect of life and rely heavily on volunteers to carry out their work, there are countless men and women who serve on committees and boards of public institutions such as parent–teacher associations, school governing bodies and community organizations. In the course of their work, many of these people learn a great deal which can be significant academically if it is articulated systematically. Increasingly, in some countries, AP(E)L facilities are being made available to those who are interested in using them.

It follows that the assessment of experiential learning concerns older post-secondary people more readily than school leavers. Older people have experience to draw on from which they may have learned something significant. But the lines are not quite so easy to draw. Shifts in emphasis in best practice for adolescent young men and women still within the statutory attendance boundary could well change that. Legal adults have no monopoly of learning from experience. Then experiential education would be the topic, and there are references to that in the chapters which follow.

For some, however, experiential learning is broader than either experiential education or assessment. It describes a mode of learning which has profound educational implications. The first edition of *New Directions for Experiential Learning* was produced by the Council for the Advancement of Experiential Learning (CAEL) in 1978. In the first chapter, entitled 'Learning by experience – what, why, how', Morris Keeton and Pamela Tate wrote:

> Experiential learning refers to learning *in which the learner is directly in touch with the realities being studied.* It is contrasted with learning in which the learner only reads about, hears about, talks about, or writes about these realities but never comes in contact with them as part of the learning process. (Keeton and Tate 1978, p.2)

Traces of that pedagogical principle run through some of the contributions which follow, even though the focus for this book is experiential learning, uncertificated learning and its assessment and the way the interest in it has spread around the world over the last 15 years. That is the story. And it will be clear already that it has to be a story about activities which lie in the border zone between the world of formal education and the worlds of employment and living. How could it be anything else, given the proposition that learning matters wherever, however it takes place?

That can lead to epistemological discussions about the relationship between the knowledge revealed through AP(E)L and knowledge as understood by traditional academic institutions. Necessarily, that involves the curriculum. And since for the most part it is traditional academics who control the curriculum, tension can arise between them and AP(E)L practitioners. For some, that means moving beyond the notion of AP(E)L as an educational approach which can empower individuals to seeing it as a means of promoting social justice, through democratizing the curriculum. In its turn, that implies challenging traditional forms of institutionalized education on the grounds that currently it tends to exclude some sections of society rather than including them. Traces of these arguments appear throughout several of the chapters in this book.

There are two other factors which run through some of the national stories which follow. The first is that wherever AP(E)L is notably successful there is a reliable advice and guidance service available to potential candidates. That is true whether candidates participate from within employment or in formal education institutions. With something as unfamiliar as AP(E)L is to them, most adults need help in understanding what it is they are undertaking, and indeed whether it is suitable for them. So, skilled advisers are an essential part of any AP(E)L programme. And that leads to the second point: staff development. For AP(E)L to work properly, there have to be staff who understand thoroughly both its theory and practice if individual men and women are to be given the service they deserve. But it is more than that. There is a strong connection between good advice and good assessment. Since the validity of the entire AP(E)L exercise rests on sound assessment, the need for good staff development and preparation is a requirement. It is not an optional extra.

There is another very important point about assessment. It also is to do with equity, and is put simply. Assessments of prior and experiential learning should be neither more nor less rigorous than assessments of formal classroom learning. It is a necessary point to make for quite proper reasons. Academics are concerned about academic standards and quality. Rightly so. However, AP(E)L can confront academics with unfamiliar problems. They are asked to make judgements about the level and scope of knowledge and skill, with supporting evidence submitted by persons they have not taught and may not even know. There can then be a natural tendency to worry about standards and about the judgements they make. And in the interests of quality they may apply more strigent criteria than they would for their regular students. What is more, they may not even be aware that that is what they are doing. So the bottom end of assessments for AP(E)L must be the same pass/fail level as for students taught in the institution. At the top end, recognition of exellence must be at a common standard.

Plotting the spread of interest in AP(E)L is an informative mapping exercise. Developments followed different paths in each country included here. They reflect their different systems of post-secondary education, differing histories and structures of government, differing cultures and, indeed, different economies. It began in the USA. There the story is atypical of the others. Its mix of private and public institutions of higher education exists without centralized control but alongside charitable foundations which have a long-established tradition of making substantial investments in innovation in education. At a time when lifelong job security was breaking down, PLA and related schemes for adults to return to study emerged in ways which are utterly different from elsewhere. Demography played its part. But by 1974 there were more than a dozen institutions of post-secondary education catering primarily for 'non-traditional students', each one shaped by a strong individual leader or set of advocates, firmly committed to the cause of serving older men and women. Among them were: Empire State College in New York State; Thomas Edison State College in New Jersey; Minnesota Metropolitan University in Minnesota; the College of Community and Public Service in the University of Massachusetts; the School for New Learning in DePaul University in Chicago; the School of Lifelong Learning of the University of New Hampshire; and Evergreen State University in the State of Washington. While these fully accredited institutions continue to this day, providing a highly respected service, by 1974 there were anxieties about the quality of some of the programmes offered in 'centres' or some units of the University Without Walls, and suspect 'degree mills', which were not recognised officially and issued certificates puporting to be degrees and diplomas, and offended against all the quality accurate procedures which are standard practices in universities and colleges. The fear was that when academic credit was awarded for life experience, rather than what had been learned from that experience, it could give the academic enterprise a bad name.

As the result of a Carnegie Commission on non-traditional education, The Cooperative Assessment of Experiential Learning (CAEL) was funded as a project from 1974 to 1977. Its remit was to find out whether valid and reliable ways of assessing extra-college learning were feasible and, if so, to produce valid and reliable ways to assess such learning at affordable costs. PLA was the result, backed up with an impressive array of research publications.

From the USA, the ideas enshrined in PLA came to England in 1979/80, with powerful encouragement from CAEL, which by then had become the Council for the Advancement of Experiential Learning. That period coincided with British government policies for the beginnings of what turned out to be a huge increase in the participation rate for higher education (from some 7 per cent of an 18 plus age cohort to some 40 per cent by 1999); initially, this was largely through increasing student numbers in what were then the polytechnics and through widening access beyond the traditional school leaver entrants. Again, demography featured but not as dramatically as anticipated. So, during the early 1980s, in some quarters it was possible for an enthusiast to talk about AP(E)L without being labelled a scary loony, although unlike the USA there was no group of supporters to draw on from institutions dedicated to adult learners. Even so, the message got heard. However, it was years before government sat up and took notice. Scotland was different. There, education and other publicly funded services are administered through the Scottish Office, rather than through different departments in Whitehall for England. This means that it is far easier to get collaboration across different categories of services than in England. So, once AP(E)L became respectable by the late 1980s, Scottish initiatives could combine education with health, employment and agencies for economic development.

By the mid-1980s, CAEL's contacts with the Canadian provinces of Ontario and British Columbia sowed seeds for subsequent development, while at the instigation of a strong enthusiast, well placed for advocacy, CAEL undertook consultancies in the province of Québec to train staff and prepare some CEGEPS (community colleges) for action. But a strong lead by an individual set things in motion. Notably there, in addition to Québec, developments had strong provincial government backing if they were not initiated by those governments themselves. France picked it up from Québec about the same time. The initiative came from the national government with an eye on the rising costs of higher education provision and on the needs of the economy. In the early 1980s, an expatriate Englishman teaching in Australia had made persistent inquries about AP(E)L in Britain; and by the late 1980s, Australia was introducing its own versions of PLA, influenced again by consultation visits by Australians to the USA and CAEL. There, too, a combination of needing to increase participation rates, widening access, costs and the economic necessity of boosting vocational skills created an atmosphere where consultative papers could pave the way for PLA developments.

Sometime in the early 1980s, a chance meeting at a conference in London with the Director of the National Council for Education Awards in the Republic of Ireland aroused his interest in AP(E)L. It coincided with some policy developments there and led to some consultancy visits, which in turn led to the Director and his senior colleague participating in a study tour to the USA arranged by the Learning from Experience Trust. It was another example of the fluke of timing, which in this instance lies in part behind the story told in the Irish chapter.

New Zealand was different again. It began as a quasi-legal requirement. The establishment of the New Zealand Qualifications Authority (NZQA) in 1989 was based on a statute which made it mandatory for institutions accredited to it to provide schemes for recognition of prior learning (RPL), as it is called there. Action then began in that country after one of the NZQA's staff made extensive visits to both the UK and the USA to find out at first hand how AP(E)L was being handled.

In South Africa, since the election of the Mandela government in 1995, from ministers downwards, employers, trade unions, community organizations and voluntary bodies proclaim that, without the extensive deployment of RPL, one vital route will be closed towards achieving the intentions of the policy of National Transformation. There, too, the influence of both the UK and USA is evident. The Ford Foundation's officer for South Africa, who seeks through CAEL to initiate PLA schemes there, was involved in some of the early CAEL activities. The Foundation funded visits for groups of South African personnel to both countries for initial investigations. Consultative visits, funded by the Kellogg Foundation and conducted by the British Learning from Experience Trust, have served the same end. Now under the auspices of the Joint Education Trust, the

Workers Higher Education Project is testing the validity of the ideas for qualified teachers, for rural agricultural workers and for middle managers, and it is poised to launch a major employee development programme in the telecommunications industry.

So in 20 years the idea has flown across both hemispheres and west to east. In each case there are significant, even unique, differences in the ways it has taken root. And the expectations are that it will fly further afield, particularly in developing countries.

As the story unfolds through the entries from nine different countries, there are several factors to watch out for. The first is most obvious: the reaction, role and actions of formal education institutions. Predictably, it has been mixed. Long-established universities, steeped in academic disciplines and research, are understandably sceptical about the entire idea of applicants having no need of a full curriculum, because they have mastered some of it beforehand without any reference to the university. And those with long application lists feel they have no need to bother about additional categories of students. Demographic shifts in some countries lessen the strength of that argument. So does competition. In the USA, as competition for students in the later 1970s led some to a loss of traditional enrolments, an increasing number of private colleges, often Catholic, needed to attract adult students to balance their budgets, and state colleges needed older students to sustain enrolments to demonstrate they were meeting their mission for public service. In some countries, government interventions played their part as well, as when funding incentives were related to policies designed to widen access to higher education. But it is noticeable that few four-year institutions in the USA with substantial graduate schools have taken to PLA. With significant exceptions, such as Nottingham and Liverpool, the same is broadly true in the UK. And in Canada, France, New Zealand and Australia there has been, and continues to be, considerable resistance.

It is different in newer universities and other degree-teaching institutions. For them, the assessment of experiential learning has been seen in part as adding a strand to recruitment policies. It has enabled them to demonstrate that they are widening access. And not necessarily directly. Institutions which established close liaison arrangements with other colleges in their catchment area recognized the value of including provision for AP(E)L for older students as helping to create a federal structure to their service, whether it was formalized or not. Although to correct the balance, as the role of universities changes as society changes, some well-established universities are following the same path. And most recently, in Britain, the establishment of the Institute for Learning and Teaching in Higher Education has given a fresh impetus to AP(E)L.

For further education colleges in Britain, community colleges in Canada and the USA, the tertiary-advanced further education colleges in Australia and the polytechnics in New Zealand, AP(E)L presents a different story. An important part of their brief has always been to serve older students and enable them to acquire vocational qualifications. Living in a credentials age, harnessing AP(E)L to enable people to improve their paper qualifications and so their job security or even job prospects, was a natural development. But in most countries, governments tried to enhance the skills and knowledge of the workforce by introducing, in one form or another, occupational qualifications. Sub-degree institutions were seen as agencies for promoting them, amidst rhetoric about maintaining a healthy competitive economy in the global market. AP(E)L was an important element in pursuing that goal. In South Africa, the role of community colleges is seen in similar terms, but the problems posed by trying to develop them are quite different.

These institutions in Britain and their equivalents in America, raise a different issue to be aware of in the succeeding chapters. In some cases, such as community colleges in the USA, they are bracketed within higher education. In others, such as the further education colleges in Britain, they are not. Essentially, this is the result of government nomenclatures which then relate to different financial systems of support from the public purse. And to a greater or lesser extent, those institutional labels can affect government policies and interventions for promoting schemes for AP(E)L. So the most helpful way of thinking about the extent of AP(E)L activities in any one country is to include all post-secondary education institutions as providers, actual or potential.

Then there are employers and the professions. Employers first. Ask most male employers what they know about the range of capabilities of the company's employees and the answer will be – not much. Women tend to be more knowledgeable about that than men, which is no surprise. But the generalization is relatively sound. The consequence is that many employers are without essential information when reorganization comes, or 'downsizing' in the current jargon, because they do not know what skills and knowledge they have within their current workforce. When the potential benefits of AP(E)L are pointed out to employers, most of them can see the point. But they are not very good at turning that point into action. In any case, they need help in designing schemes for implementation. This issue crops up repeatedly in the stories which follow.

A variation on this is work-based learning (WBL). Developing the skills and knowledge of the workforce has become a critical matter of survival for many companies. Failure to keep up with the speed of technological change can mean going to the wall. So continual skill enhancement connects with the black or red figures in financial statements. Some major companies have seized this, realizing that consciously building on existing capabilities is the best way of promoting additional learning. And AP(E)L offers a way of determining an individual's baseline for further learning. It is also a sure-fire way of increasing an individual's motivation for further learning. Again, examples of this appear in subsequent chapters.

Professions are in somewhat the same position, except that they have statutory requirements to comply with on matters of professional standards. In some countries where professional accreditation requirements involve teaching institutions complying with curricula laid down by the profession, tensions can often arise when it is proposed that AP(E)L can serve in place of some taught courses. Conversely, in other countries, the nursing and social care professions seem to have incorporated AP(E)L in their mainstream thinking. There are considerable variations in practice and attitude about these matters between the countries represented in this book. And in each case profession's role in guarding as gatekeeper the probicity of its members, affects the issue; who is in and who is out.

An anecdote can bridge employers and the professionals. A hospital consultant had a patient whose work involved AP(E)L. In best bedside manner, the consultant asked politely about his patient's work. Fumbling for an answer which would short-circuit a long-winded and complicated response, the patient asked the consultant to think about the nurses and ancillaries on the wards he visited. Could he then, the patient asked, identify some unqualified men and women who were better at their job than some of those who were officially qualified? Readily, the consultant said he could. And according appropriate recognition to those unqualified is what AP(E)L is about, the patient explained. The consultant could see nothing wrong with that. But then, the patient went on, suppose a theatre sister showed about the same competence as a junior doctor – would, could, should the same recognition apply? Ah, said the consultant, that would be entirely different. But why? Those questions, too, appear later on in different chapters.

For universities and colleges, that question raises another. As public guardians of academic standards, what learning does an academic institution recognize publicly? Suppose an AP(E)L candidate can demonstrate, academically, significant learning in a subject area which is not in the institution's curriculum. What does the institution do? Does it say that because that field of learning is not part of the curriculum, it cannot countenance awarding credit for it even though it accepts that it is up to university standards? Or does it accept the learning, because it matches the academic requirements for what it does teach, and devise ways of accommodating it? This leads into the issue of independent study.

Some institutions founded in the USA specifically to serve older men and women, such as Empire State College, developed independent study as the guiding principle for their academic work. On the basis of the learning which students brought with them, the college negotiated with them a programme of study which met the requirements for degree-level work. So assessing prior learning – including experiential learning – was the principle which informed all their work. And it was deployed for graduate as well as undergraduate study. Some universities in Britain have developed similar schemes at both first-degree and graduate levels. Obviously, independent study relates to some schemes for WBL.

This notion, which runs beyond independent study, is based on a recognition and acceptance that in modern technological societies learning occurs in almost limitless ways outside formal education institutions. It follows that institutions that accept this are asserting that it is their business to recognize learning wherever, whenever and however it takes place, provided it meets the necessary criteria for academic study. In effect, that expands the role of academic institutions, as they use their authority to make public statements about university standards concerning learning acquired without reference to them.

It does something else. It questions what constitutes acceptable knowledge for assessment in higher education. Course-content knowledge confronts implicit knowledge, as is clearly acknowledged in France. As Michel Feutrie remarks in his chapter on France, this is an ideological matter. He claims that a university which accepts AP(E)L has changed itself, even though it may not realize it.

In this way, assessing prior and experiential learning becomes a catalyst for change and institutional development. Any university or college which incorporates such schemes finds itself confronting, in a different context all the issues which are the staple diet of academic discussions. Admissions, learning and teaching styles, student support, assessment, progression – all can appear in a different light. It focuses attention on issues about learning outcomes and on procedures which accomplish what they are intended to accomplish. It relates, therefore, to the huge pressure on institutions to clarify what they actually do and how they make all their activities transparent in ways which are readily understandable by would-be applicants, their parents, the secondary schools they attend, employers and taxpayers. So the simple observation that people can learn without necessarily being taught has potentially dramatic implications. In one way or another, these themes appear in subsequent chapters.

The consequences of that simple observation has to be set alongside the rapid changes occurring in the societies of all the countries discussed in this book, affecting patterns of employment and the feelings of insecurity which are now widespread, the huge increase in the numbers of women in full-time and part-time employment, and the effect of all that on domestic and family lives. For post-secondary education, that has become very serious. It means that increasing numbers of older people who, for whatever reason, wish to study need to be able to do so as part-time students. And not necessarily older people, either. Younger people, who used to think of higher education as a chronological extension of schooling, now look around the world as they see it, reflect on the rising costs of university and college as funding systems change the balance between state subsidy and personal money, and often decide to put off decisions about further study, preferring to find some employment instead. Like their elders, they are likely to find that, when they need to study for some qualification or other, circumstances almost dictate that it will have to be by part-time study. In which case AP(E)L is likely to feature increasingly for them as a time and money saver. This is having a significant effect on the way institutions organize their work, and the likelihood is that that tendency will intensify. This is evident from some of the chapters which follow.

Government interventions have played an important role in AP(E)L developments in most of the countries represented in this book. There is a common denominator to these interventions – employability and the economy. As competition increases fiercely, between companies and between countries in the fast-changing world of the global economy, the skill and knowledge levels of individual employees and their continual enhancement becomes ever more important. By now, this is almost as trite as it is obvious. Employers are continually lectured by governments that they should enhance their own training programmes. This has been matched at one level by governments' interventions, designed to tackle this problem by introducing occupational standards linked to vocational qualifications across the whole range of employment. In some cases, by tying the completion of the vocational qualifications to the funding systems for publicly supported education institutions, governments have added a stick to the carrots. At a different level, governments have tried various ways of trying to encourage universities to be more responsive to the world around them by introducing schemes for credit accumulation which offer greater choice to students in what they study and when they study it. Most recently, 'lifelong learning' has become the banner under which these sorts of activities are included. And since enhancement implies building on what exists already, in one way or another AP(E)L has to feature in assessment procedures for promoting the cause of vocational qualifications.

Cost is another motive informing some government interventions. Public policies in all these countries have been to expand participation in higher education, sometimes with financial incentives for widening access. In France, this is more or less explicit. Expansion has become almost a litmus test for a country's ability to compete internationally. Whether that is as good a test as seems to be assumed is another matter. But assessing experiential learning for credit towards a higher education award can mean shortening courses of study within a college or university. That can mean reducing the cost to the public purse of graduating an individual.

So, promotion by governments of AP(E)L features prominently in many of the chapters which follow. But here there is an intriguing paradox. In the country which was the seedbed for AP(E)L, government has done little or nothing to promote it. The federal structure of government in the United States means that individual States, rather than Washington, have power to intervene in educational matters. And only in few States have State governments taken the initiative in utilizing schemes for AP(E)L. So, whereas in other countries government schemes make for some coherence in provision, in the USA it is companies which have been the prime developers, aided and abetted by non-governmental bodies such as some employers' associations, some labour unions and CAEL.

Throughout these international developments in AP(E)L, there has been a steady shift from the original thrust to widen access to formal study for individuals towards enhancing the employability of as many people as possible. Education principles have been absorbed, some would say suborned, even prostituted, in national economic preoccupations. And more recently, there is another detectable shift. Instead of billing AP(E)L as some peculiar animal which needs bringing in from the cold and treating cautiously, in Britain, for example, some see it as one form of assessment in the battery of techniques commonly used. In part, this is a consequence of the steadily growing acceptance that learning now occurs in many different places outside formal education. Assessment of learning then becomes more important than its source. Assessment moves centre stage. Serious attempts to promote lifelong learning seem bound to promote further this second shift.

These, then, are some of the markers to watch out for as the chapters which follow tell their countries' own stories, about the why, when, how and what next about AP(E)L developments. Have an idea, and if it is timely, it will fly. Timing is everything with ideas. And the accounts which follow show how, in different countries, at different times and for different reasons, the idea of AP(E)L flew round the world from the late 1970s.

References

Keeton, M. and Tate, P. (1978) *New Directions for Experiential Learning*, volume 1. London: Jossey-Bass.

CHAPTER 2

Recognizing Learning outside of Schools in the United States of America

Morris T. Keeton

Why recognize non-school learning?

Good teachers have always tended to start instruction from their sense of what their students already know and can do. Historically, this practice has been quite informal. A bright student is spotted, and the teacher leaps at the opportunity to bypass normal steps and challenge that student with more difficult, more advanced work. No formal permission is requested of authorities. No record is made of the recognition of the earlier learning that may have occurred at home or by accident.

By the opening of the 20th century in America, this informality in recognizing starting points for learning at post-secondary levels began to be dysfunctional. The numbers of students were rising precipitously. Students were more and more different from one another in their preparation and backgrounds. To cope with these changes, a set of selective colleges banded together in 1900 to form the College Entrance Examination Board (CEEB), the aim being to devise a way to identify students best qualified to succeed in these demanding institutions.

By the 1970s, the problem of appropriate placement and admission standards had become further complicated in the USA by the growing numbers of mature adults who wanted to return to college, but did not want to go back over things they already knew. Between 1968 and 1973, some 13 new colleges, either free-standing or within established institutions, were created to accommodate these adults and other 'non-traditional students'. The latter included young students rebelling against the teaching methods and curricula of existing universities. In the early 1970s, the Carnegie Corporation of New York, a public foundation, and the CEEB set up the Commission on Non-Traditional Study (CNTS) to study these emerging students and to advise what should be done to serve them and society better. Among the Commission's recommendations was that a way be found to assess and appropriately recognize 'extracollegiate learning' that was deserving of college credit (Cross *et al.* 1973).

Why, then, recognize such learning? The reasons include equity for adult learners, efficiency in instruction, and cost savings for the public purse. Equity, because fairness requires that admission to college studies be based on the knowledge and abilities individuals bring, not on the question of where or how those qualifications were developed. Efficiency, because such recognition prevents the waste of time and money incurred in repetition of what the adults already know. And cost savings, because this needless duplication of effort is thus avoided.

What caused this movement? Three movements converge

Why a movement *should* occur and what *caused* it to occur are quite different matters. Reviewing the events from 1900 to 1973 to understand the origin of CAEL (Cooperative Assessment of Experiential Learning, an organization devoted to finding a way to do valid and reliable assessment of extra-college learning at affordable cost), sociologist Zelda Gamson (1988) found that three movements had converged to create the need to act on the CNTS recommendations:

1.   the adult education movement beginning as early as the Chatauquas of the 19th century

2.   the growing sophistication of assessment since the origin of the CEEB

3.   the non-traditional higher education movement.

The adult education movement had grown greatly in numbers served and, more significantly, in the variety of things being learned. From basic literacy and learning for fun, the movement had expanded to include work skills, political affairs, news of the day, and a growing range of hobbies and problem-solving tasks of daily life. Some of these kinds of learning overlapped what is taught in college. The assessment movement had made it ever more feasible to measure and define what had been learned in these non-formal ways. And the non-traditional higher education movement had built demand for certification of what had been learned. Demand, capability and achievement combined to call for socially sanctioned assessment and recognition.

But why these movements? What forces conspired to support their development and their convergence to give birth to the prior learning assessment and recognition movement?

Causes behind the causes

At least six changes in American society played into the movements that generated a CAEL-like activity:

- changing demands for qualified workers in the post World War II economy of the United States
- a changing demographic make-up of the school-going populations
- the opportunity for profit making in the assessment business after World War II
- the transformation of access to higher education from a privilege to an economic necessity for thousands of Americans
- changing family patterns that sent women back to college for second careers and supplementation of household income
- changes within college populations (in the mix of ages, ethnicity and learning styles).

Also, cultural changes led to demands for greater learning options, autonomy among students and new values (emerging from the critiques of racism, sexism and discipline-centred instruction). Doubtless, other changes fed into this ferment, but this list illustrates the degree of dissatisfaction with things as they had been.

Assessment of prior learning takes root

The earliest documentable work in prior learning assessment and recognition at college level occurred in Antioch College (early 1940s) and the American Council on Education (mid-1940s), but the major force in advocacy was CAEL. The CAEL Project (1974–1977) initially focused on showing that valid, reliable and affordable assessment of non-school learning was feasible. The Carnegie Corporation, initial funder, later joined by the Ford Foundation, the Lilly Endowment, and the Fund for Improvement of Postsecondary

Education (FIPSE), insisted on the project's being led by a coalition of a prestigious testing organization, the Educational Testing Service of Princeton (ETS), and a set of colleges and universities that included some institutions experienced in using experiential learning to enhance education and in assessing its yield. ETS was to assure psychometrically sound research. The post-secondary institutions were to assure that the results would be used by teaching institutions. The combination of funders and ETS, with its own in-kind support, supplied the needed $2.1 million in financial support.

Twenty-seven institutions took part in the validation study within the CAEL Project. The study yielded a set of 'principles of good practice in assessing experiential learning'. In addition, a Faculty Development Project had trained three cadres of faculty assessors, and an Institutional Models Project, funded by FIPSE, had enabled a dozen colleges and universities to work out ways of integrating the prior learning assessment (PLA) service into their ongoing operations. Initially, the national accrediting authorities 'viewed with alarm' this practice of giving credit for learning outside of college; but after I met with them, as chair of CAEL's Steering Committee, and explained the CAEL policies, the association of regional accreditors amended its policy to one of 'welcoming the practice [of recognizing non-school learning with academic credit or advanced standing] provided the CAEL principles of good practice are followed'. Coming this far had taken three years, from 1974 to 1977. It will be clear from this brief account of the forces that generated the movement for recognition of extra-college learning that the movement was the work of many minds and hands. As Norman Evans' recital in Chapter 1 of the differences among the developments in the United Kingdom, the United States, Australia and other countries attests, the story in the USA was comparatively complex, involving numerous organizations and dozens of contributing individuals.

From roots to flourishing growth

To move the assessment and recognition of learning prior to matriculation from idea to accepted practice, however, required more than a showing of soundness, feasibility and official toleration. The task required an ongoing organized effort, campaigning and, ultimately, market demand. As ETS declared victory for the CAEL Project (in June 1977) and left the field to the educational institutions, they created a free-standing Council for the Advancement of Experiential Learning (CAEL II, we called it) and resolved to hang together rather than separately. I accepted their invitation to become its Executive Director, subsequently becoming its President and Chief Executive Officer.

A first success in this campaigning was made possible by the Kellogg Foundation, which in 1977 awarded CAEL $975,000 for a programme of 'Institutional and Professional Development' (IPD). The IPD offered workshops and consulting services throughout the United States. Aiming to engage 200 universities within three years, the IPD had enrolled that number in less than six months. To cope with the demand, acting now as CAEL's Chief Executive Officer, I enlisted by December 1977 ten 'regional managers', who initially served as volunteers with their institutions' support. After May 1978, with further Kellogg Foundation support, they were assisted with their costs in a modest degree. In the following 13 years, that foundation invested more than $10 million in CAEL's work.

At this stage in its work (1977–1982), CAEL undertook to underpin the respectability of its effort with a strategy of scholarly publication. In its 1974–1977 phase, it had already produced some 54 publications, largely printed and distributed free to users by ETS, but including a hardback book entitled *Experiential Learning: Rationale, Characteristics and Assessment* (Keeton *et al.* 1977). Beginning in 1978, CAEL and Jossey-Bass collaborated in the production of five annual sets of four books, each under the name *New Directions for Experiential Learning* (Keeton and Tate 1978–1983). CAEL also issued a newsletter that appeared several times per year and continued a series of national conferences twice yearly from 1974 to 1977 and annually thereafter, except for a period in which four regional conferences were tried out in an ongoing training and marketing programme.

As CAEL was in the process of spinning off from ETS management (1976–1977), word arrived that other longer-established associations supporting experiential education were troubled that CAEL, though the newest kid on the block, was getting a lion's share of funding. As Chair of the CAEL Project Steering Committee, I invited the association leaders to a meeting at the O'Hare Hilton (Chicago) to discuss their concerns and the possibilities for collaboration. The effort eventually led to a merger of the Society for Field Experience Education and the National Council for Internships, becoming the National Society for Internships and Experiential Education (NSIEE). CAEL, NSIEE, the Partnership for Service Learning, and the Cooperative Education Association formed a project that for several years met annually and worked on co-operative efforts, some of which elicited grants from FIPSE and other sources. In 1994, CAEL and NSIEE joined the International Council on Experiential Learning in the largest conference in the history of the field (with an attendance of some 1576 persons).

Early on, it was realized in CAEL that higher education in America does not change primarily in response to rational argument, but will respond to a combination of sound rationale and market demand. Accordingly, an effort was made to reach out directly to learners, especially to adult learners who had the greatest amount and depth of learning from experience and the greatest need to save time and money in advancing their learning and their credentials. FIPSE supported a project of telephone counselling for prospective students. The armed services showed early interest in promoting the use of PLA by their members. DANTES – the Defense Activity for Non-Traditional Education Support – has continued to facilitate this activity and now contracts with ETS for servicing DANTES Subject Standardized Tests. CAEL tapped into newspaper columns offering personal advice – a single column by Sylvia Porter that offered a free list of colleges giving PLA service forced CAEL to add two full-time staff members to handle the incoming calls for a period of three weeks. But no amount or variety of efforts adequately cracked the problem of increasing demand from CAEL's perspective.

Change casts the dice

It was not in CAEL's plans to proselytize abroad except in Canada. In 1979, nevertheless, Norman Evans was urged by his host, John Strange, then Dean of the College of Public and Community Service of the University of Massachusetts, to sit in on a CAEL conference. Evans conceived the idea of adapting the CAEL processes to the needs of British higher education for opening access to universities among able individuals who were not normally seen as 'qualified'. The sequel is treated by Norman Evans who tells that story in another chapter.

Crisis and a secure future

From its beginnings, CAEL had depended on external support to operate at a level essential for generating the change in American higher education that it sought. While it charged membership dues for both institutions and individuals, and collected conference and workshop fees and publication income, the dues never yielded more than 9 per cent of the annual budget, and the fees and subscriptions only a slightly larger share of income. For most of the period from 1974 through to 1984, over 80 per cent of CAEL income was obtained as grants from foundations and government agencies with earmarking for specific projects.

In early 1982, as Phase I of a project called LEARN (see below) was winding down, the end of assured external funding was in sight for CAEL. I was obliged in December to give notice of a cut of its central staff to five persons (from a level of 20) and to prepare for a decision whether to disband or to function as a very small entity with a budget of about $200,000 per year. In January 1983 and in September 1984 two developments occurred that turned the crisis into long-range stability. First, the Kellogg Foundation, after some two years of consideration of the request for Phase II support, funded a further five years of Project LEARN, initially for $4.2 million for an integrated set of 15 component projects and in time for an additional $2.3 million. Second, the Ford Motor Company and the United Auto Workers (UAW) contracted with CAEL, under Pamela Tate, CAEL's lead consultant for its College and University Options Program (CUOP), for the first of what became an ever-growing array of Employee Growth and Development Programs (EGDPs).

Project LEARN

Project LEARN was a partnership between CAEL, the Educational Testing Service, a national counselling association, and 14 regionally led successor institutions to those that led the earlier IPD. The ETS project would develop the computer-managed System of Interactive Guidance and Information for Adults (SIGI for Adults). The counselling project, led by Cynthia Johnson, engaged the other 14 projects plus nationwide associations of counsellors in addressing the evolving needs of adult learners. Each of the other projects was attempting to further CAEL purposes by assisting institutions to improve the responsiveness of area colleges and universities to the adults returning to learning in college. As Project LEARN gained momentum, the UAW–Ford CUOP (September 1984–June 1986) was being implemented under CAEL central management with its own liaisons from Ohio, Michigan, Indiana, Illinois and Kansas. By 1986, the Mountain Bell Telephone–Communication Workers of America–International Brotherhood of Electrical Workers Pathways to the Future Program, a second employee growth and development service, began in seven states of the Mountains and Plains Region under the leadership of Elinor Greenberg. Midway into Project LEARN, Discover Inc. was engaged to develop a software program to assist adults in organizing and presenting the evidence for their gaining credit for prior experiential learning. In time, American College Testing acquired Discover Inc. and used its CAEL software for a rival service to that of ETS's SIGI for Adults. Both programs continue to be widely used throughout the United States.

Project LEARN provided major direct services to some 750,000 adults and greater or lesser services to 2.5 million. In addition, it served more than 100,000 educators of the United States, Canada and Great Britain an estimated average of three or more times each (workshops, career advising training, publications, etc.).

An external evaluation commissioned by the Kellogg Foundation credited CAEL with influencing five major changes in American higher education (rated from 4.2 of a possible 5 to 3.5 in level of influence). Significant influence (2.5 to 3.4) was reported on 11 other changes. The five areas of greatest influence were:

- increasing the use of prior learning assessment
- enabling information and advocacy services for adults to become more widespread
- developing alliances between educational institutions, businesses and labour organizations
- helping colleges and universities to become more sophisticated in the use of assessment techniques
- increasing awareness among adults that learning is ongoing throughout life.

Changes in PLA use: 1991 and 1996

CAEL arranged for surveys in 1991 and in 1996 on the extent of provision of different forms of PLA services in the United States. The evidence is that the number of accredited institutions providing PLA has increased since Project LEARN in all forms except challenge exams, which have held steady at 72 per cent of respondents from 1991 through to 1996, as summarized in Table 2.1.

	1991	1996
Table 2.1 Extract from CAEL's 1996 survey report (CAEL 1999, p.30)		
Standardized		
Advanced placement	90%	92%
CLEP	88%	89%
American College of Teaching Proficiency Examination Program	35%	37%
DANTES	52%	62%
Challenge		
Challenge exam	72%	72%
Guidelines		
ACE PONSI/CREDIT	33%	43%
ACE armed forces	75%	78%
Individual assessment		
Individual assessment	50%	55%

Employee Growth and Development Programs (EGDPs)

CAEL's partnerships with industry and labour (the EGDPs) were intended to help workers sustain their employability in a time when downsizing had got under way in the automotive and telecommunications industries and was spreading to other sectors of the economy. The end of lifetime jobs with a single employer was being forecast and often even acknowledged with great reluctance by some labour unions. The EGDPs offered benefits, often to laid-off workers, or those about to be laid off, as well as to active employees. The benefits were a smorgasbord, different with each employer–labour combination, sometimes offered by non-unionized employers. The benefits included a selection from prepaid tuition, career and educational counselling, workshops on how to cope with college, placement services, advocacy with education providers, delivery of classes at worksites, and workshops on a variety of worker interests from investing to running one's own business. The UAW–Ford project offered options to more than 100,000 workers, and Mountain-Bell for more than 29,000, later as US West Comm-unications to a 14–state workforce of some 70,000.

In a typical EGDP, the employer would deposit tuition and other benefit funds with CAEL. CAEL would identify a list of legitimate education providers at the needed levels and would arrange with each for prepayment of its tuition once students were properly enrolled. CAEL also organized advocate groups within some of the workforces – fellow employees who would help one another make best use of the EGDP benefits. In some areas, the projects tripled the level of employees enrolled in college from the participating enterprises.

A feature of the EGDPs was that they saved the employers on their net personnel expense while enabling workers to raise their qualifications or get into new jobs in ways they could not otherwise afford. Workers saw the projects as helping with their long-run employment security (not necessarily continuing the same job or with the same employer). The ways in which employer costs were saved differed from project to project. In some instances, the employer was reducing the size of the workforce and was able, through the EGDP, to do so at less risk of litigation and at lower net severance costs than by earlier methods. In other instances, the EGDP reduced the turnover rate in an overly churning workforce by offering benefits (e.g. community college certificate programme tuitions) that held the workers' commitment for longer periods. Where the compensation package was bargained collectively, employers generally regarded use of part of the package for education more as an investment, with future benefits in morale and enhanced worker skills, than as a pure expense.

Though EGDPs have not penetrated the majority of American employers, CAEL was by the mid-1990s servicing projects for more than 60 employers of anywhere from 17 to 70,000 employees. These employees were dispersed through 40 states. From the early two sectors of automotive and telecommunications enterprises, the PLA service had been adopted also in financial services, electronics, manufacturing, consumer services and healthcare organizations. In the early 1990s, a concerted effort was made by CAEL to form coalitions of small businesses that, by pooling activities, could support a critical mass of services and staff, often with foundation support, to yield a viable venture. The partnerships were called 'joint ventures', not in the traditional sense of the term in economics, but as shared efforts by education, business, labour and, sometimes, the

State government. A benchmarking study on best practices among adult learner-friendly institutions is currently being mounted by CAEL in partnership with the American Productivity & Quality Center.

CAEL publications

From its beginnings at ETS, CAEL published actively. Already mentioned is the *New Directions in Experiential Learning* series. A first purpose of the series was to disseminate the case for more extensive use of hands-on learning in academia and for recognizing extra-college learning that was of college level in accordance with CAEL standards of good practice. The series also helped to make the point that CAEL was a professionally sound higher education association. In addition, CAEL produced books on training vouchers, levers for change in employment and training, how to develop career centres and other aids to employability. The following books are available – Lois Lamdin: *Earn College Credit for What You Know*; Susan Simosko: *Assessing Learning: CAEL Handbook for Faculty*; Urban Whitaker: *Assessing Learning: Standards, Principles, and Procedures*; Sheckley, Lamdin and Keeton: *Employability in a High Performance Economy*; Barry Sheckley and Morris Keeton: *Improving Employee Development: Perspectives from Research and Practice*; CAEL: *Prior Learning Assessment: A Guidebook to American Institutional Practices*.

American Council on Education and Adult Learners

The American Council on Education (ACE), the association of presidents of all types of non-profit institutions of post-secondary education in America and the chief spokesperson with the federal government for higher education, preceded CAEL in some of its work for recognition of adult learning and has been an active partner and supporter of CAEL from the outset. Dr Jerry Miller represented ACE as a liaison member of the CAEL Steering Committee during its initial project days and later in the years of CAEL II (1977–1979). The Center for Adult Learning and Educational Credentials of ACE, under Dr Henry Spille and his successor, Susan Porter Robinson, has expanded its services. ACE has updated the General Educational Development (GED) Tests, measuring equivalency with the major and lasting outcomes of a high-school education, and has expanded access to those services. The Center has developed a crosswalk with the National Adult Literacy Survey from that survey's results to those of GED Tests. Through the Commission on Higher Education and the Adult Learner, ACE has also influenced the National Governors Association in its members' understanding of the interplay between education and the economic well-being of their states.

ACE established its publication of credit recommendations for educational offerings in the armed services beginning during World War II. Its PONSI programme (now called CREDIT), in which corporate training programmes were evaluated and provided with credit recommendations, was begun in 1974. The ACE services were complemented by its policy declarations and its lobbying for acceptance of these enabling services throughout the decades since the 1940s. In addition, the formation of the Servicemembers Opportunity College in 1972 has been a major force favouring colleges' use of prior learning assessment and related adult learner services. SOC now has 1300 members, public and private, two- and four-year throughout the United States.

ACE has played the lead role in combating degree mills in the USA. Those institutions have trodden on many an accrediting principle in their history, but on none more damagingly than on the principles of good practice in assessing non-school learning. ACE and CAEL again joined forces in 1993 in publishing the policy paper, *Adult Degree Programs: Quality Issues, Problem Areas, and Action Steps*, that treated this scourge in a joint effort to combat this and other forms of malpractice.

It was natural, then, that ACE should have formed the Commission on Higher Education and the Adult Learner in 1981. Then still Chief Executive Officer of CAEL, I was invited to chair that Commission and was able to bring to it some financial support from Project LEARN. An early and continuing effort of the Commission was that of documenting the many ways in which federal and state legislation and its modes of implementation created obstacles that blocked or greatly hindered adults' efforts to return to schooling in post-secondary education. A first working paper was developed by Michael Goldstein of Dow Lohnes & Albertson in 1981. A fuller publication was written by Larry Gold in 1990, and the core of the findings of the two authors were included in Chapter 7 of *Employability in a High Performance Economy* (CAEL 1993).

The Commission's work culminated in a 1988 conference on enhancing the productivity and employability of the American workforce. This was co-sponsored by ACE, CAEL, the National Governors Association, and the College Board. Hosted in Little Rock by then Governor Clinton of Arkansas, the conference drew representatives of some 24 state governments, four of which later undertook follow-up projects in collaboration with CAEL (Indiana, New York, Georgia and Illinois).

Other public policy activity by CAEL and the NSIEE had preceded and helped lead to the formation of the ACE Commission. Pamela Tate, my successor as President, succeeded in substantially strengthening CAEL's work on public policy by her work with foundations.

Prior learning assessment goes global

It was not in the CAEL agenda, initially, to sow the seeds of assessment and recognition of extra-school learning abroad. Mention has already been made of Norman Evans's initiative in applying the idea in the UK. A second arena that caught the idea from CAEL on its own initiative was Canada – first in Québec, later in Ontario and British Columbia, and then throughout Canada.

CAEL had in 1978 held one of its annual conferences in Toronto. At that time, it was thought that regional managers might be enlisted in one or more locations in Canada and that a bi-national collaboration might develop through CAEL. For a variety of reasons – limited financing, differences between the educational systems of the two countries, possibly other causes – this idea did not take root. Probably the desire of Canadians to form their own movement underlay or so complemented the other causes as to make a separate development in Canada inevitable.

In the United States, universities had been at least equal partners with liberal arts colleges and community colleges in sparking the experiential learning movement. Not so in Canada, where most universities are still on the sidelines of a development now strongly encouraged by both provincial and federal governments. Robert Isabelle took the initiative in Québec, attending a 1985 CAEL conference in New Orleans and then obtaining province support for a CEGEPS (community colleges) province-wide project in which advisers, assessors and programme managers were trained to introduce PLA services. After a number of years of active co-operation, the central staffing of this effort ended. Isabelle was also able to generate an EGDP with General Motors Canada and the United Auto Workers that worked to the satisfaction of all partners as long as it had federal assistance.

Also in the 1980s, CAEL responded to a request from the Prime Minister's office in British Columbia by nominating Susan Mancuso and Urban Whitaker (regional managers) to assist. They provided training and consultation as that province launched its PLA work.

Beginning in 1990, the First Nations Technical Institute (FNTI) initiated a series of annual PLA conferences that continues to the present. Paul Zakos was the energizing force in this effort, with FNTI providing substantial annual subsidies. Initially drawing largely from Ontario, the FNTI events began to draw nationally – with British Columbia, Nova Scotia and New Brunswick all active. By 1994, the Ontario Ministry of Education, which had been actively interested early on, drew the support of Human Resources Development (HRD) Canada, which in turn engaged the Canadian Labour Force Development Board (CLFDB). CLFDB, with HRD support and encouragement, have mounted the most successful of Canadian meetings in 1995, 1997 and 1999 conferences.

In another chapter of this book, Deborah Blower tells the Canada story and describes the extent of PLA services now available.

Relationship to AAHE on assessment

Following the work of a National Institute of Education Study Group, reported in *Involvement in Learning* (1984), the American Association for Higher Education (AAHE) initiated a series of annual conferences on assessment and quality. These conferences were focused on instruction in the everyday campuses of America. They were of special interest to CAEL because a key barrier to adequate assessment of prior learning up to then had been the inability of colleges and universities to articulate their assessment standards in regular classrooms. 'Use the same standards you use in your courses,' CAEL had said. But what if you had no picture of those standards? What if they differed widely among institutions? What if they even differed widely among faculties and departments in the same colleges?

In the early 1990s, the regional accrediting associations in the United States began to articulate and later implement policies requiring that their member institutions make plans for assessing and documenting their students' achievements as learners and for doing so in language understandable across institutional lines. This effort is, though almost a decade has passed, still in its infancy but seems to be gaining momentum.

Developments at CAEL under Pamela Tate

In January 1990, Pamela Tate took the reins as President of CAEL. She had been the driving force behind CAEL's 'joint ventures' with business and labour to develop employee growth and development services.

She has brought the level of CAEL outlays in this work from some $2.5 million to well above $18 million by 1999. This enlarged activity has included a substantial proportion of activities helping laid-off workers (in 'downsizing') to craft career transition plans and locate retraining opportunities. Concurrently with the increase in workforces served, that this effort has generated, have been the new activities in public policy at federal and state levels and the projects initiated with state governments in implementation of those policies. In Greater Metropolitan Chicago, the MacArthur Foundation has given major funding to CAEL for these services, with a special emphasis on forming coalitions of small businesses to make the EGDP services affordable to them through their pooled resources. The financial implications of these developments for CAEL have also been heartening, bringing its annual income well above $14 million for each of the past two fiscal years. This result has also given CAEL sufficient resources for innovation in its work with colleges and universities. It has initiated a consulting service for colleges and a national project to establish best practices in serving adult learners.

Where next?

In addition to the work of ACE, AAHE and CAEL, a number of spin-offs are now at work in fostering assessment, some in relation to the outcomes of normal collegiate instruction, and some bridging that kind of effort with the recognition of prior and extra-college learning. Examples include: the New England Educational Assessment Network (NEEAN); some profit-seeking enterprises that help prospective students assemble documentation for their claims of prior learning; a support group formed by Northeastern Louisiana University; and one-time projects such as the 1997–1998 APQC–UMUC Benchmarking Study on Assessing Learning Outcomes. (APQC is the American Productivity & Quality Center and UMUC is the University of Maryland University College.) The PLA 'movement' in the USA thus has a dimension even larger than what CAEL, the American Council on Education and their members have.

Changing secular trends

The forces likely to affect the future of prior learning assessment in the USA differ from those that caused its earlier successes. The following is a list of questions that bear on that future – not answers as to what will be. Nor is it clear to what extent these same forces will exert a similar influence around the globe.

- Will the expected disproportion of new entries into the US workforce on the part of women, ethnic minorities and immigrants also have a bearing on the need and uses of prior learning assessment and employability programmes? If so, at what levels (entry to high school, entry to college, higher levels) will that impact be greatest?

- Will rising prices for higher education interact with greater demand for workers-to-be with college education so that pressures build for increased access to higher education and for economies on entry by use of prior learning assessment? Or could the new technologies that facilitate production with fewer and less well-educated workers make for a reduction of the numbers needing higher education and its credentials?

- A rising sophistication about qualifications needed for different kinds of work might work against the present enthralment with higher education qualifications. Will this sophistication lead to colleges' accommodation with altered curricula? Or will it reduce demand for college altogether?

- Is the movement toward voluntary national occupational skills standards an expression of scepticism about the relevance of college credentials for work? Prior learning assessment might be used to help business develop non-collegiate credentials, or it might be used to help translate the two kinds of qualification from one system to the other or to lead to college curricula that build practical as well as theoretical knowledge. How will the dynamic of these developments affect the kinds and volume of use of prior learning assessment and the division of labour in that work between higher education and employers?

- The globalization of economic competition and the acceleration of travel, communications and the movement of goods and services will probably open up new types of qualifications required (e.g. skills in multiple languages and accurate empathy across diverse cultural divides). Prior learning assessment could then be used to aid appropriate placement for this more complex array of needs. The service might apply for paid work, voluntary roles, rewarding retirement plans, and other uses. How is this scenario likely to play out?

- To what extent will educators' decisions about these matters affect the competition within higher education, and between it and outside entrepreneurs, in shaping the significance of prior learning assessment in the future?

Conclusion

CAEL was founded on two rather simple common-sense ideas: that what a learner knows and can do should be recognized appropriately no matter how or where it was learned and that hands-on experience of things being learned about and worked with can enhance that learning. These ideas were certainly not new in 1974: many good teachers had made use of them before, and a few institutions had incorporated their use into their educational strategies. It has, therefore, been strange that so much inertia and opposition have been encountered in the work of furthering the application of these ideas in higher education. At the same time, the response chronicled in this book, as the use of these ideas has spread to a number of countries, well-developed economically and less so, has gone far beyond the expectations of those who gathered in Princeton in the autumn of 1973 to debate the feasibility of a CAEL project.

References

CAEL (1993) *Employability in a High Performance Economy.* Chicago: CAEL.

CAEL (1998) *Prior Learning Assessment: A Guide to American Institutional Practices.* CAEL: Chicago. Dubuque, Iowa: Kendall/Hunt Publishing Group.

Cross, K.P., Valley, J. and associates (1973) *Planning Non-Traditional Programs.* A publication of the Commission on Non-Traditional Study. San Francisco: Jossey-Bass.

Gamson, Z.F. (1988) *Higher Education and the Real World: The Story of CAEL.* Wolferdoro, N.H.: Longwood Publishing Group.

Gold, L. (1990) *Campus Roadblock: How Federal Policies Make it Difficult for Adults to Go to College.* Washington, D.C.: Public Policy Advocates.

Goldstein, M. (1981) *Issues of Public Policy Affecting Adult Learning at the Postsecondary Level.* Unpublished paper for the Commission on Higher Education and the Adult Learner, American Council on Education: Washington D.C.

Keeton, M.T. and Associates (1977) *Experiential Learning: Rationale, Characteristics and Assessment.* San Francisco: Jossey-Bass.

Keeton, M.T. and Tate, P. (eds) (1978–1983) *New Directions for Experiential Learning.* San Francisco: Jossey-Bass.

National Institute of Education and Study Group (1984) Involvement in Learning: Realizing the Potential of American Higher Education. Washington, D.C.: National Institute of Education.

Sheckley, B.C., Lamdin, L. and Keeton, M.T. (1993) *Employability in a High Performance Economy.* Chicago: CAEL.

CHAPTER 3

The Evolution of AP(E)L in England

Norman Evans

This account of the development of AP(E)L in England runs through five sections: preparing the ground; seeding; first growth; first harvest; and second planting. If the seasonal metaphor suggests a neatly planned gardener's operation, that was not the case. Within what was essentially an ever-changing and evolving dynamic, happenstance, coincidences and flukes of timing were far more significant, initially, than carefully worked out plans. Plans came later. Later still, circumstances took over. And throughout, timing was the most important factor.

The story began almost like a child's fairy tale, where wonderful, unexpected things happened as dreamlike possibilities. Then reality and hard graft broke in. Government policies for post-secondary institutions created circumstances where it was possible to think strategically about implementation, developments then abounded, and, again, unexpectedly and extraordinarily, nearly 20 years after the story began, yet another government initiative seems to be kick-starting a third cycle of activity. Not that there was a clear linear development. Rather, AP(E)L was inserted patchily into a number of changes in higher and further education institutions and became something of a catalyst for some of them. The fairy tale, with its strong autobiographical strand, running through highways and byways to begin with, turned into intentional strategic planning – until institutions and government took over as the story quickened.

Preparing the ground

Ground preparation began in a most unlikely way. While Principal of Bishop Lonsdale College, a large teacher training institution, in 1977 I found myself, as a stand-in for a member of staff who fell ill, accompanying some students on an exchange programme with Keene State College in New Hampshire. Waiting for some appointment there, I chanced upon some buff-coloured documents which turned out to be research publications of what was then the Cooperative Assessment of Experiential Learning (CAEL) project. They documented valid and reliable procedures for assessing the learning which adults had acquired themselves without any formal tuition, and for turning it into academic credit at one level or another.

This was both intriguing and alarming. Intriguing, because I had long believed that many people had far more knowledge and skill than their qualifications might suggest, but had no external evidence to prove it. CAEL showed how to prove it. It was alarming because I was about to undertake a research project on the Bachelor of Education (BEd) degree for serving teachers. Suddenly, I was confronted with an appalling dilemma. I knew two things about the BEd and they argued with one another. There was no degree regulation for the BEd anywhere in the country which allowed teachers exemption from sections of the course where they had learned some of its content from experience. Yet my experience told me that there were many teachers who enrolled on that degree course and who were bored silly and dissatisfied because they were expected to learn from courses what they had learned already from experience.

This idea would not go away. How could it become possible to do what the Americans were doing already? Two years later, happenstance struck again. A chance meeting with John Strange, Vice-President of what had by then become the Council for the Advancement of Experiential Learning (CAEL), led to a discussion, in a friend's house in Cambridge, Massachusetts, about the theory and practice of the assessment of prior and experiential learning. He listened to my idea of trying to find ways of introducing the assessment of experiential learning to Britain. With a gleam in his eyes, he dreamed out loud of transatlantic collaboration. With mounting excitement, he said he thought CAEL could help. The upshot was that he persuaded his President, Morris Keeton, to get small grant from the Kellogg Foundation to enable me to travel across the United States trying to find examples of procedures that would satisfy the stringent requirements for assessment which would have to be met in any British institution, assuming I could find one to introduce AP(E)L. Additionally, I was equipped with all CAEL publications, and then found myself officially designated as one of some ten regional managers of CAEL. The fairy tale was being acted out. A collaboration began which continues to this day.

Happenstance again. I needed a base from which to try to turn the idea into action. Sir Charles Carter had retired from being the Founding Vice-Chancellor of Lancaster University and had become Chairman of the Management and Research Committee of the Policy Studies Institute. He heard me out, asked what we should do and arranged for me to become a Senior Fellow from September 1980, on the understanding that after six months I would have to become self-supporting.

The next step was to test the viability of the idea with influential people and see what support might be forthcoming. Richard Hoggart, then Warden of Goldsmiths' College, and Morris Keeton, who came specially for the occasion, led a seminar at the Policy Studies Institute to sound out possibilities with an audience of senior staff from higher and adult education and some employers. Afterwards, a small group met fairly regularly to try to work out what action might be taken. It was obvious that AP(E)L could serve as an access route to higher education. It was more difficult to see how AP(E)L could lead to the award of academic credit. Equally problematic was to see how the work experience component of sandwich courses could be converted into assessable learning which could count towards the award of a degree.

Simultaneously, employers were sounded out. Sir Peter Parker, then Chairman of British Rail, wrote to his fellow heads of nationalized industries to see whether they were interested in the idea of AP(E)L. As a result, Edgar Wille, head of management training for the National Coal Board, joined Peter Hobbs, then Personnel Director for Wellcome, Penny Childs from Legal and General Insurance and Stephen O'Brien, Chief Executive of Business in the Community, for a series of meeting to puzzle out how AP(E)L could be put to the use of business and industry. For that, the timing was wrong: we got nowhere. Later it was right.

Those early discussions identified two factors which subsequently proved essential for AP(E)L to be effective within higher education. The first was modularization. The second was learning outcomes, or learning intentions as I have come to call them to differentiate them from behavioural objectives.

Take AP(E)L for credit in history. It was quite obvious that although someone might prove to have substantial knowledge about, say, King Edward the Martyr or the fall of the Bastille, it would be extremely difficult to allow such credit in relation to a history course which was constructed as a three-year programme and which did not include either that period or that event. In other words the content of long courses posed almost insuperable problems for AP(E)L. However, if courses were shorter, say one term in length with less content credit for AP(E)L became feasible. So this part of those discussions was a precursor to organizing academic programmes to facilitate schemes for credit accumulation. Fairly rapidly, during the later 1980s, credit accumulation through the modularization of courses was urged on universities from government agencies, and many projects were funded to promote it. It was a route to greater flexibility with greater student choice in composing programmes that suited them better than the single or joint subject courses which until then had been the staple diet for learners in higher education. It was also a means of enabling institutions to become more responsive to the changes occurring in the world around them. American institutions had much to teach about all of this.

Learning intentions (learning outcomes) became an extension of credit accumulation. Credit accumulation offered students greater choice in selecting their courses and programmes. To make well-informed choices, they needed more information about what was on offer than previously when signing up for, say, chemistry, law or archaeology. The obvious way to provide this information was to attach to syllabus descriptions of courses a set of learning outcomes detailing what students were expected to have mastered by the end of the course. Slowly but surely, as with credit accumulation, this notion was accepted in a growing number of institutions.

AP(E)L benefited greatly from this shift in institutional behaviour. Those early discussions had fastened on the idea of learning outcomes as an assessment tool for assessing prior and experiential learning. Instead of trying to read across from claim to syllabus description, learning outcomes could serve as a check-list for assessment. And, again, this proved to be the precursor of subsequent developments throughout the system.

Meantime, as I was travelling the USA and gathering useful materials, I was writing *The Knowledge Revolution* (Evans 1981) – the rather pretentious title was invented by the publisher. Just back from one of my trips, at lunch, Brian Groombridge, Professor of Adult Education at the University of London, said I ought to read a review of my book written by Jack Mansell, then Chief Officer of the Further Education Unit at the Department of Education and Science. It said that if people had not read it, they should. I rushed back to the Policy Studies Institute (PSI) in Castle Street, read the review, and on impulse phoned Jack. I asked if that was what he said, what was he going to do. I walked across Westminster Bridge, said I needed a project to keep me going, and half an hour later I walked back with just under a £10,000 commission to do a survey of admissions regulations and practices in further education colleges to see how far, if at all, AP(E)L was being used.

So the happenstance continued. That work took me into countless colleges for investigation and discussion, so the first line of disseminating the idea was done. *Curriculum Opportunity* (Evans 1983) was the result. The Further Education Unit (FEU) published some 10,000 copies in three editions. It went to every higher and further education establishment in the country and to some employers. It meant that a marker had been put down under the imprimatur of a government publication. Notice was served nationally that AP(E)L needed to taken seriously.

Curriculum Opportunity was followed by a small pamphlet trying to recommend the idea to employers (Evans 1984a). But then, equally important and of huge significance for higher education, what was then the Council for National Academic Awards (CNAA) joined in. Its Development Services Unit asked for a project to do the same thing, but limited to its own associated colleges and polytechnics. Not only did that secure more funding, but it was the first step of trying to promote AP(E)L in degree-teaching institutions. That work resulted in CNAA publishing and distributing to every university and polytechnic, and also to further education colleges, copies of *Access to Higher Education: Non Standard Entry to CNAA First Degree and DipHE Courses* (Evans 1984b). Another national marker was put down, this time under the academic authority of the body responsible for about half of the first-degree courses in the country.

Meantime, things were moving in further education. Alun Davies, then Chief Inspector for further education for the Inner London Education Authority (ILEA), recognized, as did Jack Mansell, that AP(E)L could be a catalyst for effecting institutional and curricular change in the colleges, which they knew had to happen soon. He encouraged some of his seconded staff in ILEA's Curriculum Development Unit to find out more about the theory and practice of AP(E)L and to promote it in some of London's colleges. More happenstance – this initiative coincided with another. Through contacts with Rockland Community College in New York State,

USA, I was handling the assessment of the experiential learning acquired by Rockland students while doing community service work in London under the auspices of Community Service Volunteers. This meant recruiting assessors. Mainly, they came from the further education service in London, including the Curriculum Development Unit. After a rudimentary training, and recruited once a year for several years from 1983, they had first-hand experience of scrutinizing documentary evidence of what these students had learned from their CSV experience.

The fact that ILEA took such a determined interest in AP(E)L was important nationally. As the most powerful and well-resourced local education authority in the land, it tended to influence others by example. So, while networking carried the word to many further education colleges in London, it spread that word further afield. And as some London staff moved to appointments in different parts of the country, initiatives burgeoned. Through regional meetings and conferences where staff met one another, AP(E)L entered the language of discussion. It was particularly attractive for those responsible for access courses. Quickly, they found the power of the idea as it boosted personal confidence, strengthened motivation and whetted appetites for further learning.

Seeding

Thus, the ground was ready for seeding in different areas with the hope of cross-pollination. In 1982, I managed to get a small grant from the Wates Foundation to launch the first taught course in AP(E)L in the country. It became a test bed for subsequent action. Jointly, Goldsmiths' College and Thames Polytechnic offered Making Experience Count to adult learners who did not have the requisite qualifications for entry to higher education. It was planned as a 12-week course, with four hours a week. Its sole purpose was to enable participants to reflect on their experience, document what they claimed to have learned from it and produce evidence to support their claims. Students were told there were six possible exit routes for those who completed the course. It was perfectly acceptable for some to conclude that they had had enough formal education and, wanting no more of it, to say thank you and goodbye. It seemed highly likely that the course could help people get jobs or improve their prospects in their current employment. Some might well reckon that they wanted more study, but that they needed something like a pre-preparation course because they did not feel ready to tackle an access course for higher education. Access courses themselves were another option. But some might be able to demonstrate that they were quite capable of coping with a degree and go on to find a place to study for one. There were two other possibilities. They might discover that a course in further education leading to a national qualification was what suited them best; say, one awarded by the Business and Technician Education Council or the National Nursery Examination Board. And as a remote possibility, some might even demonstrate sufficient knowledge and skill to merit admission with advanced standing to a degree course. The possible applications of AP(E)L were articulated.

Making Experience Count was the first exercise in portfolio-assisted assessment, and it continued to be offered in the course catalogue of those two institutions for several years. Each course resulted in some students either getting a place on a degree course or enrolling on an access course or a further education course. Some found their portfolios valuable in obtaining promotion in their job, moving to a different job, or getting one in the first place. As such, it became something of a resource centre, a kind of working laboratory, as other institutions visited Making Experience Count (Storan 1998) to take stock of AP(E)L and how to do it.

Having established Making Experience Count as a demonstration model showing that AP(E)L was not only possible, but viable and acceptable in two very different higher education institutions, the issue became how to promote similar activities elsewhere. The idea of study tours to the USA became the instrument for quite systematic preparation for wider action. A strategy was emerging. Morris Keeton included a component called the Scholar Exchange Programme as a staff development programme for the UK in a second project funded by the Kellogg Foundation called Project LEARN. The idea was to take key people in higher and further education in Britain to visit American universities and colleges to see at first hand how they handled schemes for AP(E)L. It was an invitation-only programme. People invited to participate were either heads of, or very senior staff members from, higher education institutions, or those concerned with public policy (and there tended to be an overlap between the two), or academics occupying influential middling positions with the authority to introduce innovations. The overriding criterion, though, was that all had to come from institutions where its head accepted AP(E)L in principle without necessarily understanding its implications.

This was an outstandingly successful programme. By varying the amount of subsidy from the funds available according to the willingness and ability of institutions to pay a share of the costs, and then running study tours on a full-cost basis, by the end of 1996 some 160 academics and administrators had participated. That was ten times the number contracted for in the Kellogg Foundation grant. Why and how that increased number occurred is documented in an evaluation funded by Kellogg, and is published by the Learning from Experience Trust as *Learners All – Worldwide* (Craft, Evans and Keeton 1997). But, in simple terms, the reason is that from vice-chancellors down people said that the experience was seminal for them and helped to promote significant aspects of institutional change. It meant that dotted around the country, in an increasing number of institutions, there were people excited by the possibilities they could envisage when incorporating versions of AP(E)L.

At about this time, Edgar Wille persuaded a colleague in the Midlands to conduct an experiment with six volunteers from his office in the National Coal Board. Tutored by John Buckle from Sheffield Polytechnic, they prepared portfolios of their learning and successfully used them for entry to post-secondary qualifications or career advancement. So the first step was taken in employment. As with Making Experience Count in an academic institution, it proved the point that within industry and commerce AP(E)L had much to offer. It is important to add that no money changed hands for this exercise. Without funding of any kind, all concerned gave their time, expertise and effort voluntarily.

There was a very important interplay between the study tours programme and CNAA's last bit of seeding AP(E)L for higher education. It prepared the way for the dramatic innovation it introduced in 1986, which in turn provided what were then polytechnics with great scope for their own development, which they carried through a few years later when the polytechnics became universities. This produced *A Learner's Introduction to Building on Your Experience* (Buckle 1988).

In 1985, CNAA commissioned a project to 'negotiate, establish, monitor and appraise schemes for the assessment of prior experiential learning (AP(E)L) in polytechnics and colleges' (p.1). The report of this project was published as CNAA Development Services Publication 17: *The Assessment of Prior Experiential Learning* conducted by the Learning from Experience Trust (Evans 1988). The preface said: 'This was an important piece of work whose outcomes and future extension will be significant across higher education and for all those concerned with access to higher education.' The preamble (p.1) included this:

> For these purposes AP(E)L refers to ways of making valid and reliable judgements about ... the knowledge and skills acquired through life and work experience and study which are not formally attested through any educational or professional certification. It can include instruction based learning, provided by any institution which has not been examined in any public examinations systems.

That put the seal of academic authority on AP(E)L in Britain. The institutions which agreed to take part and the contributing disciplines were as follows:

- City of Birmingham Polytechnic – production engineering (p/t) and business studies (p/t)
- Bristol Polytechnic – business studies (p/t)
- Essex Institute of Higher Education – MEd (p/t)
- Newcastle upon Tyne Polytechnic – associate degree scheme
- Polytechnic of North London – evening degree (p/t)
- Sheffield Polytechnic – social studies (p/t) and business studies (p/t)
- Stockport College of Technology – mechanical engineering (p/t)
- The Polytechnic, Wolverhampton – computing and information technology (p/t and f/t)
- Middlesex Polytechnic – modular degree scheme (p/t and f/t)
- Thames Polytechnic – continuing education.

The intention was to cover the entire curriculum range by including mathematics, physics, chemistry and biology, but that proved impossible. An attempt was made subsequently to remedy that, but for complicated reasons it was not very successful. However, it produced an important insight into ways of helping students with AP(E)L. An admissions tutor for science worked patiently through interview and paper guidelines with some applicants with good laboratory experience, but failed utterly to convince them that they might know something of the syllabus already. Then she decided to walk them round laboratories asking them to identify any object or process they recognized. Thus she began to elicit from them the store of knowledge and skills they had acquired through their work. This turned out to be a very important illustration of the fact that there are many approaches to identifying uncertificated learning.

The basic issue in all AP(E)L work is to enable people to produce statements about the knowledge and skill which is locked up inside them and to produce evidence to substantiate their claims. Individuals can react to this requirement in many different ways. There can be guideline documents which take would-be AP(E)L candidates through the procedures to be followed, step by step, in straightforward language. There can be interviews to lead into the procedures. There can be formal classes. But for some, the entire prospect can be daunting, especially if their formal education left them feeling inadequate as learners, and they had little or no experience in trying to put ideas on paper coherently. So the lesson that that science admission tutor learned and was there for everyone to note was this – for AP(E)L to do its job properly, there has to be a battery of techniques available for enabling candidates to do themselves justice.

That relative failure apart, three things emerged notably. The first was half-expected: that it was part-time study where AP(E)L fitted quite naturally. AP(E)L for academic credit superceded access. But what was not expected was the clarity with which this emerged: 'Given the opportunity to articulate for themselves their current learning attainments, adults make use of that information about themselves in variety of ways. Some use it as in the brief for the project, to obtain admission to degree courses, and in some cases credit towards those courses. However others use this evidence of their prior learning to obtain employment, for career advancement, for changing career direction or finding contentment as and where they are' (p.2).

The CNAA (Evans, 1988) report began with six guiding principles.

1. The student makes the claim – this was to protect academic staff from being drawn into doing the students' work for them.

2. AP(E)L concerns learning not experience – without this there could be no academic integrity.

3. Identification comes before assessment – this was to clarify the need for organizing statements of learning fit for submission for assessment.

4. Assessment and academic responsibility – this was to insist that academic staff should use any procedure they thought most appropriate to arrive at a satisfactory judgement about the evidence before them.

5. The nature of evidence – this was to insist that any form of evidence was admissible, whether written or spoken or by observation or artefact, provided it directly supported the claim and it met the classical view that assessment should be appropriate to what was being assessed.

6. Two academic functions – this was to separate the academic task of helping students to prepare their material for assessment from the other academic responsibility of making judgements, and so avoid any possible confusion between advocate and judge.

The report then went into detail about what institutions actually did, under a number of chapter headings: 'Approaches to the identification of prior learning'; 'Approaches to assessment'; 'The variables affecting the characteristics off any AP(E)L scheme'; 'The differences between disciplines'; 'Involving the students'; 'Involving the staff'; and 'AP(E)L as a catalyst'. On the way, it commented on the characteristics of the participating students. And the appendices recorded the procedures adopted by each institution.

Under 'Issues arising', the report tried to look to the future. It commented on the curricular issues which could arise from enrolling students who brought significant learning with them. It floated the idea of AP(E)L as a validated course, carrying academic credit for the endeavour of preparing material for submission. It glanced at the potential problems AP(E)L might present for professional bodies. It raised questions about: student guidance; mainstreaming AP(E)L activities; the concept of progression; resource implications; leadership; regulations; and, above all, staff development.

All in all, therefore, CNAA Development Services Publication 17 recorded the successful use of AP(E)L in ten different institutions, for different purposes in different disciplines, and put an authoritative academic imprimatur on the entire exercise. Of critical importance, it demonstrated that academic credit could be awarded to degrees ranging from computing and information technology, through to business studies, social studies and different humanities disciplines within modular degrees. But it was more than that. It served as a resource book for anyone in any institution who was considering designing an AP(E)L scheme.

This became self-evident during the four dissemination conferences which CNAA funded during the year following the publication of the report. Altogether, staff from some 120 different institutions attended those regional conferences. The questioning was tough and direct. The scepticism was voluble and stringent. But the job was done. The word was out. AP(E)L was a perfectly proper academic enterprise for institutions to undertake if they wished to do so. The foundations were well and truly laid for higher education. What is more, they were laid by professionals themselves.

The study tours had a seminal role in serving as a supporting staff development programme throughout what became the two and a half years of the project. During that period, one and often two senior academics from each of the participating institutions had a week's experience of seeing at first hand how American colleges and universities dealt with AP(E)L and the variety of purposes it could serve. And all this occurred at precisely the time when British institutions were beginning to seek ways of extending their activities to all forms of off-campus activities. Association with nearby further education colleges, collaboration with business and industry, tailor-made programmes for particular constituencies of older students, the hunt was on for extensions to the range of academic services.

During each study tour week, the four or five men and women from different institutions talked incessantly about what they were finding out and what seemed possible to use in their own home university, polytechnic or college. Senior people in the host institutions concealed nothing when it came to questions about academic quality, about the pros and cons of disaggregating study programmes with the consequent dangers of losing coherence and of getting too close to business partners, about the resistance to AP(E)L from sections of academics, and about the problems of financing the necessary student guidance services needed to support the entire enterprise. Each group had plenty to talk about in the week. In trains, airports, planes, over meals, in bars – it never stopped. And, as many revealed in an evaluation of the programme in 1995–1997, the experience gave them the confidence to attempt initiatives they would not have otherwise undertaken. As remarked earlier, the programme continued with the same functions for academics and administrators for another ten years.

During the last years of the 1980s and well into the 1990s, the Trust arranged a reverse flow of some 20 senior American academics to this country. Morris Keeton himself came several times, so did John Strange and Barbara Buchanan from the College of Public and Community Service; Bessie Blake, Dean of the College of New Resources at the College of New Rochelle; Bill Craft, Vice-President of Bunker Hill Community College; and Steve Brooks, Director of the Philadelphia Center. All of them were hosts to study tour groups, so their visits to Britain created an important two-way traffic of ideas. The idea was to put each one in orbit to undertake a week-long series of seminars round the country, funded by contributions from the institutions which received them.

During these early years of growing interest, there was one group of people who were sceptical of, sometimes downright hostile to, the very idea of uncertificated learning being certificated. They were adult educators. They believed passionately in the power of experiential learning. But, correctly, they saw the risk that people who reviewed their life experiences, to unearth what they had learned from it, might find at the end of their efforts that, in relation to their hopes, their learning counted for nothing. Were that to happen, they argued, it would seem to imply that their lives were worth nothing too. And for people who had had to bear earlier disappointments about their capacity as learners, it was hard to think of anything more disastrous.

This was a very serious point. It epitomized the debate between those who put emphasis on experiential learning as a powerful mode of education and those who, while agreeing with that, saw the assessment of experiential learning as a way of empowering individuals. The answer to the anxiety was that initial advice on AP(E)L was essential. That advice needed to take the form of saying whether or not it seemed likely that the range of lifetime experiences they could recall would generate statements of learning which did indeed merit academic assessment. Further, to guard against possible sense of failure, if the AP(E)L route did not seem appropriate, at the earliest stage that advice should include suggestions about what might be a more suitable route to additional learning for that particular person at that particular time. Later, of course, under the banner of lifelong learning, this argument tended to disappear. But at the time it was a very important reminder that AP(E)L needed the most sensitive handling.

These conversations cropped up continually during a succession of access projects run by the government-funded Unit for the

Development of Adult and Continuing Education (UDACE) and supported by the Further Education Unit. A committee convened by UDACE to examine barriers to access included local education officers responsible for adult education, and people from further education colleges, voluntary bodies and from the emerging new institutional development, the open colleges. Open colleges were devoted precisely to the underlying principle of AP(E)L: that people needed the opportunity to benefit from whatever learning they had acquired, irrespective of how they acquired it. For open colleges, the rider was that they offered opportunities to people who would not dream of going anywhere near a formal institution. Too scared, too diffident, too unsure of their own worth, carrying a sense of failure from school, they needed to be able to approach someone somewhere who did not represent the more terrifying face of authority. So all this discussion about barriers meant that, while AP(E)L was beginning to put down roots in higher education, seeds were being sown in further and adult education.

However, seeding in further education establishments presented quite different issues from those in higher education. Their history determined what initiatives they could take. Using AP(E)L for access was fine in principle, in line with the drive for wider participation; but access to what? Access courses leading to entry to higher education were obvious. Beyond that, it was problematic. Historically, further education colleges had a strong vocational bias with concentrations of courses in engineering, construction and business-related subjects, where the syllabuses and examining systems were prescribed by bodies such as the City and Guilds Institute, the Technology Council and the Business Education Council, and with courses for scores of other vocational qualifications, as well as the Ordinary and Advanced levels of the General Certificate of Education (GCE). They taught what they were required to teach by the various examining boards. There was little scope for AP(E)L. In any case, because the academic organization of colleges was departmental, with courses and programmes running in discrete parallel lines, almost belonging to separate entities, introducing AP(E)L had to be a departmental matter. Some heads of department were understanding and sympathetic to the underlying principles and were prepared to move cautiously where they found staff willing to accept unfamilar tasks. Many were not. Gradually, however, the debate moved on to the vexed question of modularization, with all the overall management problems that such a shift in academic organization posed. But there was little point in musing over whether AP(E)L related to the college as a whole, to programmes or to individual courses, with the attendant questions of admissions, guidance, assessment procedures and, above all, staff involvement, until there was some compelling reason for doing so. Compelling reasons were about to come.

First growth

1986 was a nurturing year for AP(E)L, and the nurturing came through the establishment of two separate systems. The first came from the stunning achievement of CNAA in establishing its Credit Accumulation and Transfer (CATS) Registry. The other was the work of the newly created National Council for Vocational Qualifications (NCVQ). Unfortunately, they were not the same. They were seeking to serve different purposes: the academic and the occupational and vocational. The problems of getting an effective relationship between the two were, and have continued to be, acute. The result was that, while AP(E)L flourished impressively in some higher education institutions as an integral part of their mainstream provision, in further education colleges, to the dismay of some, AP(E)L tended to be forced into a rather narrow instrumental version, tied to externally determined occupational competencies.

But, for higher education, 1986 saw CNAA take centre stage. George Walden, Minister for Higher and Further Education, attended the press launch of the ATS Registry to make public congratulatory announcements. And the vital element in that press launch was the rule book. The regulations for the CATS Registry included clauses which helped transform the face of higher education throughout the British Isles. The regulations said that credit accumulation was expressed by establishing that 360 credit points were required for graduation, with 120 credit points needing to accrue for each of the three years. There were stop-off points at the end of years 1 (with a certificate) and 2 (with a diploma). At a stroke, this freed individual students from the requirement to follow a course of study for three years without interruption. Furthermore, since the regulations stipulated that the smallest amount of credit which was allowable for credit accumulation was 4, being the equivalent to one week's continuous study, they brought into the sphere of higher education whole rafts of post-experience development courses provided by employers and the professions.

All this was underpinned by clauses in the regulations referring to AP(E)L. Academic credit which was awarded for prior and experiential learning was countable for bachelor's degrees and master's degrees. This last was the most dramatic regulation of all in a booklet which went immediately into the public domain. Any degree-teaching institution now had an authoritative reference point for whatever flexible systems and patterns of learning for higher education awards they chose to introduce. The way was open for forms of collaboration with employers and the professions which, academically, simply had not existed before. The higher education world would never be the same again in Britain.

In retrospect, it is almost incredible that this revolution occurred so quietly and smoothly. There are differing accounts of how it happened. This is my own. The central figure is Edwin Kerr, Chief Officer of CNAA. He was fascinated by the concept of AP(E)L. He came on one of the earliest study tours. Whilst sitting on the grass outside the American University in Washington DC waiting for a cab to take him to Dulles Airport, as a computer man himself he said: 'They are giving credit for prior and experiential learning in computer studies in years 1, 2 and 3. If they can do that, why can't we?' That was after examining some of the portfolios of students and making his own judgements about the credit awarded. So he was an early convert to AP(E)L in 1983, and a more influential advocate could not have been found then. He served on the University Grants Committee's Working Party on Continuing Education as well as on a comparable working party for non-university institutions, and in both he urged the case for AP(E)L.

Norbert Singer was Director of Thames Polytechnic. After his conference speech in 1984 on part-time degrees available in the London area, much of the discussion was about the need for a more effective information service about the full range of possibilities for part-time study, so that the general public knew what the institutions were doing to extend their services. But many contributions from the floor turned on the problems of credit accumulation within individual institutions. Issues like transferring from full-time study to part-time and vice versa, and switching from one study area to another. Knowing by that time a good deal about American systems, I suggested afterwards to Norbert Singer, who had been on the first study tour, that surely what was needed was a credit accumulation system which ran across institutions, not merely within them. Knowing that he was on the key academic committee of CNAA, I went on to say that CNAA was the only body in the country which could introduce such a development. Did he think that CNAA would do anything about it? The upshot was that I took a draft letter about the possibility to Edwin Kerr and asked whether he would be prepared to act if he received it officially. He told me to get it signed by two polytechnic directors who served on that key committee. So off went the letter duly co-signed by Norbert Singer and Ray Ricketts, Director of Middlesex Polytechnic. Now, it may well be the case that others had been pressing for the same initiative, but I do not know of them. Clearly, it cannot have been a new thought for Edwin. What I do know factually is the account just given.

From that point on, Edwin took personal command. He got CNAA approval to establish a consultative group drawn from the polytechnics, and this included the Master of Birkbeck College and two Regional Directors of the Open University. He steered discussions through heated opposition from some polytechnics who claimed that such a scheme would rob them of students who would otherwise come to them. In the end, there was one convincing argument, one matter of principle for operating such a scheme and one convenient argument. The convincing argument was that some students wanted combinations of subjects to study which were not available within any one institution. Why should they be denied such an opportunity? They needed to be able to transfer from one institution to another if that was the only way of meeting their curriculum requirements. The point of principle was that anyone enquiring at the CATS Registry would, wherever possible, be referred to a polytechnic offering what the applicant wanted. And the argument of convenience to allay the fears of suspicious polytechnics was that the scheme was a trial, a pilot for the London area only. In 1985, CNAA then approved the proposal and authorized a budget to run the new Registry, which opened a year later once accommodation problems had been solved.

So in May 1986, CNAA's Registry for Credit Accumulation and Transfer was launched. And it had all happened without any government initiative at all. No doubt government could have stopped the development, for certainly senior civil servants knew what was going on. But they had no hand in developments. Given all the more recent, rather frantic, interventions government has taken upon itself, this action seems all the more remarkable.

Almost before the ink was dry on the regulations, some polytechnics up and down the country began to develop their own credit accumulation schemes with AP(E)L services to boot. Middlesex, Newcastle, Sheffield, Thames and Wolverhampton

Polytechnics led the way. And from that point on, with government urging the adoption of credit accumulation schemes, often supported by funded projects from the Department of Employment, CNAA's regulations became the template for all subsequent developments; sometimes with variations, but the structure was secure.

And there were incentives. To encourage wider access and increase the participation rate in higher education, government gave polytechnics higher target figures for admission and funding to support them. In a variety of ways, AP(E)L became one means among many for achieving that expansion.

Nothing comparable was available for further education. Whereas the CATS regulations gave polytechnics a licence to undertake whatever academic innovations they chose, provided they secured CNAA's approval (even though they had no power to award their own degrees since all such degrees were awarded by CNAA itself), further education had no such scope for initiative. There was no similar national structure within which to develop. Through access courses, AP(E)L was beginning to feature in some colleges as part of their regular provision. But beyond that, they were constrained by the regulations of the examining bodies, and so were their students. The only route for them to develop AP(E)L schemes was through collaboration with degree-teaching institutions themselves. And this is what some began to do. Working with polytechnics which were interested in developing feeder courses to fuel their expansion, many further education colleges designed foundation courses alongside access courses, and sometimes AP(E)L featured in them.

The Further Education Unit continued to support developments. It funded some projects in colleges and local education authorities. It commissioned two further publications. *Assessing Experiential Learning* (Evans 1987) was a survey of activities in some eight institutions. *Aspects of Assessing Experiential Learning – Case Studies* (Evans 1987) was a detailed account of what the eight institutions actually did with students. And most important, it commissioned work on possible developments for credit accumulation within a framework of qualifications.

But NCVQ introduced a quite different AP(E)L role for colleges. By the mid-1980s, the government, the Confederation of British Industry (representing employers) and the Trades Union Congress were convinced that some urgent measures had to be taken to increase the general skill level of the workforce. Anxieties about the national economy demanded it. Hence, 1986 saw the establishment of the NCVQ. It followed a 12-month Task Force on the Review of Vocational Qualifications, chaired by George Tolley, who previously had set up the Open Tec for the MSC (Manpower Services Commission) and before that was Principal of Sheffield Polytechnic. His remit was to try to make coherent sense out of the qualifications offered by 300-plus awarding bodies, large numbers of which featured in further education colleges' provision. The then Secretary of State described them as 'a bewildering variety of courses with a multitude of strange initials'. The idea was to create a national framework. The problem was to establish a ladder of progression between them, so that people wishing to switch from one vocational route to another did not have to begin from the bottom all over again, because one body did not recognize a qualification offered by another. Some standardization was needed. And that is what NCVQ was told to do. The implications for further education, and AP(E)L as well, were to be dramatic.

If standardization was necessary, so was some means of making it less confusing for individuals to find their way through the vocational qualifications jungle. Some national framework was necessary. But if the country was to achieve the target of a better-qualified workforce, access to vocational qualifications also had to be simplified. The solution was to put the learner at the centre of planning, rather than leaving it to individuals to find suitable courses.

Putting standardization, a national framework and a learner-centred system together amounted to an attempt to turn upside-down the education and training provision of the country. And this is what NCVQ set out to do.

NCVQ, now incorporated in the Qualifications and Curriculum Authority, was neither an examining nor a curriculum body. It was a verifying authority for certifying those qualifications offered by awarding bodies which merited the award of a National Vocational Qualification (NVQ). It did that through using occupational competences. They were its chosen tool for achieving standardization. Industry lead bodies for every conceivable activity were commissioned to produce definitions of occupational standards through designing competences at four different levels, which constituted the national framework. It was then open to awarding bodies to submit their qualifications for kite-marking with the appropriate level of NVQ.

But assessment was the critical element, and it involved AP(E)L. It had to. It was the essential ingredient for achieving a learner-centred system. NCVQ disaggregated courses of study from assessment. It was interested in one question only for the assessment of individuals. Does this person meet or not meet all the criteria which determine his or her competence for this particular element or unit for this NVQ? In other words, assessment was a yes or no issue. And since NVCQ was not concerned with how someone had become competent, assessment procedures had to incorporate some version or other of AP(E)L. In theory at least, it had to be a 'walk in off the street' set of procedures. If someone claimed to have a particular competence, and wished to present themselves for assessment, there needed to be procedures available to determine the validity of the claim.

So here was a national structure for AP(E)L in further education, but it continued the constraints of the past. And it coincided with the incorporation of colleges by government decision, removing them from local education authority control and making college governing bodies responsible for the financial viability of their colleges. The questions for further education colleges were how to respond and how to make use of the structure on offer. Difficulties abounded. Participation, either by colleges or awarding bodies, was voluntary. NCVQ had no overt powers to require compliance. However, money counts. Awarding bodies wanted to secure examination fees as income from further education colleges; and, in any case, it was not in their interests to ignore government rhetoric about the need to introduce NVQs as soon as possible. So there was plenty of incentive for them to seek NCVQ's kite-marking of their qualifications. But different awarding bodies had different regulations for assessment, so colleges had to learn to cope simultaneously with different versions of AP(E)L procedures. This was costly, both in time and money. Also, colleges soon found that NVQs began to feature in funding systems. The more NVQs achieved by students, the more secure was income. Targets for achieving NVQs appeared. Failure to meet set targets meant forgoing income.

All this posed huge organization and management issues for the colleges. Courses had to be reconfigured to align them with sequences of NVQs attached to them through the kite-marking procedure adopted by NCVQ. Assessment procedures had to be devised, backed up with advice and guidance systems. Above all, staff had to be coaxed, trained and prepared for what, for many, was an entirely new, and sometimes resented, way of working. And external pressures to move down this line mounted.

As part of its efforts to increase the general skill level of the workforce, the government introduced Training and Enterprise Councils (TECs). There were 82 of them. Each had a board of senior business figures in the locality. Their brief was to 'unlock the potential of individuals, companies and communities' in order to promote economic and business growth in their area. Each TEC was set education and training targets, measured by the number of NVQs they registered. Their funding was related to those numbers of NVQs achieved. Since further education colleges could be contracted to deliver NVQs through networks involving employers to reach those targets, they, too, began to find that income was influenced heavily by tallies of NVQs.

Additional pressure to accommodate AP(E)L in all its guises came from the Further Education Funding Council (FEFC). Like polytechnics, further education colleges were removed from the control of local education authorities and became self-governing incorporated institutions responsible for their own financial security. Under these new arrangements, the FEFC made it clear that colleges would need to supplement their annual grant with funds they raised themselves. Since they could earn substantial income from providing education and training courses contracted with TECs, they found that failure to meet target numbers of NVQs meant reductions in the income they had budgeted for. These target requirements complicated attempts by colleges to combine with employers as they did for TECs. And who pays was the continually nagging question. Because of these complications, colleges found they had to ask themselves whether or not they could actually afford to run courses with NVQs attached. Many principals and governing bodies concluded that loss-leaders were a tricky aspect of the market economy they found themselves living in.

Thus, while colleges were more or less forced into reorganizing themselves to cope with these financial uncertainties, the educational reasons requiring them to adapt to the changing circumstances of individuals came into focus as well. AP(E)L had very limited space to develop. And it did so in a structure where it was hooked onto a thoroughgoing attempt to revolutionize education and training provision through requirements to meet NVQs based on occupational competences, but when the older functions of the colleges for post-16 qualifications continued. And, financially, it was connected to a contemporary version of the 19th century's payment by results. It was not an altogether happy evolution.

The irony for further education is that while it worked under all those constraints, it was notably successful in developing very impressive schemes for open and distance learning. But apart from using AP(E)L in collaboration with higher education, the only direct provision was in the training of AP(E)L assessors for NVQs.

First harvest

1986 saw the beginning of growth producing harvest. It also saw the establishment of the Learning from Experience Trust with £70,000 start up funding from the Rowntree Foundation. Sir Charles Carter and I decided that developments in AP(E)L meant that it was time to leave the research base in the Policy Studies Institute and create a small, independent educational charity to act as a ginger group to help speed things along. With Carter as Chairman, and Shirley Williams, former Secretary of State at the Department of Education and Science, Sir Richard O'Brien, the first Chairman of the Manpower Services Commission, Frank Whitely, Deputy Chairman of ICI, Andrew Rutherford, Warden of Goldsmiths' College, Stephen O'Brien, Chief Executive of Business in the Community, and Edwin Kerr as Trustees, and myself as Director, the Trust began to make its contribution to nurturing AP(E)L development. It did so with the clear intention of working on the borderline between formal education and the wider world of employment and all the other activities adults busied themselves with. And it worked within a very modest budget. Over the thirteen years from 1986–1999 its total income was about one and three-quarter million pounds.

The creation of CNAA's CATS Registry gave the Trust the chance to put into action at higher education level the brief that it gave itself from the beginning: to work on the borders between formal education and the world of work and life. Having been part of the planning group for CNAA's CATS Registry from the beginning, I had a clear view of the kinds of collaboration which could hardly have been contemplated earlier. The MSC agreed to fund two separate but related projects. One was called the Validation of Companies' In-House Courses. Its purpose was to run an academic slide rule over in-house courses provided for their employees by several major companies. Where they met the necessary criteria, they were given a credit rating. Once that credit rating was approved academically, they were duly validated by CNAA in the same way as if they were courses submitted by education institutions for validation.

The other was called Learning Agreements for Employees (Dearden 1989). This was more complicated. The idea was to build a learning programme for individual employees based on what they were already doing, enabling them to progress academically. Twenty-four volunteers from Wimpey Restaurants, Jaguar Cars, JBS Computers and the MSC itself participated (six from each). Each employer was linked with a member of staff in the relevant discipline from a nearby polytechnic as an academic supervisor. This was hotel and catering management for Wimpey, linked to Oxford Polytechnic; engineering for Jaguar Cars and Coventry Polytechnic; computer studies with Wolverhampton Polytechnic for JBS Computers; and business studies and Sheffield Polytechnic for the MSC. There was a three-way negotiation: to agree a learning programme which (a) was of value to the employer, (b) met the interests and intentions of the volunteer employee and (c) was acceptable as likely to produce evidence of academic work meriting credit towards a degree under the CATS regulations. What was to be learned, how it was going to be learned and how it was to be assessed was all recorded in the learning agreement as a formal document and signed by the three negotiators.

But there was more to it than that. Credit for AP(E)L could also be awarded to the volunteers where they could produce acceptable evidence. And credit could also be awarded for any in-house courses which had been validated, as through the project just mentioned. This meant that the employers each had six employees who could attract academic credit from three different sources. It also meant that, when the volunteers had completed their learning agreement, they would have accumulated credit points towards whatever qualification they were seeking, so that they knew what further work they would have to undertake for graduation.

Inevitably, there were problems to overcome, and uncertainties to attempt to solve. Naturally, the employees wanted to know how much credit they were likely to earn from both the negotiated agreement and their AP(E)L. Beyond a general prediction, which might or might not be accurate, it was impossible for the supervisors to give a satisfying answer. Then the question of time. What would happen, they wanted to know, if their work assignments meant that they did not have the time to complete the learning agreement by the agreed date? The difficulty of that was that the project was for 14 months only, so there had to be some judicious adjustments to the various sections of the activity. And there was the delicate matter of the amount of support each employee enjoyed from the employer.

Those teething problems amounted to several lessons on how best to conduct such an enterprise. It was notable that the progress made by each volunteer reflected the amount of support forthcoming from the employer. No surprise really, but it indicated that it was irresponsible and potentially damaging to employees to launch any such scheme unless the employer was thoroughly committed in advance. It was clear that any AP(E)L claims ought to be dealt with before tackling negotiations for a learning agreement. And, as with any other innovation designed to help individuals attain their intentions, there needed to be well-informed advice services to make sure in advance that their efforts were going to be on target.

Despite those difficulties and uncertainties, the 24 volunteers came out of the project with success marked up positively against their names. Some non-graduate employees at Jaguar went straight through to complete a master's degree with Coventry Polytechnic. Wimpey's employees linked their work to an internal development programme and suffered, unfortunately, from internal staff changes. MSC staff variously used their credit towards a diploma in management, degrees in business studies, and one for career advancement. This civil servant was promoted on the strength of the portfolio of work presented to superiors, as they saw no need for further qualifications. And while volunteers from JBS Computers went on to further study at Wolverhampton Polytechnic, the Managing Director explained that the exercise revealed that those he thought his weaker employees turned out to be the strongest as learners and prompted him to review his appointment criteria.

Both these projects were firsts. Nothing like it had been attempted in the country before. As such they were firsts – successful sign-posting routes for the future. Very quickly, the principles were put to work more widely. Government took a hand. Having been shown what was possible and how to set about it, right away the MSC funded four additional projects on 'work-based learning' (WBL), as it came to be called, which added Oxford and Coventry to the list of institutions pioneering their own schemes. That was merely the first raft of a succession of projects extending over the following 12 years, costing millions of pounds of development money. Many projects like those on WBL connected directly with AP(E)L. Others concentrated on advice and guidance, student support, flexible curriculum arrangements and credit frameworks. There was a huge programme called Enterprise in Higher Education. AP(E)L, or flavours of it, featured on many of those programmes and projects. All can act catalytically within their institutions. And all were part and parcel of the policy being pursued by the Department of Employment: to do everything possible to encourage higher education to become more responsive to the changing world from which students were coming and to the changing world of employment they would enter. It promoted a WBL Network. Employability was the target. Enhanced productivity and a better prepared workforce was the subtext all the time. And the millions which went into funded projects were from time to time supplemented by extremely well and expensively produced dissemination reports.

And it all began with those first projects on Learning Agreements for Employees and the Validation of Companies' In-House Courses, undertaken by the Learning from Experience Trust in 1986/87. It seemed a telling confirmation of the role of charitable bodies: to attempt something which official bodies were not doing and then, having shown what can be done, leave it to official bodies to develop things fully.

Hence, the possibilities created by CNAA for development were promoted energetically by the Department of Employment, which, as the MSC became the Training Commission and then the Training Agency, was later merged with education, becoming the Department for Education and Employment. Scores of universities were funded to develop schemes, most of which involved AP(E)L in one form or another.

From this point on, the Trust's role changed from being an initiator to that of a minor player, as institutions and the Department of Employment found ways of exploiting the opportunities that CNAA's CATS Registry had created. WBL projects which incorporated some form of AP(E)L burgeoned. Middlesex, by then a university, moved from being the first institution in the land to offer credit for AP(E)L in a higher education award to showing how to exploit the curriculum opportunities offered by WBL, both internally for its own students and externally in partnerships with employers in the UK and beyond.

The Trust continued to try to promote things further. There was a second and larger effort on the validation of companies' in-house courses. Under the title of 'Potential of AP(E)L in Universities' there was an attempt to reach into established universities. That involved Goldsmiths' College, the University of Kent at Canterbury, and Nottingham and Warwick Universities. As with the CNAA project, the thrust was to encourage each institution to devise, introduce and operate an AP(E)L scheme.

The most astonishing result of that project was at Nottingham. Before it was able to award academic credit to AP(E)L candidates, its charter had to be changed. That meant taking recommendations through a succession of committees right up to the Privy Council itself. And, if that was not enough, it introduced to its list of courses, open to all its students, a formal taught course on AP(E)L. There was a double significance in these moves. The first indicated the fundamental issues that some universities had to deal with if they were to become more responsive to the world around them. The second demonstrated the willingness of a highly respected research university to move when it was able to do so. Both points were very important for the Department of Employment to face, since it was disposed to be highly critical of what it perceived as the reluctance of the older universities to react favourably to its various initiatives.

Academic credit for WBL in non-vocational undergraduate degrees was another initiative of the Trust in 1992/3. The idea was simply to take one term of the twelve in a three-year programme for students to spend four days a week in a work placement, working to a learning agreement duly negotiated and signed by student, employer and academic, and one day a week in the home institution for seminars and debriefing. The students' learning was then assessed and the amount of credit granted was the same as if they had been attending formal classes. Chester College of Higher Education, Liverpool John Moores University and Liverpool University collaborated in the project (which resulted in Work Based Learning for Academic Credit 1993). Its success meant that each institution incorporated the scheme in its regular provision. Most recently, the University of East Anglia has adopted a variation of the scheme and intends to enrol on it 500 students annually as part of their degree studies.

The Trust also tried another route to engage employers. This was to take as read that learning went on at work, but to try to find ways of converting it into intentional learning. Supervisors seemed the likely best instrument. In co-operation with GEC Alsthom, GEC Marconi Communications and GEC Management College, supervisors were taken through procedures for identifying their own strengths and weaknesses and then set the task of applying the same procedures to some of those for whom they were responsible for supervising. The project was beset with difficulties arising from the economic recession which hit the companies hard. But it was relatively successful in demonstrating the truth of the assertion that, on the whole, companies knew little about their employees, and that when they did know more about them they could make better use of them (Braham 1993).

This was confirmed amply by the Ford Motor Company. It needed to increase rapidly the number of its graduate engineers. It developed a number of different schemes with different universities. AP(E)L ran through many of those schemes. The head of training for the company had no hesitation in saying that without AP(E)L his budget could not have funded the number required on full-time courses. It was benefiting from what those non-graduate engineers had learned already which enabled him to meet the targets set by Ford top brass management. In the process, too, initiatives taken by some of the non-graduate learners as part of the WBL element in the degree programme saved the company considerable sums of money.

Social work was another area for development, the prime question being: how to enable experienced social workers to acquire a post-experience qualification without attending courses which, like as not, would purport to teach them much of what they knew already, and would not necessarily enable them to tackle what they thought they needed to know? Answer: consult them and their employer – essential that – on what they anticipated they needed to know; express it in terms of learning outcomes; provide a mixture of academic tutorial support and supervisor support; and, using their work-based learning as a launching pad, let them tackle in their own good time the learning they needed to acquire and assess it through procedures for AP(E)L. Something similar developed for experienced nurses and associated activities in the National Health Service.

There were other schemes. Some TECs included AP(E)L in their employee development programmes. Drawing on its experience from evaluating Ford's Employee Development and Assistance Programme, the Trust helped Kent TEC develop its own version of an EDP which included AP(E). The Trust designed a do-it-yourself package for those with disabilities. It promoted another initiative for school governors to capitalize on what they learned from being governors and for those who wished to use it for a formal qualification.

All this is merely indicative of the scope for development which the example of CNAA's CATS Registry created. There was a great deal of activity going on in different parts of the country. Polytechnics, before and after they became universities, not only incorporated AP(E)L in many of their degree schemes, especially part-time programmes, but they began to do their own validation of companies' in-house courses and introduce collaborative schemes with employers corporately, both public and private. Once CNAA was abolished in 1992, they were free to develop how they thought best.

One intriguing result was that the Open University established the OU Validation Services, based on some of the activities of the former CATS Registry of CNAA. Some of its accredited institutions include AP(E)L in their services for students, and this represented an additional strand for development.

Costs were always a problem for AP(E)L. Right from the beginning, great emphasis was put on the amount of time taken by academics to assess learning claims. With experience, tutors soon learned ways of short-circuiting the more protracted procedures. But with the budget reductions imposed year after year came increasingly the creation of cost centres for different parts of an institution's overall service. Hence, AP(E)L came under financial scrutiny, and charges were introduced at many universities and colleges for some parts of the process. This was not the case where AP(E)L preparation courses were included in an institution's regular course provision. Then, full-time students benefited accordingly. But as part-time students were billed for their tuition, so they came to be billed for parts of the AP(E)L service. How far this deterred would-be applicants is pure guesswork. Certainly, it was seen as an obstacle by some.

All this was relatively straightforward in higher education. The structure was there. The rules were clear. If an institution saw good reason for using AP(E)L, it could do so. Unfortunately, until recently there never has been reliable information nationally of the extent and range of AP(E)L throughout the land in higher education. A generally accepted estimate is that roughly one-third, or some 40 institutions, are, one way or another, using AP(E)L in their mainstream work.

The story here is less clear cut for further education. The Trust tried to make a contribution. The Rowntree Foundation funded a project called the Youth Training Scheme into Higher Education. The idea was to use AP(E)L to enable young people enrolled in the Youth Training Scheme to produce evidence which could be submitted for admission to a higher education course. It was modestly successful, in that two of its ten participants gained admission to a polytechnic. The Trust undertook a survey of procedures adopted by some further education colleges for the FEU. The FEU also funded a project – to try to work out what sort of student services were going to be essential for AP(E)L to work properly in further education (Johnson 1992).

Many colleges reorganized themselves internally as a response to the student-centred policy promoted by the NCVQ and then by General National Vocational Qualifications when they were introduced as alternatives to the General Certificate of Secondary Education (GCSE) and Advanced level GCSEs. Some negotiated successful schemes with major employers to provide access to NVQs in both the public and private sectors. Again, in using NVQs many worked closely with their local TEC.

Financial pressures did something else to AP(E)L. It had to be financed somehow. Under the general idea of 'unbundling' services offered to students, price tickets were attached to the various stages in the procedures for applicants successfully completing their AP(E)L claims. An initial advice session could well be free; but, thereafter, further guidance, assistance in preparing a claim and assessment itself had to be paid for. Inevitably, this meant that whereas widening access and creating greater opportunities was in principle the fundamental purpose of AP(E)L, financial obstacles confronted some who wanted to use them. Add this to the complications already referred to, and it is reasonable to say that the practice of AP(E)L did not expand in colleges at the speed which many had hoped for.

Some colleges adopted AP(E)L procedures in the arrangements they made with universities for teaching some courses in degree programmes or which were accredited for teaching at degree level. But, for the greater part, further education colleges were constrained to apply AP(E)L to NVQs and experience the difficulties referred to earlier.

During all this time, one of the frustrations was that no one in government or funding councils has accepted the importance of collecting information about the range, scope and volume of AP(E)L activity. This is all the more surprising when a succession of centralizing governments have busied themselves with delving into every aspect of higher education without seeming to have grasped the strategic importance of AP(E)L for plans for widening participation even further and its financial implications.

As a comprehensive study of extending access, choice and mobility, David Robertson's *Choosing to Change* (Robertson 1994), a report to the Higher Education Quality Council, offered a thoroughly detailed account of credit accumulation and transfer in all its various guises, internal and off-campus, including AP(E)L, but there was no reliable information about the extent of AP(E)L practices in the system. By default, therefore, the Trust, using is own very limited resources, undertook two modest surveys of its own. Under the title *Curriculum Opportunity: AP(E)L in Higher Education. The Characteristics and Achievements of Some University Students*, reports were issued for the years 1993/94 and 1994/95 (Dearden and Evans 1994; 1995). The first, based on results drawn from ten institutions known to be active with AP(E)L, showed that 786 students had graduated with some AP(E)L component in their degree results. The second used results from 12 institutions showing some 1528 had followed suit, and that from a further four institutions details of another 500-plus students were offered, but not in form which could be collated with the rest. It is impossible to know how far that information is representative nationally. It does show, however, that to a significant extent AP(E)L is being mainstreamed in higher education. That is because every one of those degree results was subjected to the same quality assurance requirements as those applying to regular taught courses.

Second planting

For higher education, this next phase came in a quite remarkable and totally unexpected way. In effect, all higher education institutions are now being urged to apply AP(E)L to their own academic staffs.

This has come about because in July 1997 the National Committee of Inquiry into Higher Education (NCIHE), chaired by Sir Ron Dearing, now Lord Dearing, published its report (Dearing Report 1997). Recommendation 13 read:

> We recommend that institutions of higher education begin immediately to develop or seek access to programmes of teacher training for their staff if they do not have them, and that all institutions seek national accreditation of such programmes from the Institute of Learning and Teaching for Higher Education [ILTHE].

Recommendation 14 was for the establishment of the Institute for Learning and Teaching by the representative bodies in consultation with the Funding Councils.

The government accepted these recommendations. What follows are some fairly extensive quotations from official documents to indicate the full significance of this institutional development for AP(E)L.

The NCIHE's reasoning for the recommendations, given in paragraph 8.76, was to:

> ...raise the status of teaching across higher education, help the UK to become world leader in the practice of teaching at higher levels, and emphasise the importance of learning. This should be a national objective to enable the UK to compete effectively in the next century in a world where the quality, relevance and effectiveness of education and training systems will underpin future prosperity.

In anticipation of these recommendations, the Committee of Vice-Chancellors and Principals convened a planning group, which in January 1998 issued a consultation document. This included a draft of a national statement as a basis for planning programmes for accreditation. When referring to various routes whereby successful completion of the requirements of an accredited programme could be achieved, paragraph 1.18 said:

> ...these [routes] could be work-based, course-based, involved one-on-one mentoring, distance or open learning, the assessment of prior (experiential) learning (AP(E)L), or various combinations of those or other modes.

The next paragraph (1.19) went on:

> It will be important to enable staff to gain membership of the Institute wholly or partly by way of demonstrable experience and qualifications and to cater for people moving from one HEI [higher education institution] to another while following an accredited programme. On way of doing this would be to draw on and adapt as necessary the experience of schemes of assessment which recognize individuals' prior experience and learning. (Some of the schemes are known by the term 'accreditation of prior (experiential) learning AP(E)L', but this is using the word 'accreditation' differently from its use in the present paper. However, the AP(E)L approach deserves very serious consideration as one possible type of pathway.)

And there you have it: suggestions for a second planting of AP(E)L throughout all higher education. In May 1998, a Final Report recorded that there were 176 responses to the questionnaire which followed that consultation paper; 117 from HEIs, 42 from associations and national bodies, and the rest (17) from individuals.

Two questions were these: Is the approach of accrediting a wide range of programmes and pathways, including AP(E)L, practicable?

Will this give sufficient scope for institutions to devise their own solutions to meeting the national statement in their own way?

There was general agreement that it did. There followed the usual discussion of the difficulties posed by AP(E)L – cost, time taken – but most emphasis was put on the need for training in those institutions without experience of AP(E)L. In paragraph f.1.1. this was because 'it was recognised that internal assessors would have to be trained and that procedures would need to be well-structured, rigorous and fair. AP(EL) should not be seen as a soft option, an easy route to membership. It was suggested that in due course the Institute should draw up guidelines on AP(E)L.' It was also suggested in some responses that 'no pathway should be based on AP(E)L alone', emphasis being put on 'the sharing of experience and ideas with others similarly placed'. paragraph f.1.2

So in 11 years it is full circle. One hundred and sixty-seven HEIs on the Funding Council's list are being asked to take AP(E)L seriously for their own academic staff. Perhaps now, in 1999, CNAA's Development Services Publication 17 (Evans 1988) needs to be taken off the shelf and read again. And it would be as well to look at the Guidelines issued by the Higher Education Quality Council before it too was scrapped and replaced by the Quality Assurance Agency.

One can only guess at the harvest this second planting will produce. Given the current emphasis on lifelong learning, it seems not improbable that, as some academics in some institutions go through an AP(E)L procedure towards membership of the ILTHE, they will recognize its value for others. Domino-like, their views of pedagogy and curriculum may change. Their experience could lead to a wider recognition and acceptance that learning in the workplace, and indeed through life experience in general, can be significant and often viable academically. Collaboration between education and the world of work could be strengthened. Student-centred learning could become the touchstone for academic teaching. Lifelong learning could be brought nearer to realization.

How far further education will feature in this second planting is unclear. Those colleges which are now engaged in undergraduate teaching will either seek accreditation for their own teacher training courses or, more probably, will make use of the programmes offered by their higher education collaborators. The big issue for them, however, is whether future schemes for enhancing the skill base of the workforce will open the way for a second planting in them for AP(E)L.

Right at the end of the chronological account, the government has given another surprise twist to the AP(E)L story. At last, it is taking seriously the need for reliable national information about the range and extent of AP(E)L activities throughout the system. It has funded the Trust to conduct the inquiry. Early indications are that, of the 138 HELs polled, 107 responded, of which 70 said that their institutions had AP(E)2 policies and 11 were thinking about it. In the second stage of the inquiry, 52 institutions responded, out of the 62 which said they would participate, of which 42 showed some AP(E)L activity. The reason for this sudden interest appears to be that the Treasury is anxious about the financial implications of the Prime Minister's recent commitment to a participation of 50 per cent compared with the current figure of around 40 per cent. Somewhere in the official mind, AP(E)L probably connects with lifelong learning as well. So it is almost as if AP(E)L is moving into a third phase in higher education. First came getting it going with the government as an interested observer. Then came giving it a run for its money with the government as supporter. And now boosters for further development are coming from the government itself.

If the combination of the thrust for AP(E)L through the Institute for Learning and Teaching and the mapping/survey initiative looks like a second planting, it is anyone's guess what the second harvest of activities will look like. One thing is certain: the landscape of AP(E)L will have changed.

So, as with many fairy tales, for AP(E)L in England, the story which began in 1979, has a relatively happy ending with the promise of another tale to come. No one could have predicted it. Common sense might have suggested that in time it was bound to come.

References

Braham, J. (1993) *Learning for Success*. London: Learning from Experience Trust.

Buckle, J. (1988) *A Learner's Introduction to Building on Your Experience*. London: Learning from Experience Trust.

Craft, W., Evans, N. and Keeton, M. (1997) *Learners All – Worldwide*. London: Learning from Experience Trust.

Dearden, G. (1989) *Learning while Earning: Learning Contracts for Employees*. London: Learning from Experience Trust.

Dearden, G. and Evans, N. (1994) *Curriculum Opportunity: AP(E)L in Higher Education. The Characteristics and Achievements of Some University Students*, 1st edn. London: Learning from Experience Trust.

Dearden, G. and Evans, N. (1995) *Curriculum Opportunity: AP(E)L in Higher Education. The Characteristics and Achievements of Some University Students*, 2nd edn. London: Learning from Experience Trust.

Dearing Report (1997) *The National Committee of Inquiry into Higher Education: Report of the Committee.* London: HMSO.

Evans, N. (1981) *The Knowledge Revolution.* London: Grant McIntyre.

Evans, N. (1983) *Curriculum Opportunity: A Map of Experiential Learning in Entry Requirements to Higher and Further Education Award Bearing Courses.* London: Further Education Unit.

Evans, N. (1984a) *Exploiting Experience.* London: Further Education Unit.

Evans, N. (1984b) *Access to Higher Education: Non Standard Entry to CNAA First Degree and DipHE Courses.* London: Council for National Academic Awards, Development Services Publication.

Evans, N. (1987) *Assessing Experiential Learning.* London: Longman, for Further Education Unit.

Evans, N. (1987) *Aspects of Assessing Experiential Learning – Case Studies.* London: Further Education Unit.

Evans, N. (1988) *The Assessment of Prior Experiential Learning.* London: Council for National Academic Awards, Development Services Publication 17.

Johnson, M. (1992) *The Assessment of Prior Learning and Learner Services.* London: Further Education Unit.

Robertson, D. (1994) *Choosing to Change.* London: Higher Education Quality Council.

Storan, J. (1988) *Making Experience Count.* London: Learning from Experience Trust.

Contributors from Chester College, Liverpool John Moores University and Liverpool University (1993) *Work Based Learning for Academic Credit.* London: Learning from Experience Trust.

CHAPTER 4

Canada: The Story of Prior Learning Assessment and Recognition

Deborah Blower

Introduction

This chapter begins by taking inventory of Canada's experiences with prior learning assessment and recognition (PLAR) – reflecting on where we have been, what we have done and what we have learned as a result of substantial projects and PLAR implementation in many sectors. PLAR began in the 1980s; and since the early 1990s, it has burgeoned in many directions. PLAR implementation is occurring on both a national and provincial level, within secondary and post-secondary education, particularly in the college system. Its emergence in workplace training models, business and industry, community-based organizations and professional accrediting/regulatory bodies indicates both a growing interest and a commitment to PLAR practice. Although PLAR is implemented differently in many jurisdictions, the ultimate goal has been to provide individuals with the opportunity to obtain recognition for learning – no matter where, when or how it was learned – through fair, equitable, transparent, flexible and accessible ways.

PLAR is basically a process of identifying, documenting, assessing and recognizing learning that has been acquired through many means of formal and informal study, including work and life experience, training, independent study, volunteer work, hobbies, travel and so on. The PLAR process examines the learning an individual has acquired as it applies to the individual's particular goals – whether that be academic credit from an educational institution, job entry/advancement in the workplace or demonstration of competency for occupational/professional certification. Flexible assessment practices, such as portfolio review of direct and indirect evidence, demonstration or challenge processes (i.e. written/oral examinations, projects, assignments, performance demonstration, product assessments, interviews), standardized tests and programme review, are currently used to determine what learning has occurred. Qualified specialists in education or the workplace assess the learning evidence.

Throughout Canada's PLAR history, terms such as experiential learning, credit for prior learning and prior learning assessment (PLA) have been used. Although the most common term used today is PLAR, both PLA and PLAR have been used in this chapter to reflect the terminology of the various stakeholders. In closing, the chapter briefly explores the challenges Canada faces with PLAR implementation and recommends possible solutions, some currently underway, to ensure the sustainability and future growth of PLAR in Canada.

Historical development

Although PLAR has been practised informally for many years, it began in a more formal sense at the post-secondary level, in the college system as a means to grant academic credit for learning achieved outside of the educational system. Earliest use of PLAR practice was in the Diploma Nursing (1980), Dental Assisting (1981) and the Early Childhood Education (1983) programmes at Red River College of Applied Arts, Science and Technology in Winnipeg, Manitoba. Early PLA activity was driven by the institutions' desire to meet the needs of mature learners who were returning to college with significant learning from work and life experience related to their programmes of study, and the professional bodies' immediate need for qualified practitioners (Blower 1997). Two Ontario colleges, First Nations Technical Institute (FNTI) and Mohawk College, also began PLA in the early 1980s.

Québec was the first province in Canada to begin province-wide PLA implementation. In the mid-1980s, at the recommendation of the Jean Commission of Education, Québec introduced a PLA system at the secondary and CEGEP (college) level. This initiative, funded by the Department of Manpower and Immigration – Canada, focused on four priorities: the development of PLA methods and tools for the establishment of experiential learning programmes in all Québec CEGEPs; the implementation of PLA in the CEGEP system; the implementation of a provincial research and development structure to provide the CEGEPs with technical and financial assistance to ensure co-ordination and liaison between the institutions; and to improve the relationship between CEGEP programmes and labour market needs (Isabelle 1987). From the onset, training in PLA methodology was a priority. Key organizations in the USA namely, the Council for Adult and Experiential Learning (CAEL), the American Council on Education and the Education Testing Service – and Québec PLA practitioners provided training and services for the development of extensive policies, processes and resources to further PLAR in Québec's CEGEPs. Building on the Québec expertise and the PLA activity occurring in the UK and USA, other provinces in Canada began to formally implement PLAR.

During the early and middle years of the 1990s, while pockets of PLAR activity were developing in post-secondary institutions across the country, a few provinces began provincial post-secondary PLAR initiatives. Of note here, is that the development of PLAR took a provincial rather than a national direction. Canada is one of the few countries in the developing world that does not have a national education system. Education is a provincial jurisdiction. Each of the ten provinces and two territories has its own educational standards, policies, procedures and programmes designed to meet the needs of its learners. Individual provinces have created excellent models that have allowed PLAR to develop within the specific infrastructure and needs of each Canadian province. The challenge has been to ensure that transferability and portability of credentials are available for individuals within the provinces and across Canada.

In addition to Québec, five other provinces (Ontario, New Brunswick, Nova Scotia, Newfoundland, British Columbia) have implemented province-wide PLAR initiatives, including development of policies and implementation strategies at the secondary and/or post-secondary levels, specifically in the college system. The government of Ontario, early in 1993, began the implementation of a comprehensive PLAR system in all colleges of applied arts and technology. This three-year implementation initiative was the culmination of the Ontario government's research and consultation on the PLAR process. Today, all 25 colleges in Ontario have PLAR in place, including policies and procedures, assessment practices and training for faculty advisers and assessors (Ontario Council of Regents 1994).

In 1994 and 1997 respectively, New Brunswick and Nova Scotia instituted provincial PLAR policies for their college systems. To date, the colleges provide PLAR processes and services, and the system is enhanced with a learning outcomes approach to college programming.

Between 1995 and 1997, the government of Newfoundland and Labrador conducted a province-wide initiative to facilitate the implementation of PLAR in the public college system. This initiative included the development and delivery of comprehensive training to college personnel, the development of provincial guidelines for institutional policy, and the development and distribution of marketing tools and strategies to raise awareness of PLAR. In 1997/98, the government also conducted a project to facilitate the implementation of PLAR within apprenticeship training in both public and private colleges.

The province of British Columbia (BC) has tackled the implementation of PLAR in the most far-reaching way. Beginning in the early 1990s with policy guidelines and standards for colleges, institutes and universities, BC has moved forward with its implementation strategy to the extent that the 26 post-secondary institutions provide programmes and services to support the flexible assessment of prior learning. At the heart of BC's system is the Centre for Curriculum, Transfer and Technology (C2T2), which co-ordinates and supports the development of the initiative across the province. The C2T2 continues to provide extensive training opportunities to ensure that high-quality PLAR services are offered by the institutions. A Provincial Steering Committee on PLA provides leadership, direction and advocacy to the provincial initiative. An Institutional Coordinators Working Group, comprising of individuals from each institution responsible for implementing PLAR, supports the objectives of the Provincial Steering Committee on PLA and reports to C2T2 (Matthews 1997).

With funding from the provincial ministry, a PLAR system and extensive involvement from knowledgeable PLAR practitioners, BC has moved quickly with implementation. The work of many, including international PLAR consultant Susan Simosko, has fostered this development and a new vision for educational reform. Simosko, in *Prior Learning Assessment and Educational Reform: A Vision for Now* (Simosko 1995), outlined critical issues for creating system-wide change in BC so that PLA was not marginalized as a stand-alone service. Simosko envisioned assessment and learning as part of a continuous process for learners – who were active partners in the learning process and were supported by faculty who would serve as both advisers and assessors. The BC model includes a variety of flexible assessment practices that measure learning against clear, assessable learning outcomes for courses and programmes. There is an emphasis on ensuring quality in the process and technically sound assessments (Simosko 1997). These characteristics of the emerging BC system exemplify a model of best practice for all of Canada.

In other provinces, such as Alberta, Saskatchewan and Manitoba, many PLAR projects and initiatives are also under way.

PLAR at the national level

During the early and middle years of the 1990s, a number of national organizations, including Canada's federal government, recognized the importance of PLAR and began to provide support for its continued development. The federal government body Human Resources Development Canada (HRDC) has been extensively involved in marketing PLAR through promotion and information-sharing materials. HRDC has consulted with provincial governments to identify activities and areas in which HRDC might participate to further the development of PLAR, and has facilitated the development of training partnerships for learners and industry that include PLAR. HRDC has examined the practices used to grant advanced standing in apprenticeship training, and has identified potential uses for PLAR practice. The federal government's most significant work has been the continuing support to national sector councils to promote the integration of PLAR into occupational standards initiatives and sectorally sponsored training.

The involvement of HRDC in the PLAR movement has supported the development of projects and provided a national perspective in the promotion of PLAR. HRDC continues to provide support through funding for such activities as: biennial national PLAR conferences, sectorally sponsored pilot projects, publication guides for PLAR partnerships and, most recently, a research study on PLAR activity in seven Canadian colleges.

The Canadian Labour Force Development Board (CLFDB) has made PLAR one of its priority areas for policy development. CLFDB is a national advisory body made up of: labour market partner organizations including employers, workers and unions; groups seeking equality (i.e. women, aboriginal people, visible minorities and people with disabilities); and training and education services (schools, colleges, universities and training institutions). Early in 1994, the CLFDB began consultation with all labour market partners to determine how Canada could improve its labour force development system. CLFDB was intent on determining solutions that would make efficient use of available resources and skills, and make it easier for individuals to secure education and training, to get a job and to move more easily from education or training programmes to work.

In 1996, after extensive consultation and research, CLFDB, believing that increased use of PLAR could benefit all Canadians, proposed national PLAR standards. These 14 minimum standards, available on the CLFDB website (**http://www.plar.com.english. html**), are fundamental to the systematic implementation of PLAR in Canada. The CLFDB believes that the application of these standards on a nationwide basis will achieve the following six important public policy goals: efficient use of resources; development of a lifelong learning culture; advancement of social justice; co-ordinated and consistent labour force development; reform of education and training systems; and effective management of change (CLFDB 1996, 1997). Today, these national standards provide a framework for an effective PLAR system and serve as widely accepted voluntary principles for the establishment of good PLAR practice. In furthering its commitment to PLAR, CLFDB has developed a PLAR Quality Audit Tool, designed for organizations and institutions implementing PLAR, to compare PLAR services against the national PLAR standards. The quality audit assesses PLAR services from the point of view of users, to determine how well the service meets consumer needs in an accessible, relevant, efficient and productive way.

Other CLFDB projects include: the development of a Skills Knowledge Profile Tool currently being tested with various community groups; a research project report, *Reaching Our Full Potential: Prior Learning Assessment and Recognition for Foreign Trained Canadians* (CLFDB 1999); and research on a Canadian strategy for the recognition of workplace training. The CLFDB organized the 1997 National PLAR Forum, attended by over 600 delegates from across Canada, and, with its partner organizations, the recent 1999 National PLAR Forum in Vancouver, BC.

Nationally, both HRDC and CLFDB continue to advocate for the development of PLAR by providing project leadership and funding that enables PLAR issues to be addressed and policies and systems to be facilitated across the nation. Their involvement helps to ensure that PLAR remains on the national agenda.

PLAR in Canada's secondary and post-secondary education system

Secondary schools

The secondary school system (i.e. Grade 7 to 12) has in recent years become involved in PLAR. Three provinces – British Columbia, Ontario and Québec have established provincial policies and initiatives in PLAR in this area. As part of the Ontario Secondary School Reform, PLAR policy was announced in January 1998 that will allow adolescents and adult learners to access challenge processes for credit in Grades 10–12. British Columbia, through its province-wide PLAR strategy, provides challenge processes for Grades 10–12 and equivalency assessments for external learning activities with no maximum limit set. The Québec government has instituted policies, assessment tools and provides funding for PLAR in 50 vocational education programmes. Assessments are also available in non-vocational programmes (Van Kleef 1998). Adult learners will have access to a greater number of credits through both challenge and equivalency credit processes in these provinces. Other provinces in Canada have policies which allow learners to challenge one or two credits in specific grades, often with a set maximum per grade level. Some standardized testing, such as the General Educational Development (GED) test, provides learners with the opportunity to demonstrate equivalent secondary school learning.

An interesting PLAR practice used in the secondary school system is that of portfolio development. In Manitoba, since the mid-1990s, a number of secondary schools require students to develop a portfolio detailing and providing proof of their knowledge, skills and abilities throughout their senior school years. These students graduate with usable skill portfolios that can open the door for entry into post-secondary education or the workforce (Blower 1996).

Post-secondary – colleges

Canada's college system has taken a leadership role in the development and implementation of PLAR. Significant policy implementation in some provinces has greatly increased the number of institutions and the number of learners involved in PLAR activity. There has been substantial development of PLAR policies and processes, system implementation and training of facilitators, advisers and assessors. In the college system, the introduction of PLAR has often served as the catalyst for the development of learning outcomes-based curricula. Learning outcomes-based curricula, describing what a learner will know and be able to do at the end of a course or programme, provide the parameters for the development of flexible assessment processes and the learners' subsequent proof of the learning. The learning must be current, relevant to course or programme and of sufficient breadth and depth to ensure college-level learning. Through a variety of individualized flexible assessment methods, learners demonstrate learning and receive credit recognition in college programmes.

College learners accessing PLAR benefit from increased confidence in their own abilities, increased motivation to continue learning, the elimination of duplicate learning, and savings in time as well as tuition costs. The colleges benefit as they are able to serve a more diverse population, increase institutional efficiency by eliminating the need for unnecessary training, more appropriately place learners in programmes, and increase recruitment and retention in college programmes. PLAR offers the colleges a wonderful opportunity to partner with business, industry and the community. Many partnerships have been initiated, with PLAR as the driving force.

Perhaps one of the most significant benefits of PLAR implement-ation has been for college faculty. The implementation of PLAR practice has provided faculty with the opportunity to broaden their understanding of flexible assessment and to rethink their approaches to learning and teaching. College policy development ensures that faculty and other staff involved in PLAR receive training in best practice and have the opportunity for continued professional development. Québec, Ontario, New Brunswick, Newfoundland and British Columbia have developed intensive province-wide training for college faculty covering a wide range of topics, including: local/provincial policies for PLAR implementation; advising and supporting PLAR candidates; marketing PLAR services; conducting PLAR orientations; flexible assessment practices; developing PLAR materials; and portfolio development. These training sessions, offered on-site or through distance education by qualified PLAR practitioners, are supported with well-developed PLAR resources and help to ensure quality practice in flexible assessment.

Many excellent examples of best practice in PLAR, including partnerships with industry, business and the community, abound within the college system. If Canadian colleges are able to access sufficient funding, continue to develop flexible assessment practices, implement PLAR in fair, equitable and transparent ways and provide the 'top up' training that may be required as a result of assessment, then PLAR practice will increase in the college system.

Post-secondary – universities

Universities in Canada are debating the merits of PLAR and its implementation. PLAR has been practised informally for years in the university sector, but the process, other than the opportunity for challenge examinations, for the most part, has not been formalized. Most PLAR in the university sector occurs in the continuing education (non-degree credit programmes) area and to a much lesser extent in degree programmes.

During the past few years, increasing numbers of universities across Canada have begun to adopt PLAR policies and processes. For example, in British Columbia, universities have received funds from the Ministry of Education, Skills and Training for the development of policies, programmes and services to support flexible assessment practice. There are examples of PLAR use for flexible admission in part-time degree programmes and provision for credit for non-traditional learning. One BC university uses an outcomes-based learning approach and includes flexible assessment of prior learning in its programmes. Athabasca University in Alberta is a leader in PLAR at the university level. This open university, specializing in distance education, established the Centre for Learning Accreditation in 1996 to evaluate and recognize learning from experience, training workshops and self-directed study for university credit.

Other groups supporting PLAR in the university sector include the Canadian Association for University Continuing Education (CAUCE), an organization for professional development in university. In addition to research and promotion of PLAR, CAUCE supported the development of a handbook that promotes the learning outcomes-based approach to university programmes and provides an overview of PLAR practice (Collins 1996). The Council of Ontario Universities developed a policy supporting PLAR at universities and currently co-ordinates and supports PLAR pilot projects funded by the Ontario Ministry of Education and Training. Universities in other provinces have received grant funding and are investigating the feasibility of PLAR implementation. For the university sector, until PLAR has proved its worth, most implementation will be on a project-by-project basis.

PLAR in the workplace, regulatory bodies and other professional organizations

Workplace

Since the mid-1990s, PLAR has evolved to include partnerships between education, business, industry and labour. These partnerships forge the development of strategic alliances to promote workforce development. PLAR is used for academic credit within the partner institution(s), for labour entry and job promotions, and provides the opportunity for employees to develop lifelong learning strategies and plans. PLAR in the workplace can involve flexible assessment of an employee's learning as it relates to specific criteria, as well as a process of programme evaluation whereby training programmes from the workplace are assessed for their value by another organization (i.e. educational institution, regulatory body, etc.).

Often, PLAR is the catalyst for the development of workplace and institutional partnerships because it provides benefits for all parties. Currently in Canada, these partnerships include business, industry, sector councils, educational institutions, industry education councils, provincial apprenticeship boards and community organizations. These partnerships require close co-operation, commitment and active participation from all partners in the development and implementation of PLAR.

Excellent examples of partnerships with PLAR as a key component have been implemented in the steel, mining, telecommunications and aerospace industries. For example, the Canadian Steel Trade and Employment Congress (CSTEC), a joint initiative of the United Steel Workers of America and 34 steel-producing companies in Canada (CSTEC 1996a); and 21 colleges/CEGEPs from six provinces (Québec, Nova Scotia, Ontario, Saskatchewan, Manitoba, Alberta) have jointly developed a national Steel Industry Training Program (SITP) to deliver training for steel industry workers. The SITP provides recognition and credit equivalency to workers in the steel industry for their prior learning, including that from work and life experience. The recognition of prior learning offers significant time and cost savings, both to workers and employers, and acts as an important incentive to further cost-effective investments in training. The SITP uses a flexible approach to assessing and recognizing prior learning. Several assessment methods (including portfolio development, demonstration processes and programme review) have been developed jointly by CSTEC and the participating colleges/CEGEPs to meet the needs and resource constraints of the steel industry and its workers. A one-day PLAR training session and the modularization of a portfolio development course are critical components in making PLAR both accessible and affordable to employees and employers (CSTEC 1996b). The Mining Industry Training and Adjustment Council (MITAC), a national sector council, has adapted the CSTEC model; in 1998, MITAC (in partnership with industry and the colleges) began to introduce a national training programme utilizing PLAR processes for mining industry employees across Canada.

These examples, and others such as the Return to Learning programme in Ontario, sponsored by Northern Telecom and local branches of the Canadian Auto Workers Union, are providing access to PLAR and achieving positive results for employers and employees.

Regulatory bodies and other professional organizations

Since the early 1990s, regulatory bodies and professional organizations have been interested and involved with PLAR. Some examples of organizations using PLAR include: Ontario College of Midwives, Ontario College of Nurses, Certified General Accountants Association of Ontario and the Credit Union Institute of Canada. These organizations recognize the value of lifelong learning where individuals must constantly re-skill and retrain to remain current in our rapidly changing and mobile society.

An excellent example of a national strategy to enhance worker mobility, and assess worker competence against a national standard, is the Canadian Technology Human Resources Board (CTHRB) TechnoFile project. The CTHRB, established in 1995, is a partnership of employers, practitioners and educators who publish and maintain industry-defined national Canadian Technology Standards for technicians and technologists. As part of their mandate to assist Canadian industrial and occupational organizations to resolve human resource issues, the CTHRB has developed a national programme to meet the diverse needs of technicians and technologists. This TechnoFile project includes:

- CTHRB's national PLAR policy and PLAR guidebook, developed by the Alberta Society of Engineering Technologists and PLAR experts and practitioners from across Canada (CTHRB 1998a). These PLAR policies conform with national and international principles identified by CLFDB and CAEL. The PLAR guidebook provides direction for validating agents involved in the development and implementation of PLAR.

- The Technology PROfile – an on-line three-part portfolio document designed for technicians and technologists to maintain during their careers.

- The TechnoFile – a unique on-line database for technicians and technologists to manage their career records and validate their competencies against the national technician/technology standards. Validation of skills against the Canadian Technology Standards can be completed through an accredited validation agent (CTHRB 1998b).

In September 1998, the CTHRB in partnership with the Canadian Association for Prior Learning Assessment developed the validating agent process to ensure transferability and acceptance across Canada and quality assurance in assessment practice. This project provides numerous benefits for technicians and technologists trained in Canada and abroad.

PLAR advocacy organizations

Canada's greatest strength in PLAR lies in its advocacy organizations and its core of dedicated PLAR practitioners committed to the implementation of fair and credible PLAR practices. The Canadian Association for Prior Learning Assessment (CAPLA), a national association for the advancement of PLA, was formed in 1994 and officially incorporated in June 1997. Its Canada-wide membership includes individuals and organizations from educational institutions, business, industry, labour, government and the community. CAPLA's mission is to work towards the development of educational services which are flexible and responsive to the changing needs and circumstances of adult learners. CAPLA advocates for continuous learning opportunities and formal acknowledgement of previous learning. Utilizing the skills and resources of its members, CAPLA provides a consultation and training service, maintains a website, distributes a quarterly publication (*The Hub*) hosts an annual PLAR conference and offers members access to an extensive resource library.

During the past year, CAPLA, with funding from HRDC, has initiated research on the development of national benchmarks for the assessment of prior learning. These benchmarks would build on the CLFDB's National PLAR Standards, focusing on the assessment process, assessment practices and assessor/practitioner training. CAPLA believes the development of standards of quality practice is essential to ensure: that assessment practices are applied consistently in all sectors across Canada; that credit and recognition of learning can be transferred readily in a standardized, flexible, cost-effective manner; that quality issues are addressed nationally; and that PLAR's impact as an instrument of educational change is fully recognized. These standards are of great importance nationally and internationally. When there is a common agreed standard for PLAR, strategic national and international alliances between educational institutions, business, industry and labour can be greatly enhanced.

Two provinces, Manitoba and Ontario, have active networks devoted to the advancement of PLAR. Both the Ontario Prior Learning Assessment Network and the Manitoba Prior Learning Assessment Network provide ongoing professional development, networking opportunities and strategies for developing and sharing resources. Members represent education, business, industry, union, government and community organizations.

One of the most interesting PLAR developments in the past few years has been the opening of two community-based PLA centres. These two centres – one in Halifax, Nova Scotia, in 1996, the other in Winnipeg, Manitoba, in 1998 – have generated significant interest in other Canadian constituencies because of their inclusive community-based model approach.

The Halifax PLA Centre in Nova Scotia, funded by HRDC, was initiated as a joint project by five Metro universities, the Nova Scotia Community College and the Native Council of Nova Scotia. Its board of directors includes representatives from community groups, government agencies, organized labour and the corporate sector. With a core staff of four, the Centre draws on the personnel of the participating institutions for its PLA advisers.

A key element of the Centre's mandate is to encourage and support the adoption of PLAR principles and practices in the Nova Scotia post-secondary system. Besides briefings, workshops and symposia, the Centre is now engaged in pilot 'portfolio development' courses at four universities in fields ranging from a graduate-level programme in public administration for mid-career civil servants, to undergraduate candidates for programmes in public relations and tourism.

The Nova Scotia Centre's most striking feature is its involvement in PLAR applications for a diverse range of clients, outside of the context of formal post-secondary education. Since its opening, over 1100 individuals have used the Centre for advising services, 'transferable skills' workshops or 'portfolio development' courses. The

Centre provides these services in workplace settings – at Canadian Forces Base Halifax, for civilian employees of the Department of National Defence, and in communities outside Halifax.

The Centre also plays a capacity-building role in the field. In the spring of 1998, it launched its first train-the-trainer 'Portfolio Development for Practitioners' programme. The Centre is also exploring the application of interactive software to provide PLAR services and programmes via the internet.

'The diversity of the client groups we work with is the most interesting and productive aspect of the Centre,' says its executive director, Douglas Myers. He continues:

> We are learning a great deal about the applicability and effective-
> ness of prior learning assessment in a wide variety of settings. We
> can also make progress in several areas, instead of simply being de-
> pendent on one. The PLA Centre seems to be a useful and
> innovative model for negotiated change across a number of agen-
> cies and constituencies. (Myers 1998)

The Manitoba PLA Centre's mandate is to raise the profile and practice of PLAR across the province and to assist advocates and practitioners to demonstrate PLAR as an essential feature of an employment transition and post-secondary education system. The Centre is incorporated as a not-for-profit entity and is governed by a board of directors. The Centre's advisory services, including the provision of PLAR information and guidance on documenting and validating prior learning through a portfolio process, are available to a wide range of clients. The Centre's developmental services focus on: assisting Manitoba organizations to develop PLAR programmes, policies and initiatives; providing training for advisers and assessors of prior learning; assisting with the development of PLAR partnerships between education and workplace; and the development of PLAR processes for self-accrediting bodies (Dedi 1998). Both centres offer a community-based model and services that are essential for furthering the PLAR cause.

PLAR for Canada's aboriginal and minority learners

Canada is a multicultural and multilingual country. One of Canada's challenges for PLAR is to ensure it is incorporated into systems which will meet the needs of aboriginal and minority learners. Currently in Canada, a number of initiatives promote this advancement. Some of the best examples of programmes for aboriginal learners are those offered at the First Nations Technical Institute (FNTI) in Ontario. For over 14 years, FNTI has been developing and refining an approach to learning which integrates the values, beliefs and traditions of the aboriginal learner. This model is based on an understanding of the aboriginal culture, a deep respect for the learner and a belief that the learning process is an important and powerful tool for individual, community and social change. At FNTI, PLAR is more than a tool which matches an individual's prior learning to an existing course – it 'is a multipurpose educational tool aimed at assisting aboriginal learners in a way which furthers the fullest understanding, maintenance and development of the whole person in the total environment' (Hill 1995, p.68). This philosophy, practice and use of PLAR began in the Human Service Worker Program in 1985. Since that time, the concept of portfolio-assisted PLAR has evolved as a core part of all programmes, with the majority of FNTI learners developing portfolios. FNTI provides training and resources for PLAR practitioners across Canada who wish to use this portfolio process. This training includes aboriginal culture and traditions, as well as the integration of portfolio development into an aboriginal learning model. Other provinces such as Manitoba and Saskatchewan have begun initiatives with aboriginal groups to incorporate PLAR into specific educational programmes offered by the colleges in partnership with aboriginal councils and organizations.

Canada has a skilled immigrant population. Many immigrants arrive in Canada with skills and abilities suitable for employment, but they may be unable to access employment because of licensing or certification requirements. A recently released CLFDB report *Reaching Our Full Potential: Prior Learning Assessment and Recognition for Foreign Trained Canadians* (CLFDB 1999) researched practical solutions on how the education, knowledge and skills acquired abroad by immigrants and other Canadians could be recognized as bias-free, timely and systematic way through effective use of PLAR. Although the CLFDB will cease operation as of 31 December, 1999 it is encouraging other groups to use the report to champion the cause and develop a national strategy to recognize the prior learning of the foreign trained in Canada. Canada also has experience in the use of portfolio development as a tool for language skill career development for 'English as a second language' learners. These portfolio courses are offered in Ontario colleges.

PLAR research and resources

New Approaches to Lifelong Learning (NALL) is a research network and project co-ordinated by the Ontario Institute for Studies in Education (OISE) and funded by the Social Sciences and Humanities Research Council – Canada. The project is researching the relations between informal learning and formal and non-formal education. Specific projects related to PLAR include: development of an online annotated bibliography for PLAR; current and future use of PLAR; and development of a 'values' document for PLAR and PLAR in Canadian community colleges. The NALL project is an innovative partnership of researchers from 21 universities teamed with partners from the private, public and non-profit sectors (OISE 1997).

Another research project, A Slice of the Iceberg: Cross Canada Study on Prior Learning Assessment and Recognition (Van Kleef *et al.* 1999) has been completed by a partnership of seven colleges/CEGEPs from across Canada and an independent consultant. Using a combination of statistical data collection analysis and focus groups, the study over a five-year period (1993–1998) examined the characteristics of over 3500 PLAR learners, the PLAR experience from both the learners and the institutions perspectives, programs offering PLAR and the costs of PLAR. The study provides valuable data on the impact of PLAR in educational institutions and lays a foundation for future research into the long-term impact of PLAR on adults and institutions. To date, no studies like this have been conducted in Canada and very few worldwide. The study partners believe that this study provides new information so that organizations wishing to implement PLAR can make informed decisions on its usefulness.

Many Canadian PLAR resources and publications are available. Some examples include: CAPLA's extensive practitioner network, resource library and quarterly publication *The Hub*; British Columbia's Centre for Curriculum, Transfer and Technology journal *Learning Quarterly* and its set of PLA training modules; portfolio development CD-ROMs and other software programs. PLAR websites and on-line conferences offer easy access to information.

Conclusion

The future of PLAR looks promising, but Canada is faced with some tough challenges. Canada has a wealth of well-developed PLAR policies, programmes, practices and resources in education and the workplace. We have a strong grass-roots network of PLAR practitioners and supporters who continue to advocate for PLAR as part of education reform and workforce development. These practitioners are creating more open and flexible learning programmes and assessments that will help to remove barriers and ensure that learning truly has no boundaries. We are collaborating nationally and internationally with partners in business, industry labour, education and government to create and deliver flexible assessment and programmes so adults can move more easily from education to the work world and vice versa. We are off to a good start!

There are, however, a number of issues that must be addressed to ensure PLAR's continued growth and viability. First, PLAR must become a priority in national public policy development, otherwise it will remain a marginalized service available only to select Canadians. We need to create a national co-ordinated effort to increase awareness and help to ensure further development of PLAR policy across Canada. Both CAPLA and the CLFDB are well positioned to lead this national movement. Canada must also collaborate internationally to ensure that PLAR has a common vision, international standards, practices and acceptance.

Second, Canada must find ways to provide the financial and human resources required for quality PLAR implementation. The upfront development work and delivery, PLAR training, advising and assessing services require significant resources. These funding resources are not available to support continuous development or delivery of PLAR throughout Canada's education sector. Although provinces provide some initial development funding, only three currently recognize PLAR in the actual funding formula for PLAR assessments within the post-secondary system (Van Kleef 1998). Not only in education but also in the workforce, financial resources and incentives must be identified. Paul Zakos, President of CAPLA, stresses the importance of identifying 'financial incentives in both the public and private sectors which reflect current economic, demographic and social realities and encourage education, employers and training providers to allocate significant amounts of their budgets to PLA, workforce development and education reform' (Zakos 1997, p.4).

Third, we must continue to provide quality assurance in our practice if PLAR is to be accepted widely. Learners, practitioners, educators, employers, etc. all need to be assured of quality in the PLAR process. It must be a credible process. The further development of PLAR practitioner competence through national standards development and training, as advocated by CAPLA, and collaboration worldwide on international standards for PLAR practice will help to ensure quality practice and sound assessments.

The PLAR process has provided many Canadians with the opportunity to demonstrate and receive recognition for the knowledge, skills and abilities they possess. Now, it is time to ensure that *all* Canadians have access to PLAR. To accomplish this, we must confront the challenges and advocate for further development of PLAR in all sectors and on a national and international scale.

References

Blower, D. (1996) *Prior Learning Assessment and Recognition (PLAR) – An Overview of PLAR Practices in Canada*. Ottawa: Human Resources Development Canada.

Blower, D. (1997) 'A lasting commitment to PLA.' *College Canada – Association of Canadian Community Colleges 2*, 4, 12–18.

Canadian Labour Force Development Board (CLFDB) (1996) *Improving Training and Access to Employment through Prior Learning Assessment and Recognition*. Ottawa: CLFDB, policy paper with national implementation strategy and national PLAR standards.

Canadian Labour Force Development Board (CLFDB) (1997) *Prior Learning Assessment and Recognition*. Ottawa: CLFDB.

Canadian Labour Force Development Board (CLFDB) (1999) *Reaching our Full Potential: Prior Learning Assessment and Recognition for Foreign Trained Canadians*. Report prepared for PLAR Working Group – Canadian Labour Force Development Board. Ottawa: CLFDB.

Canadian Steel Trade and Employment Congress (CSTEC)(1996a) *About CSTEC*. Toronto: CSTEC.

Canadian Steel Trade and Employment Congress (CSTEC)(1996b) *About the Steel Industry Training Program*. Toronto: CSTEC.

Canadian Technology Human Resources Board (CTHRB) (1998a) *Identifying Acceptable Prior Learning Assessment and Recognition (PLAR) Policy Models for the National Technology Career Credit Bank Policy Document*. Ottawa: CTHRB, a Canadian Project co-ordinated by the Alberta Society of Engineering Technologists.

Canadian Technology Human Resources Board (CTHRB) (1998b) *CTHRB TechnoFile Project*. Ottawa: CTHRB, overview paper prepared by Frances Manning.

Collins, M. (1996) 'Prior learning assessment'. Paper presented at the 'PLA: Maximizing our Learning' Conference, Moncton, New Brunswick.

Dedi, R. (1998) 'The Manitoba prior learning assessment centre project.' *The Hub 7*, 11.

Hill, D. (1995) *Aboriginal Access to Post Secondary Education – Prior Learning Assessment and its Use within Aboriginal Programs of Learning.* Deseronto, Ontario: First Nations Technical Institute.

Isabelle, R. (1987) 'Where does prior learning assessment stand in an entrepreneurial approach on the part of the colleges?' *Études et Réflexions.* Québec: Fédération des cégeps Secteur Development et Communication.

Matthews, C. (1997) 'Prior learning assessment in British Columbia.' *Learning Specialist Association of B.C. Digest 12,* 1, 3–6.

Myers, D. (1998) 'The Halifax PLA Centre.' Personal communication.

Ontario Council of Regents (1994) *Prior Learning Assessment: A Credit to the College System.* Report of the prior learning assessment advisory and coordinating group. Toronto, Ontario: Ontario Council of Regents.

Ontario Institute for Studies in Education (OISE) (1997) *Lifelong Linking of Formal, Non-formal and Informal Learning: Current Practices, Social Barriers and New Approaches.* A strategic research network in education and training detailed proposal. Toronto: OISE.

Simosko, S. (1995) *Prior Learning Assessment and Educational Reform: A Vision for Now.* Report prepared for Centre for Curriculum and Professional Development and the British Columbia Council on Admissions and Transfer. Victoria, B.C.: Centre for Curriculum and Professional Development.

Simosko, S. (1997) 'B.C. trends in prior learning assessment: Where are we going?' *Learning Quarterly 1,* 3, 7–9.

Van Kleef, J. (1998) *Prior Learning Assessment and Recognition.* Reference document prepared for Third National Forum on Education for sub-theme School to Work and Work to School Transitions. Toronto: Council of Ministers of Education Canada.

Van Kleef, J., Aarts, S., Blower, D., Burke, R., Conlin, E., Howell, B., Howorth, C. and Lamarre, G. (1999) *A Slice of the Iceberg: Cross-Canada Study on Prior Learning Assessment and Recognition.* Toronto: Cross Canada Partnership on PLAR.

Zakos, P. (1997) 'PLA, workforce development and educational reform in Canada.' *The Hub 4,* 1–3.

CHAPTER 5

France: The Story of *La Validation des Acquis* (Recognition of Experiential Learning)

Michel Feutrie

All of us learn from our activities and experiences, whether they take place at home or at work. Nevertheless, it is only recently that this form of learning has started to be recognized as being, in some way, equivalent to formal university learning. Today in France, accreditation of experiential learning has become a central issue for the government, professional bodies and unions, companies and learning institutions.

What does accreditation of experiential learning actually mean? Basically, it is recognizing that it is possible to learn outside a formal, controlled classroom context. That means attributing a certain value to such learning by formally recognizing it according to the codified system of diplomas. This allows candidates who satisfy the required conditions either to gain exemption from the qualifications normally required for entry to a programme in higher education, or to gain units, modules or credits. This opportunity has been recognized as a right for the individuals. Everybody can apply for '*validation des acquis professionnels*' (VAP).

Why has this become such a big issue today? There are many answers to this question. We are witnessing a rapid evolution in work content as a result of the organizational changes within enterprises. Work is becoming more training oriented. At the same time, there are substantial modifications to an individual's professional life. It is becoming less and less of a linear development. People frequently change jobs, and periods of unemployment are not uncommon, implying, for an increasing number of workers, reorientation and retraining. As a result, needs for long higher-level training periods arise, more often meaning higher education programmes.

But should an individual constantly be required to relearn everything? The emergence of the current preoccupation to assess and accredit experiential learning shows significant movement from arrangements aiming to answer specific problems, or those resulting from the initiatives of militant supporters, to a more economic vision which today meets a political interest and is likely to develop the schemes of continuing education of tomorrow.

This chapter, which deals only with the situation in France, will focus on four points: history and background of VAP; the implementation of the system into higher education; the results; and the perspectives.

History and background

The mid-1980s proved to be what the specialists consider the key turning point for VAP in France. However, the question of VAP cannot be regarded as really new in the French system of continuing education. A law passed in 1934 concerning engineering allowed people over 35 years old with no higher education qualifications, who had worked for at least five years on activities which are normally those of engineers, to gain the official title of engineer through the preparation and presentation of a dissertation based on their work experience. That can be seen as an early convergence of different categories of actors intervening on the political, educational and economic levels.

In 1984, people responsible for the planning of professional training and continuing education at the State level insisted on the necessity to develop VAP (first appearance of the expression) in order to increase the level of workers' competence. The development of the European Union, particularly with the greater opportunities for workers' mobility, worries the policy makers because the majority of the workforce in France has no official qualifications. They would like to offer to a large number of them the opportunity to have recognized the skills, experience and knowledge acquired on the job. And last but not least, the growth of continuing education programmes raises the question of their efficiency as they focus on the social and professional development of unemployed people from 16 to 25 years old. For this category of people, the possibility of gaining credits for training periods completed and experience gained while working has become the main issue, in order to build coherent routes towards employment.

This in turn allowed for the launching of innovative projects. They were supported wholly by the government: the 'Délégation à la Formation Professionnelle', which created in 1984 an official working group to investigate recognition and accreditation of experiential learning; and in part by the Ministry of Labour and the Ministry of Education.

The schemes set up in response to these different questions are mainly based on the research of North Americans, in particular for the French, researchers like Marthe Sansregret and Ginette Robin who have defined the principles for the Québec model of VAP. According to Liétard (1997), their approach lies on five main principles: it is possible to learn outside formal education; this knowledge must be theoretical as well as practical; no one should be required to have to relearn that which he or she already knows; everyone has the right to be officially recognized if he or she is able to prove what has been learned; it is possible to assess this experiential learning with proper methods.

Two main decisions taken during this period in France were in line with these approaches: the *'portefeuille de compétences'* (September 1985), inspired from the North American portfolios, and the decree organizing accreditation of personal and experiential learning in higher education (August 1985). These decisions from ministerial departments served as a springboard for the launch of other initiatives which, despite criticism, resistance and hesitations, gave rise to the idea of recognition of experiential learning.

The rise in general interest concerning this domain, based on the results of the first experiences, resulted in the passing of a law on VAP in 1992 which would apply to educational institutions dependent on the Ministries of Education and Agriculture. Since then, this question has been at the centre of a societal concern over the relationship between work and education.

Implementation
Existing arrangements

One of the specificities of the French scheme of VAP is that it is based on statutory documents defined by the Parliament (when the laws are concerned) and by the Ministries (when the decrees are concerned). Three important texts, one law passed in 1992 and two decrees written in 1985 and 1993, organize VAP in higher education. They offer two different, yet complementary, approaches: access to higher education programmes of study and the awarding of modules or credits within a diploma.

Assessment for access

The oldest text on the subject, a decree from 1985, allows a university to award exemption from the qualifications normally required for entry to different levels of higher education, based on personal and professional experience, to anyone over 20 who has had a break from his or her studies of at least two years. This text also allows a university to give exemptions for modules, if appropriate. The candidate must submit an application including a personal statement, comprising a complete description of any previous courses, of any qualifications obtained, of any other skills or knowledge acquired outside the formal system of education, and of his or her professional experience and any other extra-professional activities undertaken. This application is then examined by an academic committee and sent off to the president of the university for the final decision, one which can include certain conditions or restrictions. For example, the university may require the candidate to undertake some top-up studies either before entry or alongside the study programme.

In the assessment for access, a global evaluation is placed on the personal and professional route of the candidate. The process tries to identify, through the submitted documents and from interviews with candidates, the ways and methods used to solve problems and the general process of reflection of candidates while undertaking their tasks. It also tries to verify the level and scope of responsibilities. This is not a process focused on verifying the candidates knowledge by tests or formal examinations. Rather, it is a *deductive* process centred on the level of complexity of the work in question (and even more on the continual increase in that complexity), on candidates' knowledge and skills used to achieve it, and on how they correspond to the level of knowledge and ability required in the course on which the candidates seek enrolment. The decision is made, more or less, on the basis that the whole of this information submitted for assessment amounts to a representation of the capacities and abilities of the candidate in question, and that they correspond to the required level of any other given person enrolled at that level. This all boils down to what is called the 'verification of the candidate's potential' – that is to say, the confirmation of the ability both to identify what has been learnt from his or her experiences and to put it into action in a new, more complex, context. In other words, it asks the question: Can this candidate succeed in the chosen programme if given direct entry? Eventually, candidates will be asked to acquire some top-up studies either before entry or alongside the course.

The assessment for modules or credit within a diploma

The 1992 law and the 1993 decree allow a university to award modules, units or credits of a diploma course to any person having at least five years professional activity, not necessarily continuous, relevant to the course in question. The accent is placed, in these texts, above all, on the candidate's professional experience. This procedure does not apply to medical or engineering students. The candidate is asked to provide more in the case of access: a detailed description of specific responsibilities and tasks. This includes, for example: a description of professional activities, tasks and projects undertaken; working conditions; extent of autonomy; specific responsibilities; membership of team; and internal and external relations. The candidate has also to provide a description of the company worked for (sector, size, number of employees, turnover, type of equipment, etc.). If possible, it is desirable that the company confirms the documents produced by the candidate. The description of the candidate's professional activity must be accompanied by a personal presentation focused on exemplary problems that needed to be solved while working. In other words, candidates themselves will be asked to choose from their different experiences the evidence which would be the best support for their claims and to explain in written form the way in which they faced the problems they have chosen to present, the internal and external resources used (equipment, financial means, human resources), skills and abilities relied on, and how they put this all together to reach their objectives and obtain the required results. An application, developed with the help of an adviser, is then examined by an Accreditation Jury, including teachers and representatives from companies. The jury's decision is passed to the '*Jury de diplôme*', which ratifies and records the decision on the advice of the president of the university. If the decision is positive, the candidate is then regarded as having obtained the modules, units or credits in question.

The decision process is here different from that of the assessment for access, because this time it is a question of officially awarding university modules, units or credits without passing the required examinations. This consists of trying to establish a relation between on-the-job learning and academic learning. This is particularly difficult, because the two are not immediately comparable. The object is therefore to find the approximate, not exact, similarities between them. The assertion is that this can be verified through the level of expertise the candidate demonstrates, through the way given problems are solved and reacted to, through the reflexive mechanisms built to do that, and through developing the intellectual and problem-solving skills similar to those which the course will seek to develop. Therefore, it is not the candidate's stock of formal knowledge which is assessed, rather, it is the ability to prove the achievement of a level of intellectual development corresponding to that required. This calls for a long, in-depth, progressive analysis through a dialogue between the university and the candidate. Here the individual plays an active role in the process, a role which proves to be as important as the content of the application.

As for the universities, no universal agreement exists on how to carry out the process. Many defend the idea that it is up to the candidate to prove the knowledge that has been acquired. They have a tendency to design a 'classical' way of assessment, which basically means that it is the candidate's role to understand the rules of the game beforehand and to produce that which the university will accept. In this way, a candidate is expected to present a claim in a form comparable to that which is required of 'normal' students. Thus, these universities do not modify their procedures and criteria; rather, they adapt them to each candidate, individually.

VAP introduced a new approach to assessment. As Aubret (1997) explains, in the 'classic' definition of education there is basically the transfer of knowledge from someone who knows to someone who in principle does not know. By evaluation, the teacher verifies whether or not this transfer is effective; the teacher is the only judge in the game. In the VAP process, the candidate builds his or her own application with the required evidences, so deciding what goes into it and what points will be developed; the candidate plays a part in the rules of the game, intruding on the prerogatives of teachers. Thus, there is a movement from a one-way evaluation to a reciprocal, almost contrac-tual, process of identification.

Putting it into practice

VAP was put into practice in higher education at the end of the 1980s in universities that were already active in adult education. But universities are independent, so their commitment to this process and the scope of involvement in concrete action plans have varied – there is no unique model. So a working group, involving directors of human resources from various large companies, was set up based on the pioneering initiatives of some universities, with the support of the Department of Higher Education in the Ministry of Education. Its brief was to produce documents designed to help universities to define their own VAP procedures and to encourage them to invest in this field. The documents produced by this group were confirmed, validated by the Ministry and proposed to all French universities in 1994.

The proposed procedure included four steps. The advising phase, where the candidate meets and discusses with an adviser, concentrates on: examining the validity of the claim; outlining the process of assessment; helping the candidate to decide whether to apply for access or for credit; and defining the steps to follow. The application-building phase is where the candidate, accompanied by the adviser, meets the tutors of the course in question. These two phases can be repeated. The assessment phase is where the Academic Committee or the Accreditation Jury examines the candidate's application. They can ask to meet the candidate in person as well. Finally, the decision phase, where, according to the 1985 decree, the Academic Committee examines the dossier and decides whether or not the candidate can enter the programme applied for, and, according to the 1993 decree, the Accreditation Jury determines what modules, units or credits are awarded.

Follow-up organization

In order to heighten the universities' awareness of VAP, to collect good practices and to help them to overcome any difficulties, the Department of Higher Education has organized, on two occasions, 'VAP Days'. Most recently, in May 1997, this Department launched a three-part action plan aimed at the development of VAP in universities. The first part is to include VAP in development contracts that universities negotiate and sign with the Ministry every four years. The next is a training plan for different categories of actors inside the universities (management team, deans of faculties, advisers and tutors, members of juries, etc.) and the creation of a helping network to which the president of the university can refer whenever needed. The last is the forming of an evaluation group assigned to follow the entire process.

VAP in higher education: Where are we now?

The analysis of practices on VAP in different universities leads us to a two-part observation. The practices are extremely diversified, and it is fair to say that every university represents a particular case. They apply law and decrees differently and all deal with a different number of candidates. What is more, taking part in VAP means confronting an ideological question, because it challenges the traditional conceptions and representations of knowledge and how it is acquired. As a result, universities are often hesitant in recognizing experiential learning. Or at least teachers seem to be uneasy about the whole thing, because they often do not know how to deal with or evaluate this experiential knowledge, nor how to match it with academic approaches, and they are basically afraid that it runs a risk of leading some candidates to failure.

Three models of arrangements in French universities

Although the process seems to be particular to each case and each university, three varieties of VAP procedures can be singled out.

CENTRALIZATION

The main characteristic of this model is the adoption of a global procedure which applies to the entire university. It is a structure which places the Adult Education Department on centre stage. The Department takes charge of everything from welcoming the candidate to placement on courses at the university.

DECENTRALIZATION

This model is composed of two sub-models. The first is a set-up that can be qualified 'anomic'. In this scenario, teachers themselves or leaders of programmes are free, for their own courses and their own modules, to define the awarding of exemptions to candidates. The idea is this: departments prefer to define their own rules, make their own policies, thus moving away from a centralized university procedure. In the second sub-model, the procedure is spread out and divided up among different commissions in each department. Every step of the procedure, from submission to decision, is managed, guided and controlled at the department level. Teachers welcome candidates, help them to build their applications, explain the assessment procedure and then discuss and assess all this with their colleagues. Each department defines criteria for assessment differently. This model almost never sees the intervention or guidance of an adviser or the setting up of a help network for the candidate.

MANAGEMENT BY UNIVERSITY ADMINISTRATION

In this model, Student Service welcomes the candidates, helps them to build their application, explains the VAP procedure and tries to obtain a decision from the department concerned.

The past few years, however, have seen a general movement from decentralization to centralization, as university departments begin to integrate VAP into the curriculum, which basically means more guided help by an adviser for the candidate.

Results

Exact numbers can be produced concerning VAP in higher education as a result of a two-year study made by the Department of Higher Education. For the 1995/96 academic year, universities received 6334 requests for accreditation (5571 for access and 763 for the awarding of modules), of which 68 per cent were approved. For 1996/97, 10,389 requests were made (9677 for access and 712 for the awarding of modules), of which 79 per cent were approved, allowing us to conclude that interest in VAP for access is increasing. In addition, there has been an increase in the approval rate of the process, thus giving rise to a better system of guidance and counselling.

The decisions for access can be divided up as follows: 32 per cent represented the number of admissions to the *premier cycle* (the French equivalent of a two-year diploma), 47 per cent to the *second cycle* (the third and fourth years of a university programme) and 21 per cent to the *troisième cycle* (graduate studies). For the awarding of modules, the results are as follows: 44 per cent of the requests were for the *premier cycle*, 43 per cent for the *second cycle* and 13 per cent for the *troisième cycle*. In the case of access, positive decisions can be divided up into three areas: humanities and social sciences (38%); economics and management (38%); and sciences and technology (27%). The awarding of modules can be broken down as: 61 per cent in humanities and social sciences, 19 per cent in economics and management and 20 per cent in sciences and technology. Sixty-nine per cent of the candidates are over 30 and 46 per cent have more than 15 years of work experience; 25 per cent of them are executives and 51 per cent of them come from intermediate levels.

VAP within companies

The VAP procedure in universities is beginning to be echoed in companies which are looking to incorporate it into their management of human resources. Two examples illustrate this phenomenon.

In the first case, VAP intervenes as a way of closing the gap in terms of qualifications between different categories of workers doing the same job, or having similar functions. This is the case for companies which have increased the level of recruitment for certain jobs. The results of an analysis done by human resources departments show that the older workers, who have been there for some time and do not officially own the same qualification as newer employees, feel under-qualified and therefore disadvantaged. VAP thus offers them an opportunity to obtain an equivalent qualification quickly. In every case, the enterprise argues that it is a question of improving the position of these experienced workers for the job market, if at some time, for economic reasons, companies have to dismiss them.

In the second case, VAP is used as a management tool for internal and external mobility. It takes place in companies that, after having experienced periods of rapid growth and so allowing their employees to develop along with it, have had to either slow or stop their pace. They are then confronted with a double problem. First, there are those who have developed along with the company and whom the company wants to hold on to, but do not have an official qualification. VAP would guarantee them their position by having it officially assessed. Second, there are those who had less of a chance to develop within the company. VAP would assess that which they have learned if and when they decide or are forced to look for another job. Or VAP could offer them the opportunity to learn a second or third profession, or become skilled in a second or third area. So VAP becomes a particularly well-adapted means of designing training routes which will formalize experiential learning and better prepare them for the job market.

These two cases, which do not at all cover the entire range of strategies that companies' develop, demonstrate that VAP can also be a tool well adapted to companies strategies, and not only a tool for personal promotion. But this presupposes a real willingness on the part of managers in companies to embrace the concept of VAP.

Perspectives

VAP is currently at the centre of a political debate which concerns politicians, professional bodies, companies and, of course, educational institutions, particularly universities. The passing of the law on VAP incited certain reactions which offered other solutions and alternatives to VAP. These tried to separate the accreditation of experiential learning from diplomas. In 1996, the Ministry of Labour announced the establishment of a national scheme for assessment and accreditation of experience, defining and listing each professional domain by level in a hierarchical order. The objective behind this scheme was to support the accreditation of experiential learning, no matter how it could be acquired, and to rate candidates on an equal level with those who obtained qualifications through formal schooling. This scheme was never actually realized, but its intentions, which remain, did have an effect on different areas.

The current Ministry of Labour has stated that the development of VAP schemes would lie in global reform of the system of continuing education. It has announced that it would like to launch a sort of *passeport de compétences*. It is a question of putting certain markers in place corresponding to any professional skill, no matter how specialized, which can be identified within a certain professional area. According to VAP, the role of the State is to organize the creation of a scheme, to define how it will work and identify exactly what the assessment criteria will be. Also, the assessment process should be undertaken by institutions independent of, and not by, training organizations and of those who use the qualifications acquired.

In October 1998, the national professional body (CNPF – Conseil National du Patronat Français, now MEDEF – Mouvement des Entreprises de France) organized a conference (welcoming 1500 participants) which focused on the question of competence. One of the main issues was assessment. At the time of the conference, the official position of MEDEF was that the assessment of competencies remained entirely the preserve of the enterprise. In response to this, it was shown that the professional career of today is constantly evolving, more tangential than linear in development and growth, so that it is unlikely that the worker of today would remain solely at one enterprise throughout his or her working life. It follows, therefore, that it will be necessary to make the transfer of VAP possible from one company to another, from one work sector to another. For this to happen, a standard form of equivalency must be agreed upon.

At the same time, certain groups of education institutions are looking to form their own alternative schemes, offering a different approach from that of the Ministry of Education. This is, for example, the case with the network of education centres managed by Chambers of Commerce.

More generally, today's VAP trends can be placed somewhere between two poles: one which favours the creation of an assessment procedure independent of companies and educational institutions; and another which, whilst recognizing the difficulty of trying to keep VAP entirely neutral and independent of companies and educational institutions, orients itself towards developing connections between institutions having a responsibility in accreditation of experiential learning, so as to construct bridges to allow for continuing development of individuals.

As for the Ministry of Education, the question of accreditation proves to be one of its primary concerns. It has decided to make it a part of its policy on higher education. Inscribed in this policy, too, is the universities' position that learning is a lifelong process. VAP, then, becomes the missing link joining formal education and experience.

Conclusion

The accreditation of personal and experiential learning has become a fundamental element of today's society. It is an opportunity to be used, but care is essential. It is a new field to be explored, underlining the border between work and education. It requires careful analysis in both practical and theoretical domains. But, based on what has happened in France during the past 16 years, it is clear that VAP has brought great benefits to French learning institutions, particularly universities. For universities, VAP proves to be an excellent analysing mechanism. It forces the institution to evaluate itself in its role as the centre of production of knowledge and in how it delivers it. From the moment the university agrees to recognize the fact that an equivalence can be made between knowledge acquired on the job or in life in general and formal studies, that university has evolved into something different. In other words, the university becomes less of a 'distribution centre' for knowledge rather, it becomes more of a place of fine-tuning and formalizing of already acquired knowledge as a basis for further learning. In this new context, its mission is to organize and regroup the multifaceted domain of acquired knowledge from outside the university, so that it has new meaning for the individual.

VAP also calls for the university to review the organization of its internal education structure and focus more on individuals and their current needs, future goals and past experiences. VAP thus puts the individuals at centre stage. It makes students active partners in the process, bringing with them completely original and personal cases, where they must be judged individually, separate from all other cases simply because the student alone (or possibly with other people in their environment) can stand for that which is presented. In such a scheme, individuals become real actors in the field of education.

Finally, with its open and adapted programmes, VAP best represents what can become a lifelong learning process. It provides a means of communication with companies. It offers a real opportunity to establish new partnerships with them. The question is even raised in literature describing different models of management of human resources within companies. Each of them implies a strong, effective, working relationship with universities and, keeping to the global plan it envisions, the formalizing of a partnership which would even be able to go as far as creating new diplomas. The study of these partnerships shows that VAP offers them the opportunity to come into contact with new enterprises or the possibility of enlarging the field of intervention in partner enterprises concerning other areas, such as continuing education, research and placements. The company thus becomes a type of learning institution, and decisions concerning its employees on VAP indirectly mean an evaluation of its ability to train and to build competence and so of its future prosperity.

Certain people have said that VAP creates something of a break in French culture: this is most certainly true. As yet, this break is still a small one. The omens are that it is likely to get larger.

References

Aubret, J. (1997) 'Reconnaissance et validation des acquis: Sens et procédures.' *Paroles et Practiques Sociales 54–55*, 29–39.

Liétard, B. (1997) 'Se reconnaître dans le maquis des acquis.' *Education Permanente 133*, 65–74.

CHAPTER 6

Scotland: The Story of the Assessment of Prior Experiential Learning

Norman Sharp, Fiona Reeve and Ruth Whittaker

Introduction

The story of the assessment (or accreditation) of prior experiential learning (AP(E)L) in Scotland can perhaps best be told through an exploration of its cycle of development. The cycle moves through stages of innovation, reflection and consolidation, and new development as the higher education community in Scotland seeks to realize the potential of AP(E)L.

The innovation phase of the cycle commenced in the late 1980s and was characterized by pump-priming activities largely supported by short-term government funding initiatives. This resulted in *ad hoc* development which generally took place at the margins of the institutions. The reflection and consolidation phase began early in the 1990s and saw an initial lull in new AP(E)L development, with the exception of particular areas such as nursing and social work. During this period, endeavours were made to systematize the processes of AP(E)L through collaboration between institutions, with a particular emphasis on the assurance of quality and standards. Collaborative work focused on identifying commonalities and examples of good practice to support the development of institutional strategies. In the late 1990s, institutions are applying the lessons learned through this process in the next stage of the cycle – the realization of the potential of AP(E)L. The late 1990s have witnessed a resurgence of development, with a range of new examples of AP(E)L becoming incorporated within the mainstream of institutional activity.

This chapter will first consider the context in which AP(E)L development in Scotland took place, before moving on to explore each stage of the cycle. In doing this, we have drawn upon our own experience and that of other AP(E)L practitioners, as well as some systematic research evidence, mainly from the west of Scotland. We hope that this provides a representative picture of the development of AP(E)L in Scotland, but recognize that this chapter is inevitably shaped by our own personal perspectives.

The background to the development of AP(E)L in Scotland

The development of arrangements for AP(E)L in Scottish higher education needs to be located in the wider context of the move towards mass higher education which was accelerating in Scotland to an even greater extent than elsewhere in the UK (DfEE 1993). For example, between 1987/88 and 1995/96 the total age participation index in Scotland more than doubled, from 20.5 per cent to 44.2 per cent (Garrick Report 1997). As Sir Christopher Ball indicated, more would mean different (Ball 1990). Key aspects of that difference could be seen, for example, in the government and institutional policy emerging during the 1980s on wider access to higher education (Fairhurst 1991). It could also be seen in the range of government initiatives to encourage higher education institutions to be more responsive to the needs of the labour market (e.g. the Enterprise in Higher Education Initiative). The purpose of this section is to locate the emergence of AP(E)L in Scotland within this broader context of deeper and wider participation in higher education. It is useful to summarize these contextual factors in relation to: the dynamics of the labour market; the development of policy on wider access and credit accumulation; and the individual institutional contexts.

The labour market and associated higher education developments in the late 1980s

It was argued during the 1980s that predicted changes in the labour market would have a significant impact on higher education in a number of respects. First, because of demographic changes, it was widely expected that there would be a significant decline in the number of new entrants to the labour force, and that consequently the future skill needs of the economy would require to be met through the training and retraining of the existing labour force. Second, changes in the structure of the economy continued to involve the decline of traditional industries and the loss of traditional employment opportunities in Scotland. This added further to the demands for retraining in order to avoid long-term structural unemployment. Third, the pace of technological change, particularly in relation to communications and information technology, was leading to significant changes in work practice and was also contributing to demands for retraining and skills development. In general, the concept of a job for life was argued to be outmoded, and the importance of recurrent learning and employment flexibility was increasingly emphasized. In addition, a fourth important source of pressure on higher education from the labour market was the increasing professionalization in some occupational groups. This trend led to a re-examination of initial qualifications for entry to professions and of requirements for continuing professional development, which were both linked in some cases to formal recognition through additional qualifications. For example, the 1980s witnessed the redefinition of initial qualifications and of continuing professional development structures in both nursing and social work.

The Scottish Wider Access Programme and the emergence of CATS in Scotland

Many developments in relation to higher education in Scotland are characterized by co-operative and collaborative approaches (see, for example, Sharp and Gallacher 1996). This is clearly evident in the development of AP(E)L in Scotland. This also characterized the associated development of wider access and credit initiatives, both of which had a significant bearing on the nature of AP(E)L development in Scotland. By the second half of the 1980s, a small number of special access courses had been developed by a number of individual higher education institutions, which in 1988 led to the emergence of national policy in the form of the Scottish Wider Access Programme (SWAP). The SWAP arrangements offered a structure of access provision based on Scottish Vocational Education Council (SCOTVEC) national certificate modules. This was provided through three consortia involving the colleges of further education in partnership with HEIs across Scotland. The SWAP strategy was important for AP(E)L developments in a number of respects. First, this was the first major national initiative relating to higher education in Scotland which utilized explicit learning outcomes and therefore emphasized achievements rather than educational processes – an important step in recognizing the value of learning from experience. Second, SCOTVEC was itself experimenting with AP(E)L processes in the context of its national certificate programme from the end of 1987 with funding from the Training Agency and the Scottish Education Department. The development associated with SWAP in supporting wider access for many with considerable life and work experience rather than traditional school-based qualifications was key to the development of AP(E)L in Scotland, as was the growing emphasis on the demonstration of outcomes rather than processes.

The parallel development of mechanisms to support credit accumulation and transfer (CATS) in Scotland was also important in laying the foundations for AP(E)L. The first two institutional schemes in Scotland were accredited by the Council for National Academic Awards (CNAA) in 1990 in Glasgow College (later to become, with the Queen's College, Glasgow, Glasgow Caledonian University) and Paisley College (Paisley University). These were both developed in the co-operative context of the embryonic SCOTCAT Network which then produced the Scottish-wide SCOTCAT Framework in 1990 (Sharp 1991). In each of these CATS developments, AP(E)L played a prominent part in the general strategy of recognizing for appropriate academic credit and assessed learning from whatever source. This was a key principle which some institutions adopted in addressing the new demands of new student groups (referred to above). These national developments in CATS and wider access, together with the demands of new student groups, created an important framework for AP(E)L developments which were concentrated in particular institutional contexts.

Aspects of the institutional context

While there were some early developments in relation to CATS in the pre-1992 universities, the bulk of the development, and certainly the pioneering work in AP(E)L, tended to be focused in the ex-CNAA institutions. In part, this was encouraged by the Scottish Education Department with its emphasis on the vocational mission of the central institutions related to the perceived needs of the labour market. In part, it was also through the vocational and wider participation emphasis which had been promoted by the CNAA.

The dynamics of the labour market, referred to above, led to a growing emphasis on provision for adults in the ex-CNAA institutions. The 1980s saw a significant growth in the provision of 'mature student entry schemes' and other initiatives to attract adults into higher education in Scotland. A number of such schemes involved the recognition of prior learning from a wide variety of sources as demonstrating the individual's ability to benefit from higher education, rather than traditional school-based qualifications. In some cases, these pressures on higher education institutions from the labour market were explicitly supported by employers. For example, at the closure of the steel plant in central Scotland at Ravenscraig, British Steel attempted to secure the future employability of the labour being shed through a range of educational initiatives, including the assessment of prior experiential learning (see also Carmichael 1991; Osborne *et al.* 1993). Thus, the development of AP(E)L in Scotland has been shaped by pressures from the labour market and employers that have had a particular impact on institutions which have an emphasis on access and vocationalism.

Within these institutions, the academics and other staff who became most actively involved in the early AP(E)L developments tended to have strong professional interests in the creation of new forms and structures of higher education provision for new groups of participants in higher education, in particular those which had been traditionally underrepresented. In many cases, it was these practitioners who formed the core of continuing education or CATS departments or units within these institutions. These departments in the ex-CNAA institutions which nurtured the early AP(E)L developments therefore had, in the main, a very different focus from the adult/liberal education roots of the continuing education departments of the pre-1992 universities.

The context of the learner

A final factor to consider in the background of AP(E)L development in Scotland is the context of the learner. One dimension of this, of increasing importance as the 1990s have progressed, was the growing trend of consumerism in higher education, as in many other aspects of life in the Conservative UK of the 1980s. One group of new students, clients or customers of the institutions were adults who were well aware, at least in general terms, of their prior learning and future learning needs. AP(E)L and CATS appeared to offer such consumers a cost-effective and efficient way of building on their prior learning to meet their new needs. These well-informed learners tended to be already experienced in relation to tertiary education and frequently involved in continuing professional development. On the other hand, AP(E)L seemed also to offer a valuable wider access route to groups traditionally underrepresented in higher education by allowing positive learning from past experience to be recognized, as opposed to re-emphasizing failure in qualifications. AP(E)L therefore appeared to offer institutions an important new strategy for wider access (on the basis, for example, of the pioneering work of the Learning from Experience Trust (Evans 1987)) and to respond to the needs of students who could demonstrate learning from prior experience and who did not wish to devote scarce resources to repeating learning already achieved.

The innovation stage

By the late 1980s, there was therefore a range of interrelated factors which stimulated the early development of AP(E)L in Scotland. This section will provide a few brief examples of this early innovation.

Perhaps the first formal AP(E)L initiative in Scotland was the 1987 Scottish Education Department/Training Agency-funded project which enabled SCOTVEC to develop an AP(E)L system within the further education sector (Yule and Brownlie-Marshall 1991). As indicated above, this was greatly facilitated by the earlier decision by SCOTVEC to create a competence-based national certificate framework with its structure of explicit learning outcomes, performance criteria and range statements. Because of the close relationships between the further and higher education sectors in Scotland (e.g. through SWAP), this served as an important exemplar for the whole tertiary sector. This project overlapped with the creation, in 1989, of the group that was to lead the early application of AP(E)L in higher education, the SCOTCAT Health Studies Group (SHSG). This self-help group included members from the CNAA, the National Board for Nursing, Midwifery and Health Visiting in Scotland, and staff from the HEIs with CNAA undergraduate nursing provision. The SHSG developed, piloted and introduced a system of AP(E)L which formed a key component in the structure of continuing professional development for experienced senior nurses (Yule and Brownlie-Marshall 1991). Both of these examples illustrate the importance of co-operative developments in relation to AP(E)L and its early vocational thrust. These elements were also present in the Scottish Applications of Learning from Experience project (1990), funded by the Training Agency, and also the Scottish Enterprise-funded Scottish Higher Education and Employers Collaborative (SHEEC) project (1990). The former project provided, under a CNAA, Scottish Office and SCOTVEC umbrella, funding for the development and dissemination of the use of experiential learning, both planned and prior, within the undergraduate provision of CNAA institutions in Scotland. The SHEEC project, developed jointly by the University of Stirling and Glasgow Caledonian University, was designed to examine the attitudes of management, in both the public and private sectors, to the accreditation and validation of in-house education and training programmes and to AP(E)L (Carmichael 1991). The project focused on 19 employers and developed a small number of major case studies of AP(E)L and in-house accreditation in operation.

These initiatives were taken a stage further in the Scottish Enterprise-funded project on the Development of Employment-Based Access to Learning (DEAL), 1992. Through the DEAL project, Glasgow Caledonian University, the University of Stirling and Napier University, together with partner employers, developed structures which embraced the accreditation of experiential learning in the workplace (both planned and prior) within the context of a range of access and undergraduate provision (Reeve *et al.* 1995). One of the key themes of the DEAL project was to provide a model for the integration of AP(E)L, and the assessment and accreditation of work-based learning generally, with more mainstream institutional activity in relation to teaching, learning and the assurance of quality. The barriers to utilizing these approaches in the context of small – and medium-sized enterprises were then examined by a team from the University of Stirling in the Learning in Smaller Companies project (Seagraves *et al.* 1996).

In general, these early projects all demonstrated that AP(E)L processes did have much to offer as institutions addressed new challenges (outlined above). The projects reflected a very clear focus on work-based learning and collaborative development, and they were, in the main, developed within the ex-CNAA institutions. The funding which facilitated these early developments was, with the important exception of SHSG, of a short-term nature. This meant that for the duration of the funding period, relatively resource-intensive methodologies could be employed, particularly in relation to providing support in portfolio compilation and assessment. The short-term nature of developments also tended to militate against the full integration of AP(E)L with other institutional processes (e.g. in relation to quality assurance), and very often *ad hoc* arrangements were made. This early period of innovation over the late 1980s and early 1990s was followed by a period of reflection and consolidation as institutions and practitioners sought ways to take forward the benefits of AP(E)L in a secure and resource-efficient manner which was not dependent on *ad hoc* funding arrangements.

Reflection and consolidation

By the early and middle years of the 1990s, considerable development work had therefore taken place, which demonstrated that the principles of AP(E)L could be applied within higher education both to widen access and to award credit within degree programmes. However, there was a real danger that these developments would be marginalized within higher education as isolated pilot projects which would fail to have an impact beyond their period of funding. Many AP(E)L practitioners were aware of these dangers and were seeking ways to consolidate the initial development work and to move from the margins to the mainstream of institutional activity in a cost-effective manner.

Some of the nervousness of institutions regarding implementing AP(E)L more widely was related to concerns about 'debasing' the quality of their provision and the challenge of maintaining standards. It might also be the case that these fears focused on external perceptions and the danger of AP(E)L being characterized as an easy route to a degree. For new universities in particular, these were pressing considerations as they sought to establish themselves in the post-1992 environment. They were potentially more open to innovation in this area, and were keen to be seen to be maintaining their missions and responding to the needs of the local community, including employers. However, they were also concerned to establish themselves fully within the traditional higher education community as a whole. In this context, two themes emerged to take forward consolidation of AP(E)L developments: the development of quality assurance guidelines and, at institutional and practitioner level, greater collaboration and sharing of good practice.

In some senses, the focus on quality assurance within AP(E)L was a reaction to developments elsewhere in the sector, where greater openness in the learning and assessment processes was being required of institutions. However, practitioners argued that, since AP(E)L raised very fundamental questions in relation to standards, such as the meaning of 'level' within a higher education degree, it had much to contribute to these important debates. As Winter points out, the need for greater transparency when dealing with experiential learning has perhaps resulted in more comprehensive quality assurance processes than can be found elsewhere (Winter 1994).

The importance of collaborative development in Scotland has already been highlighted. For AP(E)L practitioners, and those involved in work-based learning, discussions with colleagues engaged in similar work elsewhere was important in helping to maintain the development momentum over this period, particularly where practitioners may have felt at the margins of their institution. Collaboration also created a 'critical mass' for reflection, enabling the sharing of practice and the exploration of commonality, difference and good practice. The core of these collaborative arrangements during this period of reflection and consolidation was provided, in the main, through the SCOTCAT Network and its various subject forums.

Both of these themes of concerns with quality and collaborative endeavour are evident in the development of quality assurance guidelines for the sector in Scotland. With the dissolution of the binary divide and the demise of the CNAA, the Higher Education Quality Council (HEQC) took over responsibility for credit-based learning and the SCOTCAT Scheme in 1992. At the same time, the SCOTCAT Development Forum was created. One of its first acts was to invite 'expert practitioners' from across the sector to participate in the process of drafting quality assurance guidelines for credit-based learning, including experiential learning. Draft guidelines were tested out more widely within the sector through a series of workshops held across Scotland. In a sense, this exercise aimed to distil practice, including innovative practice, into policy that could be used at the institutional level to guide developments in the sector. An important step, therefore, was the adoption of the guidelines by the Committee of Scottish Higher Education Principals (COSHEP). Thus, the desire to maintain coherence within Scottish higher education is demonstrated even in its most innovative developments. The guidelines were published in 1995 (HEQC 1995a), and these subsequently formed the basis of the UK-wide guidelines which were published later that year (HEQC 1995b). In addition to a series of general guidelines on credit-based learning, a specific set of work-based learning guidelines, including AP(E)L, had been established. Thus, for the first time, experiential learning had become recognized within important new developments for the sector as a whole. The location of AP(E)L within the work-based learning section of the guidelines reflected not only the inevitable close relationship between prior and planned learning, but also the origins of many early AP(E)L developments in Scotland (referred to above).

As a result of this early work, a special interest SCOTCAT Forum for Experiential Learning was formed in 1995, which was linked to the overall SCOTCAT Framework. During 1997, this group undertook a revision of the original experiential learning guidelines, which resulted in a number of changes that reflected the ways in which practice had been developed and refined in the intervening period. For example, the revised guidelines addressed the growth of partnership arrangements with private, public or professional organizations and higher education. They also were designed to provide illustrations of how the guidelines were reflected in actual practice across Scotland by including annotated case studies of work-based learning and AP(E)L. The revised format was an attempt to model the link between policy and practice which had characterized AP(E)L development during this consolidation phase. The experiential learning guidelines were formally published by the Quality Assurance Agency (QAA) (the successor to HEQC) and COSHEP in 1998 (QAA 1998).

Another key parallel development in AP(E)L from 1995 to 1997 was the 'AP(E)L in the West of Scotland Project', funded by the Scottish Higher Education Funding Council (SHEFC). A survey which was undertaken as part of this project illustrated the extent to which AP(E)L had developed during this consolidation phase (University of Ulster 1998). The project involved all of the universities in the west of Scotland: Glasgow Caledonian University and the Universities of Paisley, Strathclyde and Glasgow. It is reasonable to assume that the results of the survey may be representative of the position across Scotland as a whole, since it encompassed a range of institutions with different traditions and missions. The survey of programme organizers confirmed that AP(E)L activities were still concentrated in the post-1992 universities (Glasgow Caledonian University and the University of Paisley) or, in the case of the University of Strathclyde, in a particular faculty (Education) which had only recently merged with the University. In general, the pre-1992 universities, represented in the survey by the University of Glasgow, had yet to develop AP(E)L mechanisms for awarding credit. It has been argued (Davies, Gallacher and Reeve 1997) that the greater presence of AP(E)L in the post-1992 universities may to some extent be a result of the more centralized management structures of these institutions. In a top-down management approach, academic departments were often explicitly encouraged to engage in new activities such as AP(E)L. Such an explicit steer was largely absent in the older universities. The influence of the different traditions, missions and continuing education units of different institutions was one of a number of important contextual factors (outlined above).

Even within the new universities, the level of AP(E)L activity varied across the institutions. Certain areas had developed considerable experience of using AP(E)L to grant credit within their awards, such as nursing and combined awards, whilst others such as law and mathematics had not considered making AP(E)L available to students. This distribution of AP(E)L by subject area confirms the earlier report of the Learning from Experience Trust (Dearden and Evans 1995) which examined practice in 16 institutions across the UK. This does of course reflect the appropriateness of AP(E)L to the nature of the subject area. Programmes which embody the kinds of knowledge, understanding and skills that may be developed in the workplace are more likely to accommodate AP(E)L claims. The level of the award may also influence the use of AP(E)L. The outcomes of the survey suggested that AP(E)L is used more extensively at the later stages of the undergraduate degree (within 'post-experience' programmes) or at postgraduate level. This perhaps reflects the nature of experiential learning which, with its origins in particular contexts, is likely to relate to the more specialist areas of knowledge and skills that are addressed at this level, rather than to the broader knowledge base developed in the early stages of undergraduate programmes. Another important factor that influenced the availability of AP(E)L within particular programmes was the perception of the student 'market'. Where courses were oversubscribed by 'conventional' students, staff appeared to be less keen to operate what many perceived as time-consuming AP(E)L procedures. However, even in this context, staff were reporting that employers and professional bodies were beginning to exert a demand for AP(E)L opportunities.

The survey also examined the nature of the AP(E)L processes being operated. A strong degree of commonality was found which could be traced back to the early influence of organizations such as the Council for Adult and Experiential Learning (CAEL) in the USA and the Learning from Experience Trust in the UK. The influence of these organizations can be seen in the principles of AP(E)L that were adopted by the institutions (e.g. 'learning not simply experience') and in the ways in which these have been put into practice; for example, in the emphasis on using the portfolio as an assessment tool. Given this commonality between institutions, it was possible to synthesize a manual of good practice (Reeve and Smith 1996) as a means of consolidating good practice in this area. This manual also had the explicit aim of supporting staff in their attempts to develop AP(E)L systems that would be appropriate for their own institutional context.

Realizing the potential

The emergence of lifelong learning and the 'learning society' as a central theme in government educational policy in the late 1990s has given experiential learning, both prior and planned, an increasingly important role in the next wave of development in higher education. This role has been identified in a number of key policy documents. These include: the Dearing and Garrick Reports (1997); the report of the National Advisory Council on Continuing Education and Life-long Learning (the Fryer Report) (NAGCELL 1997); the NAGCELL Task Group Report on Workplace Learning (NAGCELL 1998); the Green Paper on lifelong learning (*The Learning Age*) (DfEE 1998); and the Scottish Green Paper on lifelong learning (Scottish Office 1998). The Scottish Green Paper, *Opportunity Scotland*, welcomed the plans by the higher education sector and the Scottish Qualifi-cations Authority to introduce a comprehensive Scottish Credit and Qualifications Framework by August 1999. This framework encom-passes all formal awards in Scotland – school, college, higher education, work-based and professional awards – and will build upon the SCOTCAT system. Within such a framework, the assessment of all prior learning, including AP(E)L, will figure prominently, both in terms of its role in widening access to students from all backgrounds and in encouraging participation by enabling the accumulation of credit from different sources of learning over individuals' lifetimes. Issues of access and guidance are intended to become issues of helping individuals to locate themselves within this comprehensive framework and to identify the different paths that radiate from this location.

The rhetoric of widening access and promoting flexibility of provision, which has been contained in many mission statements since the late 1980s, is now being increasingly reflected in mainstream provision. Within the credit-based qualifications framework for Scotland, the institutional context now exists to take advantage of the AP(E)L systems which began their development approximately a decade ago. It is interesting to note that, in a number of our higher education institutions, AP(E)L developments are now being demand-driven. There are a number of examples where individual departments are now asking for institutional support in providing an AP(E)L service rather than developments being driven at an institutional level. Within these institutions, the perception of AP(E)L practitioners by academic colleagues is shifting from that of 'problem creators' to 'problem solvers'. AP(E)L is, in some cases, now being viewed as the mechanism through which some part-time programmes can be run, often in partnership with employers. These are frequently professional 'top-up' degrees in areas such as nursing, social work and occupational therapy. These are clear examples of programmes designed the new student groups (earlier) referred to – a different, mature student group which demands recognition for prior experiential learning whether in terms of advanced standing within programmes or to make up a credit gap prior to entry to a programme. Programmes that present such opportunities for AP(E)L are again generally located in the post-1992 universities.

The shift from 'salesperson' to 'troubleshooter' for those staff responsible for AP(E)L within institutions can result in a potential tension between the desire to enable maximum flexibility at departmental level and the responsibility to maintain overall quality assurance for university-wide procedures. Institutional procedures that clarify to staff what the boundaries are, but enable sufficient flexibility to meet local needs, go some way towards managing these tensions. Thus, the nature of the collaboration between, for example, an AP(E)L co-ordinator and departmental academic staff becomes that of working together to try to find solutions within a common framework.

A cost-benefit analysis of AP(E)L undertaken as part of a review of AP(E)L procedures at Glasgow Caledonian University indicated largely unquantifiable, but nevertheless substantial, benefits for both staff and students. AP(E)L was considered by practitioners to be a highly marketable aspect of their programmes, both to individuals and, particularly, to employers. It was also reported as having a positive impact on current teaching and research. Staff and students reported that the experience of putting together an AP(E)L claim contributed greatly to an individual's personal development and skills of reflection, critical thinking and organization, as well as self-discipline. These clearly are valuable assets to the students when they embark on their programmes of study.

Finally, having reviewed the experience in Scotland to date, it is clear that there are a number of areas, discussed below, where further development would appear likely.

Targeting AP(E)L provision

Rather than offering access to AP(E)L across a university, even in principle, some practitioners are now suggesting that it might be more effective to target AP(E)L at programmes where the nature of the learning and market conditions provide an appropriate context. Such areas would be determined by subject area, student group, professional body or employer interest. This is likely to lead to a concentration of AP(E)L provision within part-time programmes at post-experience or postgraduate level. In this context, the intrinsic link between AP(E)L and work-based learning is likely to continue to grow.

Group support

The ways in which support is offered for students undertaking AP(E)L claims is evolving, with most institutions investigating ways of providing group support and incorporating peer group support more effectively. The use of group sessions, either on their own or in combination with individual tutorial support, appears to some practitioners to be an effective mode of AP(E)L support. Group approaches at stages where guidance of a more generic nature can be delivered to a number of students also have the advantage of enabling the students to draw upon peer group as well as tutorial support. The exchange of ideas and experiences between students has been seen to be a valued learning tool in the conventional seminar context within higher education, and lends itself equally well to the process of AP(E)L claim preparation. Group sessions have taken the form of a formal 'course', such as a 'Make Experience Count' type of programme, and more informal meetings of students. Because AP(E)L claims are by their very nature highly individualized, provision for individual support, either within the context of a group session or through tutorials, is likely to remain necessary.

Open learning materials

Open learning materials are increasingly being developed to supplement other forms of learning support. Most of these are currently paper-based materials and, therefore, relatively static. But it is likely that future developments will be in the form of computer based materials, which can be readily updated or tailored to particular contexts. Such materials are also increasingly likely to be supported by computer-mediated conferencing and other interactive mediums such as 'answer gardens'. Much of the time conventionally spent by staff in advising students on the processes of putting together an AP(E)L claim might be more efficiently used in the future when supported by appropriate open learning materials.

Variety of assessment tools

Initially, institutions provided a maximum degree of flexibility for students in AP(E)L assessment tools. The use of the 'open' portfolio route, by which the candidate, with guidance, determines the content of the portfolio and the nature of the evidence, has predominated. As indicated previously, this was largely a result of the influence of CAEL and LET in early AP(E)L developments. There is now recognition within many institutions that such flexibility has disadvantages as well as advantages.

The advantages of such flexibility are its recognition of the individual nature of the experiential learning process and of the evidence it generates. The process of putting together an 'open' portfolio can also be a valuable learning experience in itself and a journey in personal development. However, this also requires a level of self-motivation and self-discipline that many students find difficult to sustain, particularly if they have been out of education for some time and lack confidence in their academic abilities. Such students benefit from a more clearly defined structure. Some institutions are therefore currently exploring ways in which they might provide more direction for students through the development of assessment tools specifically designed for experiential learners. These would include the 'structured' portfolio route where there are explicit requirements for particular pieces of evidence to be used in the portfolio. Early consideration of these approaches indicates that this can be a more effective strategy, both in terms of staff time and student effort. Due to the nature of the subject matter or the unavailability of existing evidence, it is now apparent that many students find the portfolio route to be inappropriate. In such cases, project work or 'assessment on demand' are being found to be more suitable options.

It therefore seems likely that future developments in AP(E)L will focus on encouraging a range of support and assessment modes which will take into account differing student and programme needs.

Cycle of collaboration

The nature of collaboration in AP(E)L developments in Scotland is also changing. It has shifted from working with other AP(E)L practitioners from across the higher education sector, as characterized, for example, by the SCOTCAT Forum on Experiential Learning, to working with institutional colleagues at faculty and departmental level within the institutions themselves. Cross-institutional collaboration provided the opportunity to explore ways forward in 'mainstreaming' AP(E)L. The outcome of this exploration was the development of different institutional strategies. The feasibility of these strategies is now being tested as implementation spreads more widely through each institution. No doubt, collaboration between institutions will again be pursued to explore what has been learned from this process. Indeed, the SHEFC is actively encouraging such institutional collaboration in current educational developments.

Conclusion

Over the decade of its development in Scotland, AP(E)L has evolved from a common UK base through the work of the Learning from Experience Trust (and hence CAEL) and the CNAA. It rapidly developed its own distinct and coherent character through: collaborative development and networking; links with developments in further education; the emphasis on work-based learning; partnerships with employers and professional bodies; and its close integration with parallel developments in Scotland, in particular the SCOTCAT Network. This development has taken place within a context where an explicit and collective emphasis has been placed on the assurance of quality and standards and the identification of models of good practice.

The first stage of the cycle of AP(E)L development in Scotland, the innovation phase, can be interpreted as having turned broad policy into practice. The second stage, of reflection and consolidation, can be generalized as distilling good practice into policy. The current stage of new development continues the cycle as new policy is again being translated into more effective practice at an institutional level. The cycle of development, like the story, continues. AP(E)L is likely to be a key element in the response of higher education institutions in Scotland to meeting the lifelong learning needs of the communities which they serve.

References
Ball, C. (1990) *More Means Different: Widening Access to Higher Education*. Final Report, Industry Matters. RSA.

Carmichael, J. (1991) *Accreditation of In-House Training Courses and Accreditation of Prior Experiential Learning – An Employer Perspective*. Stirling University and Glasgow Polytechnic Joint Research and Development Project. Stirling: Department of Employment/University of Stirling.

Davies, P., Gallacher, J. and Reeve, F. (1997) 'The accreditation of prior experiential learning: A comparison of current practice within the UK and France.' *International Journal of University Adult Education 36*, 2, 1–2.

Dearden, G. and Evans, N. (1995) *Curriculum Opportunity: A(P)EL in Higher Education. The Characteristics and Achievements of Some University Students*, 2nd edn. London: Learning from Experience Trust.

Dearing Report (1997) *The National Committee of Inquiry into Higher Education: Report of the Committee*. London: HMSO.

DfEE (1993) *Student Numbers in Higher Education – Great Britain 1980/81–1990/91*. DfEE Statistical Bulletin 17–93.

DfEE (1998) *The Learning Age*. London: HMSO.

Evans, N. (1987) *Handbook for the Assessment of Prior Experiential Learning*. London: Learning from Experience Trust.

Fairhurst. J. (1991) *The Scottish Wider Access Programme*. The Scottish Central Institutions Committee for Educational Development (CICED) and the Polytechnic Association for Continuing Education (PACE): Teaching and Learning in Higher Education Series 5, No. 5. Aberdeen: CICED/PACE.

Garrick Report (1997) *Higher Education in the Learning Society*. Report of the Scottish Committee of Inquiry into Higher Education. London: HMSO.

Higher Education Quality Council (HEQC) (1995a) *The SCOTCAT Quality Assurance Handbook*. Glasgow: HEQC.

Higher Education Quality Council (HEQC) (1995b) *Guidelines for Quality Assurance of Credit-Based Learning*. London: HEQC.

NAGCELL (1997) *Learning for the 21st Century*. First report of the National Advisory Group for Continuing Education and Lifelong Learning (The Fryer Report). London: DfEE.

NAGCELL (1998) *NAGCELL Report on Workplace Learning*. London: DfEE.

Osborne, M., Yule, W., Carmichael, J. and Dockrell, R. (1993) *Accreditation of In-House Training Courses and Accreditation of Prior Experiential Learning – Some Case Studies*. Stirling: University of Stirling and Glasgow Caledonian University.

Quality Assurance Agency (QAA) (1998) *Learning from Experience. The SCOTCAT Quality Assurance Guidelines for Credit Rating and Case Studies*. Gloucester: QAA.

Reeve, F., Gallacher, J., Sharp, N., Osborne, M., Land, R., Whittaker, R., Dockrell, R. and Neal, P. (1995) *Flexible Learning at Work: The DEAL Project Final Report*. Glasgow: Glasgow Caledonian University/University of Stirling/Napier University. Glasgow: Glasgow Caledonian University/Scottish Enterprise.

Reeve, F. and Smith, I. (1996) *Accrediting Prior Experiential Learning: A Manual of Good Practice*. Glasgow: Glasgow Caledonian University.

Scottish Office (1998) *Opportunity Scotland*. Edinburgh: HMSO.

Seagraves, L., Osborne, M., Neal, P., Dockrell, R., Hartshorn, C. and Boyd, A. (1996) *Learning in Smaller Companies (LISC) Final Report*. Stirling: University of Stirling.

Sharp, N. (1991) *Changing Patterns in Higher Education: A Guide to the Development of Credit Accumulation and Transfer in Scotland*. The Scottish Central Institutions Committee for Educational Development (CICED) and the Polytechnic Association for Continuing Education (PACE): Teaching and Learning in Higher Education Series 5, No. 4. Aberdeen: CICED/PACE.

Sharp, N. and Gallacher, J. (1996) 'Working together: Further education-higher education links in Scotland.' In M. Abramson, J. Bird and A. Stennet (eds) *Further and Higher Education Partnerships*. Buckingham: Society for Research into Higher Education and Open University Press.

University of Ulster (1998) *AP(E)L and Lifelong Learning: A Higher Education Perspective*. Newtownabbey: University of Ulster.

Winter, R. (1994) 'Work-based learning and quality assurance in higher education.' *Assessment and Evaluation in Higher Education 19*, 3, 247–256.

Yule, W. and Brownlie-Marshall, M. (1991) *The Assessment of Prior Learning*. The Scottish Central Institutions Committee for Educational Development (CICED) and the Polytechnic Association for Continuing Education (PACE): Teaching and Learning in Higher Education Series 5, No.2. Aberdeen: CICED/PACE.

CHAPTER 7

The Republic of Ireland: The Story of the Assessment of Prior Experiential Learning

Denis McGrath

Introduction

The period since 1960 has been characterized by significant developments in education in Ireland. Against the background of the beginnings of significant economic growth, there commenced an expansion of the Irish education system, both in terms of investment and in terms of participation rates, which continues up to 2000.

In this chapter, it is proposed to describe these developments in so far as they define the setting for the development of policies in relation to the recognition and assessment of prior experiential learning in Ireland. Much of the development took place in the extra-university sector of higher education. The evolution of policy over a 20-year period will be described. Information will also be given in respect of the activities of FÁS (the Irish Training and Employment Authority) in applying accreditation of prior learning (APL) in various areas of industrial training.

Between 1960 and 1980, a number of important reports on various parts of the Irish education system were published. The Commission on Higher Education was established in 1960 and produced its report in 1967 (Commission on Higher Education 1967). The Investment in Education survey undertaken by the Organisation for Economic Co-operational Development (OECD 1965) took place between 1962 and 1965, and the OECD report on the Training of Technicians in Ireland was published in 1964 (OECD 1964). The Steering Committee on Technical Education was established in September 1966 and produced a report embodying a preliminary brief for the establishment of Regional Technical Colleges (RTCs) in January 1967 (Steering Committee on Technical Education 1967).

The Minister for Education, Dr P.J. Hillery, announced the establishment of comprehensive schools and RTCs at a press conference in May 1963 and the first eight RTCs were constructed between 1969 and 1971. The Higher Education Authority (HEA) was established in 1968, and in March 1969 published its report: A *Council for National Awards and a College of Higher Education in Limerick* (Higher Education Authority 1969). A National Institute for Higher Education (NIHE) was established in Limerick in 1971 and in Dublin in 1976. Both NIHEs became universities in July 1989. The National Council for Educational Awards was established in 1972 to promote, co-ordinate and develop higher education in the extra-university sector.

The RTCs offered new higher education courses which had different structures and content than those offered in universities. Two-year full-time courses leading to the award of a National Certificate were established. Those who passed with credit (average examination marks of 55% later increased to 60%) could proceed to a one-year course leading to the award of a National Diploma. In 1970, these courses commenced in a range of new study areas for which there had been no provision hitherto: manufacturing technology, polymer technology, computer science, hotel management and construction technology.

New policy agents were established. The HEA, as mentioned above, was established in 1968; it had a co-ordinating and planning role in higher education while also exercising a funding role in relation to designated institutions – mainly universities.

Participation rates and demographic considerations

In order to understand the factors influencing policy development, factors relating to participation rate in the education sector and population trends should be taken into account.

Between 1960 and 1990, the numbers participating in second-level education in Ireland increased by 167 per cent, and by 316 per cent in the case of third-level education (OECD 1965; Department of Education 1992). Major influences on the increased participation in second-level education were the introduction of free second-level education and free school transport in 1967. The share of public expenditure on education rose in the case of second-level education from 28 per cent to 40 per cent, and in the case of third-level education from 7 per cent to 22 per cent (Department of Education 1992).

The annual number of births in Ireland between 1960 and 1980 increased to a peak of 72,000 in 1980. Thereafter, the birth rate dropped until the number had reached 45,000 in 1994. The rate of decrease has since reduced and a slow reversal is expected.

The impact of the above factors on the higher education system was that government funding had to be increased and universities and colleges were obliged to accommodate increasing numbers of school leavers wishing to participate in the higher education sector. In 1998, arising from the demographic factors described above, the numbers studying for the school Leaving Certificate dropped for the first time, and by 500 candidates.

While there were many reports urging providers to ensure that the needs of adults were met (in terms of participation in the higher education sector), the universities and colleges were well able to fill all their available places with school leavers and thus did not feel any pressure to accommodate adult students. This is not to say that these institutions were not supportive of the idea of participation by adult learners in the higher education sector, it is merely to state that circumstances were such that these institutions were hard-pressed simply to provide places for school leavers (deemed a higher priority than adult students) during this period of expansion. In such an environment, it can be seen that in relation to policies designed to facilitate the participation of adult students in the higher education sector, such as the assessment of prior experiential learning, there was much discussion but little action.

The 1970s – policy development and consciousness raising

The National Institute for Higher Education in Limerick, which was established in 1971, was probably the first institution to introduce the concept of experiential learning into the Irish higher education system. At the outset, its courses were structured on a modular basis and incorporated a period of co-operative education.

During the 1970s, the National Council for Educational Awards (NCEA) set about its work of approving courses in the newly established RTCs and the NIHE in Limerick, while at the same time establishing a policy framework which would allow colleges an acceptable degree of academic freedom in designing courses consistent with a wide degree of cohesion within the extra-university sector. The early activities of the NCEA centred around the development of a 'ladder of awards', from National Certificate through to degree, and the establishment of the criteria which would underpin this policy framework.

In 1975, the NCEA published *Guidelines for the Evaluation of Study Courses* (NCEA 1975). This report introduced for the first time the concept of quantifying a learning experience by using a 'work unit'. A work unit was defined as consisting of three hours of active participation in a course by the student. This three hours of active participation was to include all learning activity. The report further stated (p.11) that 'experience gained in practical work situations, e.g. in industry, business or hospital, may receive credit as part of a study programme. One major issue here would be to determine the relevance and the level of the work experience.' Credit to be given for prior work experience in this case was to be dealt with only on a case-by-case basis, and all work experience was to be evaluated in terms of its relevance. This was the first NCEA policy document which dealt with prior experiential learning, and the effect was that it introduced the concept within the extra-university sector.

In 1973, a government committee on adult education published its report (Committee on Adult Education 1973). Among its recommendations were that adult education courses should be accredited by the NCEA. In response to this, the NCEA established the Working Group on Recurrent Education, which published its report, *Recurrent Education* (NCEA 1978), in May 1978. This working group further developed the ideas in relation to experiential learning established in the 1975 report. Work experience was to be credited and 'problems' were identified as being:

- the level of relevance of work experience to the course content (direct, indirect or general)
- the duration of the work experience
- the combined relevance and duration factors.

Work experience was to be classified into direct, indirect and general categories and a transfer factor calculated in respect of the combination of duration and relevance. In this way, a work unit allowance was to be computed, and students could be exempted from up to 25 per cent of a course depending on the award concerned.

There was little, if any, take-up by colleges in respect of the techniques established for the assessment of prior experiential learning which were described in these policy documents. It is also fair to say that the policy documents in themselves were not overenthusiastic in their espousal of this concept. It was widely regarded as a good idea at the time, but the time was deemed to be not quite right for implementation in a higher education system which was in a state of rapid change and development and was trying to cope with the increasing number of school leavers wishing to participate.

The 1980s – further policy development and consciousness raising

In 1984, a government commission on adult education published its report (Commission on Adult Education 1984); it envisaged third-level institutions having a role to play in the provision of part-time courses leading to degrees and other awards for adult learners. This led the NCEA to establish another working group on adult education, which published its report in July 1985 (NCEA 1985). This report, entitled *Towards Facilitating Awards for Adult and Continuing Education*, recommended the establishment of a credits system related to student effort and also recommended that principles in respect of the assessment of work experience, espoused in the *Recurrent Education* report of 1978, should be applied.

In April 1986, a study tour of a number of higher education institutions in the United States was undertaken by the Director of the NCEA, Pádraig MacDiarmada, Denis McGrath (author) and organized by Norman Evans, then of the Policy Studies Institute, London. This tour, which was partly funded by the Kellogg Foundation, centred on experiential learning, student mobility between institutions and distance learning. Institutions visited were: Lesley College, Cambridge, Massachusetts; New York Institute of Technology; Rockland Community College, New York State; Thomas A. Edison State College, New Jersey; and University College, University of Maryland. Much was learned during the study tour, especially about experiential learning. The concept of the rigorous evaluation of the learning gained from experience, as opposed to the experience itself, was a consistent principle being applied in all institutions visited. Procedures in relation to learning contracts, portfolio design and evaluation, mentoring and assessment were evaluated. A report on the study tour (NCEA 1986) was produced and presented to the Council of the NCEA.

In February 1987, the NCEA published a document, entitled *Awards, Range, Levels and Criteria* (NCEA 1987), which detailed most of the academic policies then in place. It had chapters on the range of NCEA awards, general guidelines and criteria for course design, course guidelines for particular levels of award, and included a section headed 'Work Experience and Experiential Learning' (as follows):

> The Council supports the concept of experiential learning and will give due allowance, in evaluating the quantity dimension of courses, to any prior or concurrent work experience required of students.
>
> The allowance to be given in respect of work experience, whether prior or concurrent, will depend on the full circumstances of the case, with particular reference to the nature and quantity of the work experience, its relationship to the course objectives, and its role in the overall structure of the course.
>
> In general, the Council has not tended to grant an allowance in respect of work experience in excess of 10% of the quantity requirements for a given level of award, although, in special circumstances, a maximum allowance of 25% has been granted.
>
> The Council is prepared to approve arrangements under which students with substantial relevant work experience prior to admission to a course may be afforded exemptions from specified parts of the course on the basis of such experience. (NCEA 1987, p.19)

This new policy restated the policy first promoted in the NCEA publication *Recurrent Education* in 1978. In summary, this was that the NCEA accepted that students should receive credit for prior experiential learning up to a maximum of 25 per cent of the quantity of learning on any approved course and on the basis of receiving individual proposals from higher education institutions. As with other reports published at that time, the absence of a scheme for policy promotion probably played a part in the low take-up of these policy initiatives by the higher education institutions. Of course, the demographic consideration still applied and institutions were primarily concerned with providing the facilities needed to accommodate the ever-increasing numbers of school leavers who were interested in entering higher education.

The 1990s – policy development, promotion and implementation
Policy development

In November 1990, at the invitation of the NCEA, Dr Morris Keeton gave a lecture on experiential learning to a seminar attended by the presidents, directors and principals of higher education institutions in

Ireland. This excellent lecture had a major effect in influencing these individuals towards a situation where the introduction of prior experiential learning became a live policy matter requiring early consideration.

In January 1991, the NCEA established a working group, with terms of reference to develop an NCEA policy, on the assessment of prior experiential learning. The working group was chaired by a former Commissioner of the Garda Síochána (Irish Police Force) and included academics and representatives from industry. It used as its basis the principles espoused by Urban Whitaker in his excellent book *Assessing Learning* (Whitaker 1989). It combined the ten principles of good practice described in this publication with the consideration of important factors in the Irish higher education system, and produced a policy which was launched by the Irish Minister for Education, Niamh Breathnach, in June 1993 (NCEA 1993).

This was the single most important development in the promotion of the assessment of prior experiential learning in Ireland. In this publication, prior experiential learning, or learning gained prior to enrolment on a course, was defined as knowledge and skills acquired through life, work experience and study, not formally attested through formal certification. Experience was defined as the input, and learning outcomes as the result, of a successful learning process. The policy specifically targeted individuals involved in employment, community activity, home duties, sport and other life or work experience. It also stated that prior experiential learning was not to be confused with concurrent experiential learning, 'which is learning planned and structured into a course as a way of achieving certain of the learning outcomes for that course' (NCEA 1993, p.2).

An important factor underpinning the policy was a reliance on learning outcomes as the output of any learning experience, irrespective of its setting. For some years, colleges in Ireland had been using learning outcomes when designing programmes; this policy was now to place a greater discipline on academics, as it could not be applied without the use of properly written learning outcomes. As much of the work of the NCEA has to do with the approval of new programmes in colleges and the review of existing ones, the NCEA insisted that credit for prior experiential learning could apply only to those approved courses which had their individual subjects or modules described in terms of learning outcomes.

In defining the extent of exemption or credit to be granted for prior experiential learning, the policy stated that applicants could gain exemption only from entire subjects or modules on courses or programmes approved by the NCEA as a result of assessed prior learning. Credits were not granted; instead, students were granted exemptions from studying or from being examined in the subjects or modules whose learning outcomes the student had met through prior experience. A decision in relation to an applicant's eligibility for exemption from an entire subject on the basis of prior experiential learning was to lie with the assessor in the individual institution.

Conscious of the fact that full-time students may pass an examination with an average of 40 per cent in a subject or module, the policy gave assessors the guideline that an applicant needed to meet a minimum of only half of the learning outcomes of a particular subject or module in order to gain exemption from that subject. Furthermore, it was stated that, normally, applicants could not be exempted from more than half the subjects or modules on a course without the prior approval of the NCEA.

General guidelines in relation to applications were laid down; they required institutions to ensure that:

- an applicant had selected in the first instance the most suitable higher education course for his or her needs

- a mentoring process was used to review the experience gained by the applicant so as to identify potentially creditable learning and to advise the applicant on the preparation of a portfolio

- having given the applicant an appropriate length of time for preparation of a portfolio (typically 4/5 weeks), an assessor was to evaluate the learning gained from the prior experiential learning described in the portfolio submitted by the applicant

- employment-based prior experiential learning was to be certified by the employer in each case.

Criteria were laid down for determining the quality of the learning as follows:

- there was to be an appropriate balance between the theoretical background to a subject and its practical application

- learning acquired through prior experience was to be transferable to contexts other than that of the learning environment within which it was acquired

- when assessing learning gained from prior experience, care was to be taken to ensure that the learning was at the appropriate academic level.

Examples were cited in respect of each of the issues involved in the policy.

Policy promotion

It was considered that one of the most important aspects of policy development and implementation was the promotion of the policy among the public at large and among academics in the institutions concerned. Considerable attention was paid to this by the NCEA in the weeks following the June 1993 launch by the Minister for Education. For example, an interview was given by this author which was broadcast on the main evening news bulletin on Irish television (RTE) on the day of the launch. There was further newspaper and radio coverage and interviews given in the following weeks. Promotional literature was produced by the NCEA and issued to the higher education institutions in September 1993.

Policy implementation

The final part of the establishment of the assessment of prior experiential learning in the extra-university sector was that of policy implementation. It was considered that a formal process of implementation of the policy was needed if it was to have any real effect in the institutions. Advice was sought in the Faculty of Work Based Learning at Middlesex University in England from Professor Derek Portwood.

In March 1994, seven academic registrars from higher education institutions in Ireland were given an intensive training course in the assessment of prior experiential learning, in a seminar designed by Professor Portwood in consultation with the NCEA, and conducted by the academic staff of Middlesex together with Professor David Justice from DePaul University, Illinois, USA. The objective of this two-day course was to provide participants with mentoring and assessment skills as applied to prior learning, and to enable them to similarly train colleagues in Irish higher education institutions. Following the course, a report was given to the Committee of Directors of Higher Education Institutions in April 1994.

In May 1994, a one-day conference on prior experiential learning was given by the 'Middlesex trainees' using materials from the Middlesex course. This was attended by 100 interested academics from higher education institutions in the extra-university sector. At the conference, invitations were issued for the submission of pilot projects on the implementation of the policy in the institutions.

In July 1994, seven pilot projects were selected and started operating in seven institutions. In September 1994, the 'Middlesex trainees' then conducted a two-day intensive training course for those academics who were going to be mentors, assessors or administrators of the pilot projects selected. The course was based on the one followed in Middlesex.

In February 1995, a one-day seminar on the findings of the pilot projects was held and the findings discussed. Following this seminar, a manual on best practice for the management and administration of APL in higher education institutions was published. This included a detailed analysis of the procedures to be followed in the implementation of NCEA policy and also incorporated a set of documents to be used when administering the policy. It included documents such as an application form, a pro-forma curriculum vitae form, documentation to be used by mentors and assessors in relation to the portfolio and exemptions to be granted, etc. These forms were accepted by the institutions concerned and adapted to suit their own situations.

Finally, in May 1995, training courses were arranged in five regions around Ireland for all those in higher education institutions who were to be involved in the assessment of prior learning. The training was provided by those already trained at Middlesex University or via the pilot projects.

Since the conclusion of that phase of policy implementation, institutions of higher education have been implementing the policy, and students have been given exemptions from subjects on courses leading to NCEA awards.

There was a wide take-up of the NCEA policy on prior experiential learning in NCEA-designated institutions between 1993 and 1998. For example, at Garda Síochána College (Irish Police Training College) the NCEA awards structure allows for students who have completed, to Merit standard, a three-year National Diploma to proceed to a one-year full-time approved course, at the end of which they may be awarded a bachelor's degree. In 1996, the NCEA approved a BA in Police Management which was submitted by the college. The NCEA accepted the case made by the Garda College that all eligible participants on the programme will have studied enough aspects of legal, policing, technical, communications, supervisory and management studies, having successfully passed Garda professional examinations at sergeant and inspector levels and with 20 years' experience in various ranks and assignments, for the programme to be deemed equivalent to a National Diploma with Merit. Participants in the programme then continue their studies, in a distance learning mode, to proceed towards a formal examination and assignment required for the award of the BA in Police Management. While aspects of this programme derogated from the NCEA policy on APL, it was decided that, in this particular case, the full extent of APL principles could be applied productively to the programme.

The Cork Institute of Technology has developed simple procedures for the assessment of prior learning of applicants for its programmes. The procedure used is described on a predesigned diskette, and students may submit their portfolios by providing the required information on the diskette provided. Employees of the pharmaceutical company Schering Plough entered 12 students for the National Certificate in Applied Biology at the Institute. Approximately one-third of the total learning experience of these students was measured using a combination of prior learning and work-based learning, primarily in the area of laboratory theory and practice as well as quality control.

Dovatron International entered 15 students for the National Certificate in Electronic Engineering. These students received subject exemptions in engineering communication and practice, and computer applications. The Institute has also started a portfolio development programme at night for 32 students who are interested in progressing to higher education programmes there.

The Institute of Technology, Tallaght, was established in 1992 in a new town on the outskirts of Dublin. It is located in the centre of an industrial area and many of its programmes have direct links with local industry. Of 110 students enrolled on a National Certificate in Mechanical Engineering course, 17 students were granted exemption on the basis of their prior learning. Fifteen of a total of 130 students of electronics were granted exemptions from the National Certificate in Electronic Engineering. The Institute has also devised modules based on the learning of employees at specific levels in the Intel Corporation. These modules constitute electives on their programme, leading to the National Certificate in Electronic Engineering. These electives were all approved by the NCEA.

For many years, forestry workers in Ireland have undertaken a variety of training programmes and have developed skills in forestry management. The Waterford Institute of Technology evaluated these skills, and a proposal was submitted to the NCEA for consideration for the award of a National Diploma in Forestry Management. This proposal was accepted. Two hundred and forty students were awarded the National Certificate in Forestry Management, and 190 students were awarded the National Diploma in Forestry Management, based entirely on their prior experiential learning, without the need for any learning in a formal academic environment. Whilst this was outside normal NCEA policy, this specific proposal was accepted as a special case.

APL and Irish universities

In recent years, the assessment of prior experiential learning has been developed in Irish universities, primarily in the newer universities, Dublin City University and the University of Limerick. The principles described above are generally applied and are often used to grant admission to taught master's degree programmes to individuals who may not hold a first degree. Students are also given exemptions from subjects on degree programmes. It is expected that the extent of the application of prior experiential learning principles in Irish universities will expand significantly as the proportion of adult students gaining admission increases.

Development of accreditation of prior learning at FÁS (Irish Training and Employment Authority)

The Certification and Standards Department of FÁS has developed and tested a number of approaches to the accreditation of prior learning for occupations in retailing, construction, childcare and, more recently, in the craft occupational area (Lambkin 1998). APL in FÁS stems from a policy of widening access to certification. It is also called 'taking credit'. It is taking credit for what you know you can do.

FÁS defines APL as a process which enables people of all ages and backgrounds to attain formal certification for experience, skills and knowledge they already possess. APL has developed in response to a demand from individuals and companies to certify skills and experience acquired over time at work rather than those acquired through formal training courses. The APL process itself involves a skills audit of the individual and the gathering of proof through assessment or a portfolio, or both. This is then assessed against the standards of performance for the particular occupation or qualification. FÁS did not develop new philosophies but drew on the existing literature and transformed it into pragmatic workable models. The same certificate is awarded irrespective of where the skills are achieved, as it is the certified skill which is important, not how it was achieved.

As a major player in vocational certification, FÁS thoroughly researched the APL concept in the development of the process and has gathered information on the APL issue in Ireland and abroad. Initially, a Euroform project using APL in the retail sector led to the development of the APL process. Since that time, the APL experience of FÁS has provided its expertise on APL in South Africa.

This work has been undertaken by the Certification and Standards Department. Project Leader Angela Lambkin and Donal Kerr, Manager of the Department, have provided their expertise to participating companies, which include the Electricity Supply Board, Quinnsworth Supermarket, Arnotts Plc, department store, Ardkeen Superstores, Waterford Chamber of Commerce, the Construction Industry Federation, the Construction Committee of the Irish Congress of Trade Unions, the South African Qualifications Authority, and the Building Industry Training Board in South Africa.

The range of FÁS activities in the APL area between 1994 and 1998

FÁS is presently participating in a European Centre for the Development of Vocational Training (CEDEFOP) project on 'Identification, Validation and Accreditation of Prior and Informal Learning'. FÁS is one of four EU states selected on account of the range of experiences in APL to date. This work is ongoing and will determine a model for APL for a Europe-wide study.

FÁS has provided APL for the construction sector in partnership with employer bodies and unions offering FÁS/City and Guilds certification to tower crane drivers, bank employees, telescopic mobile handlers and scaffolders. This work has been undertaken in conjunction with the Construction Industry Federation and the Irish Congress of Trade Unions, and will be extended to other construction occupations.

A major project to accredit Irish Electricity Supply Board linepersons to craft electrician status commenced in 1997 and is the first APL experience in the craft area in Ireland. FÁS is providing advice, training and assessment support to enable the Board to facilitate some 400 linepersons to achieve National Craft Certification as electricians.

FÁS has developed a programme of childcare (level 2) certification by APL. This certification is equivalent to National Council for Vocational Awards level 2. The certification covers the same areas as those provided on the conventional course. The programme, piloted in Navan, is currently operating in Tallaght, Waterford and Wexford. The programme operates flexible times which suit participants. Childcare (level 1) and community care – care of the elderly (level 2) APL programmes are nearing completion. Up to 700 persons are expected to avail themselves of these APL programmes in the next two years.

FÁS International Services has also completed an APL pilot project in South Africa, participating with the Building Industry Training Board, for the occupational areas of bricklaying and carpentry (1995–1996). The project in Bloemfontein involved over 300 people from nearby townships. Of these, 161 were awarded skill certificates and 19 were certified with full craft status. The pilot was successful in meeting its objectives and showed that APL (RPL – recognition of prior learning – as it is known in South Africa) could work in the vocational sector there. FÁS also trained and certified APL (RPL) advisers and assessors who can continue this work in South Africa.

FÁS *Guide to APL* – a trainer guide to APL – has been developed by FÁS to support employer-led accreditation. This guide was tested in 1997 using an employer group linked to the Waterford Chamber of Commerce.

An FÁS/Euroform pilot project, with three retail companies offering accreditation to sales assistants, employed and unemployed, was completed in 1995. A software package (expert system) to facilitate the occupational analysis element of the process has been developed as part of the project. Successful participants received FÁS/City and Guilds certification in retailing as a result of the project.

Summary

In this chapter, a description has been given of a process which commenced with consciousness-raising in relation to an educational idea and which was carried through to implementation over a 20-year period. The demographic and participation rate factors which influenced the take-up of policy on the assessment of prior experiential learning in Ireland were described, and the deliberative processes, by way of policy development and their effectiveness in the context of this background, were analysed. The use of APL in the industrial training sector was described. Finally, a description was given of the circumstances when the policy on the assessment of prior experiential learning in the extra-university sector was put in place and the policy was described in detail.

Since this chapter was written, the government has enacted the Qualifications (Education and Training) Act 1999 (Government of Ireland 1999). One of the objectives of this Act is the following: 'to promote the recognition of knowledge, skill or competence acquired through research, adult and continuing education and training and employment'.

This will mean that recognition of learning in these settings will become a statutory obligation of the new bodies to be established under this Act. This ought to be a major force to promote the accreditation of prior experiential learning in the Republic of Ireland.

References

Commission on Adult Education (1984) *Lifelong Learning*. Dublin: Stationery Office.

Commission on Higher Education (1967) *Report of Commission on Higher Education*. Dublin: Stationery Office.

Committee on Adult Education (1973) *Adult Education in Ireland*. Dublin: Stationery Office.

Department of Education (1992) *Statistical Report*.

Government of Ireland (1999) *Qualifications (Education and Training) Act*. Dublin: Stationery Office.

Higher Education Authority (1969) *A Council for National Awards and a College of Higher Education at Limerick*. Dublin: Higher Education Authority.

Lambkin, A. (1998) Personal communication.

NCEA (1975) *Guidelines for the Evaluation of Study Courses*. Dublin: National Council for Educational Awards.

NCEA (1978) *Discussion Document on an NCEA Award Structure for Recurrent Education*. Dublin: National Council for Educational Awards.

NCEA (1985) *Towards Facilitating Awards for Adult and Continuing Education*. Dublin: National Council for Educational Awards.

NCEA (1986) *Experiential Learning, Student Transfer and Distance Learning*. Dublin: National Council for Educational Awards.

NCEA (1987) *Awards, Range, Levels and Criteria*. Dublin: National Council for Educational Awards.

NCEA (1993) *Prior Experiential Learning: NCEA Policy*. Dublin: National Council for Educational Awards.

OECD (1964) *Training of Technicians in Ireland*. Dublin: Stationery Office.

OECD (1965) *Investment in Education*. Dublin: Stationery Office.

Steering Committee on Technical Education (1967) *Report to the Minister for Education on Regional Technical Colleges*. Dublin: Stationery Office.

Whitaker, U. (1989) *Assessing Learning: Standards, Principles and Procedures*. Philadelphia: Council for Adult and Experiential Learning (CAEL).

CHAPTER 8

The Recognition of Prior Learning in Australia: An Ambivalent Relationship with the Academy, Competency-Based Education and the Market

Rick Flowers and Geof Hawke

Introduction

There is still much work to be done in Australia if recognition of prior learning (RPL) is to bring about promised changes to education and training. The Australian Qualifications Framework Advisory Board (1997, p.2) succinctly summed up the changes RPL is expected to bring about: 'The rationale for RPL is three-fold: it eliminates wasteful duplication of education and training, enhances equitable access to a qualification and encourages a more constructive relationship between the culture of institutionalised education and training and the culture of the workplace and, more broadly, of life experience.'

It is now almost a decade since RPL has been actively promoted in the schools, and the higher education, vocational education and training sectors in Australia. But the available evidence indicates that the extent of RPL provision is small (Eyres 1997; Haydon 1997; Kenyon 1997). There is also little evidence that RPL has led to significantly improved access to credentialled learning for disadvantaged groups or individuals (McDonald 1995). And RPL has yet to build closer relationships effectively between those who hold dearly to traditional notions of 'academic' knowledge and those who advocate more recognition of work-based and experience-based learning. The expansion of competency-based education in Australia has been a double-edged sword for RPL. It has, on the one hand, helped build a close relationship between institutionalized education provision and uncredentialled learning in work and community settings by promulgating a system for naming and assessing learning that happens outside the classroom. But competency-based training has, on the other hand, also entrenched a rigid and narrow way of naming learning which has discouraged alternative ways of recognizing experience-based and work-based learning. By not encouraging alternative ways of recognizing learning, traditional notions of knowledge, as established within institutionalized education and training, have remained largely unchallenged.

There does remain, however, continued interest in the changes RPL is expected to bring about, and RPL assessment provision is likely to grow. Anecdotal evidence indicates that the reasons for the expansion of RPL may have more to do with providers jostling for more competitive edge, within an increasingly deregulated education and training market in Australia, than with the reasons given by the Australian Qualifications Framework Advisory Board (quoted above). A more competitive educational market, which is being actively encouraged by conservative Australian governments, is likely to create an expansion of RPL, as providers vie to offer the most generous RPL scheme in order to attract the most fee-paying students.

RPL has an ambivalent relationship to the market because there are both opportunities and constraints in a market-driven expansion. The opportunities are that expansion of RPL may encourage efforts to build closer relationships between experience-based learning, work-based learning and traditional notions of 'academic' learning. The constraints are that market forces will narrowly concentrate on arrangements with experience-based and work-based prior learning that have the most potential to attract fee-paying students versus access and equity student target groups.

Definition of terms

By recognition of prior learning (RPL) we [in Australia] mean the same thing as the British when they talk about Assessment of Prior (Experiential) Learning (APL or AP(E)L) or the North Americans when they talk of Prior Learning Assessment (PLA). With the development of more formal structures for RPL within companies has come the term Recognition of Current Competence, partly as a way of emphasising 'current' rather than 'prior', and partly reflecting the industry focus on recognising areas in which people can demonstrate 'competence' rather than 'learning'. (McDonald 1997, p.2)

RPL 'has become the standard term used by educational institutions in Australia, and refers particularly to credit given within a course' (McDonald 1997, p.2). The most common definition of RPL in Australia is that proposed by the Vocational Education, Employment and Training Advisory Committee: RPL is 'acknowledgment of the skills and knowledge held as a result of formal training, work experience and/or life experience' (VEETAC 1993, p.2).

'It felt like going for a parole interview'

In various ways, RPL policy and practice developments at the Faculty of Education in the University of Technology, Sydney, mirror RPL developments across Australia. This chapter will discuss developments in that Faculty and connect them with other educational experiences in Australia. It begins with a brief account of one of the first RPL assessments carried out in that Faculty.

Lenny was an RPL applicant who was able to make a strong case for having learnt much that was relevant to his community education degree studies from his prior experiences, largely as a prison inmate who had lobbied for, and organized, prison education programmes. When Lenny was asked to comment on the RPL assessment process, he said, with a wry smile: 'It felt like going for a parole interview.' Although the university, in this case, did recognize Lenny's prior learning, his comment highlighted the role of the 'academy' as a gatekeeper of what is to be credentialled as university-based learning. The university staff who managed Lenny's RPL assessment had mixed feelings about this gatekeeper role. On the one hand, it seems responsible that universities act as guardians of what should be judged as 'academic' knowledge. On the other hand, RPL was encouraging us to examine critically the way we were defining 'academic' knowledge, and we wondered whether we had a useful framework to assess Lenny's experience-based learning.

Lenny's prior learning was assessed in 1992, when the Faculty developed for the first time a scheme to assess prior uncredentialled learning of students who sought exemptions from course subjects. In order to make RPL assessment decisions, it was believed to be necessary to develop more detailed subject descriptions than we had at the time. More detailed subject objectives and assessment criteria were written. There were workshops and tutorial sessions to help students examine the subject descriptions and to consider whether they had already learnt some of the subject matter. Students were advised to analyse and document their prior learning by tracing achievements in previous community, family and work experiences. This approach was built on an assumption that informal and experience-based learning can be equated with formal and university-based learning. Further on in this chapter, there is a commentary on the complexities of this assumption.

The introduction of the RPL scheme in that Faculty in 1992 was driven by two broad imperatives. One imperative came from a keen desire to respond to growing calls to recognize the prior learning of mature-aged Aboriginal students; the RPL scheme was first implemented in a degree programme for such students. Another imperative was to engage with a national training reform agenda that took off in the early 1990s. RPL was asserted as a key strategy in the reform agenda which was first enshrined in the National Framework for the Recognition of Training (VEETAC 1992a). Of the 31 principles that defined that framework, five concerned RPL (VEETAC 1992b):

- **Principle 1: Competence** The recognition of prior learning will focus on the competencies a person has acquired as a result of both formal and informal training and experience – not how, when or where the learning occurred.

- **Principle 2: Commitment** It is important that training providers have a commitment to recognizing the prior learning of individuals.

- **Principle 3: Access** Every individual must have his or her prior learning recognized.

- **Principle 4: Fairness** All participants must be confident that the recognition of prior learning process is fair.

- **Principle 5: Support** Individuals ... must be given adequate support.

In the early 1990s, there seemed some promise that RPL policies and practices would expand in the Faculty and that it would encourage a deeper critical examination of what is worthwhile 'academic' knowledge and how we define it. This promise, however, faded early. An RPL assessment scheme did continue in an undergraduate programme, but it has been dominated by the more pedestrian exercise of recognizing prior credentialled learning or credit transfer applications. There has been a sense from both students and staff that assessing prior uncredentialled learning is unrewarding and too hard. Until 1999, RPL did not do much to inspire an examination of the ways we define the nature and levels of academic knowledge in our degree courses.

Why did the interest in, and energy for, RPL in the Faculty remain low, or fade? In hindsight, there are three likely reasons. In what follows, each of these reasons is discussed in some detail and connected to wider RPL developments in Australia.

First, traditional notions of 'academic' knowledge remained paramount. A widely held view among staff is that prior uncredentialled learning can be recognized as equivalent to 'practical' but not 'theoretical' university subjects. A related view is that students should not be exempted from theoretical subjects because they need this university-based 'academic' knowledge to prosper in modern Australian society. This view was expressed forcefully by some Aboriginal lecturers on behalf of Aboriginal students (McDaniel and Flowers 1995). Second, a common refrain from students and staff is that applying to have prior uncredentialled learning recognized involves more effort than it is worth. Third, federal government legislation prevented Australian universities charging fees for RPL assessments; this has discouraged the Faculty from developing more than *ad hoc* RPL assessment arrangements in its postgraduate courses.

Moving towards 2000, there is renewed interest in developing RPL arrangements in the Faculty. This can be partly explained by market-driven forces, which are discussed in the final section of this chapter. As education providers and universities in Australia are being encouraged to be more commercially oriented, it is no surprise that RPL is increasingly seen as a competitive tool. When considering market forces, it is instructive to see how work-based learning (WBL) appears to be challenging traditional notions of 'academic' knowledge far more effectively than RPL has done. WBL initiatives have been concerned in striking deals with large corporations and government agencies, where their employees can have on-the-job learning – their experiential learning – included and credentialled in a university degree course of study. The Faculty and the University as a whole have promoted WBL as a strategic priority, and actively foster debate about the implications it has for our understanding of what constitutes a university-based education (Garrick and Kirkpatrick 1997; Yasukawa and Griffin 1998). RPL also has the potential to foster this sort of debate, but it does not have the same market attraction as WBL.

The extent of RPL provision across Australia

Before discussing RPL policies and practices at a national level, the
extent of RPL provision is sketched in according to the available
information. The extent of RPL in the Australian vocational education and training (VET) sector is small. In 1995, it was estimated
that

> Australia saved a nominal 4.1 million hours of training in the VET
> sector through granting RPL and 7.4 million hours of training
> through granting credit transfer to students or trainees. This rep-
> resents considerable savings but it represents only 4.1 per cent of
> the overall hours for which students and trainees enrolled.
> (Kenyon 1996)

Table 8.1, which is based on 1997 data, indicates that there has been a
decline in RPL levels since 1995. Kenyon (1997) also suggests that
the data indicate some decline of RPL in favour of credit transfer.

Table 8.1 Percentage of all module enrolments in which students were granted RPL or credit transfer		
State	**RPL**	**Credit transfer**
New South Wales	2.56%	2.0%
Victoria	2.30%	0%
Queensland	1.50%	1.0%
Western Australia	0.97%	3.0%
South Australia	6.40%	0.9%
Tasmania	2.11%	1.8%
Northern Territory	0.31%	0%
Australian Central		
Territory	2.61%	5.0%
Australia	2.10%	3.0%

National Centre for Vocational Education Research Ltd (NCVER) (1998)

The data are derived from an arrangement whereby state and
territory VET systems are required to report annually on a wide range
of statistical matters, including the extent of recognition granted

through RPL. The data, though substantially based on enrolments in technical and further education institutes, include provision from a range of other VET providers such as community colleges, commercial providers, enterprises, etc.

As is clear from the table, there is great diversity in the extent of RPL granted from state to state. To date, no formal examination of this phenomenon has been conducted; but, amongst those working in the state systems, the most commonly accepted explanation lies in the very different ways in which RPL is treated by the states for funding purposes. In some states, little or no funding is provided to institutions which report that students have been awarded RPL. In others, differing proportions of the standard funding unit apply. Clearly, states where no funding is provided are less inclined to offer credit by RPL and are more likely to reach other arrangements with students. This includes, for example, enrolling students with exemption from formal attendance requirements or with varied assessment arrangements.

In Australia's 38 universities, the extent of RPL assessment activity is also small. While federal government statistical collection protocols make it difficult to distinguish between the number of students who had their prior uncredentialled versus credentialled learning recognized, it is nonetheless possible to make inferences about the extent of RPL activity in universities. In a survey conducted in 1996 (Haydon 1997), it was reported that:

- only 40 per cent of the universities had RPL assessment opportunities available in all their courses
- less than half of the universities make RPL policies available to prospective and current students
- specialized RPL assessment procedures have not developed widely in higher education
- 78 per cent of respondents use the same procedures to assess credit transfer applications as they do to assess prior uncredentialled learning
- specialized RPL assessment training for staff is rare in universities (11.1%).

Note: the above is seen to contrast with best practice in parts of the USA and of the UK, where such programmes are routine, and with the recommendations in the Australian Vice-Chancellors' *Guidelines on the Recognition of Prior Learning.*

The survey also commented:

Half the respondents took the opportunity to propose reasons why the development of RPL assessment in universities continues to be slow, with the most commonly identified problem being the demands which it places on the time of staff required to carry out 'customised' assessments; other issues raised by respondents included: a lack of RPL assessment expertise and training in universities; resistance by academic staff and professional bodies; delays caused by the need to develop special policies and procedures for RPL; and disincentives to grant credit inherent in the existing funding arrangements for universities. (Haydon 1997, p.7)

Up against or with the academy

This subheading highlights the ambivalent place RPL has in the educational establishment. On the one hand, there are policies and practices which champion the claim that RPL has the potential to make a significant improvement to academic notions of education and the curriculum for a mass system. On the other hand, there are those which defend traditional academic notions of education. This ambivalence or contestation is played out in universities in two ways. One way is through the negotiations about what value to accord various qualification levels. Another way is through the discussions about what are acceptable ways for knowledge from prior learning to be constructed.

Most Australian universities have traditionally not recognized for university credit any learning from course qualifications 'below' diploma level. This practice is based on an assumption that there is a neat progression in the complexity and level of learning as one moves up the hierarchy of qualifications – certificate, diploma, bachelor's degree, graduate certificate, graduate diploma, master's degree and doctorate.

RPL raises lots of awkward questions. Should RPL arrangements be conceived in this hierarchical manner? How much recognition of lower-level awards should be given for credit in higher-level courses? In response to these questions, there is a wide variety of views and practices in Australia's education system. Government, industry and union bodies have strongly encouraged universities to recognize learning below diploma level. And many universities have shifted. But in 1996, a report by the Australian Credit Transfer Agency found that only half the Australian universities were encouraging credit for certificates and had formal agreements with vocational education providers (Haydon 1997).

Traditional academic notions of knowledge are built upon an assumption, 'reinforced by the hierarchical character of career thinking, that post-school education is a two-dimensional vertically structured system, in which everyone aims to reach the highest possible level in one particular field' (Golding, Marginson and Pascoe 1996, p.ix).

A national research project about generic skills in the context of credit transfer and the recognition of prior learning (Golding *et al.* 1996) challenged this assumption. It found that many people studied because they wanted specialised skills and knowledge and were not always interested in vertical mobility. It argued:

> It is a kind of cultural cringe to assume that all technical and further education courses are necessarily at a 'lower level' than higher education … Courses and sectors are more heterogeneous than that. In recognition arrangements, qualifications at the same formal level cannot always be interchanged. Knowledge requirements are often more important than levels of achievement. (p.x)

But it will take many years to overcome this 'cultural cringe'. In the meanwhile, there is likely to be an intensified debate in Australia in the coming years about mobility across qualification levels in the context of RPL, as the education market is further deregulated. Vocational education providers are now able to offer graduate certificate courses. There are diverging views about whether such graduate certificates are to be deemed the equivalent of university graduate certificates, let alone whether they should be recognized for credit in university master's degrees.

Stuart (1995) argued that 'most of the research work that has been done around AP(E)L has concentrated on the structures for assessment of prior learning rather than questions of the relationship between the academy and knowledge' (p.162). Stuart was referring to the situation in the UK. But it applies equally well to Australia. Jones and Martin (1997) argue that RPL has been less concerned with empowerment and more concerned with gatekeeping; in other words, with checking that individuals have learnt what is deemed worthwhile by educational providers. They assert that 'RPL has the potential to value experiential learning fully and to challenge the myth … that education can only be acquired in a bastion of learning' (p.16). They continue:

To date, most of the research conducted on RPL has explored the issues surrounding the assessment process, namely the interview; whether the results of the assessment have both validity and reliability; whether the assessment system can be streamlined and the cost reduced; whether the key competencies in the workplace have been achieved; whether RPL is useful and economically viable for both industry and tertiary education, which system is the pinnacle of 'best practice'. On the other hand there appears to be a dearth of literature on the benefits of RPL empowering the individual; on RPL being a meta-cognitive process; on RPL providing the means through which the individual can critically examine their values and assumptions; on RPL and the identifying, valuing and assessing of informal and incidental learning; on RPL as a catalyst for change in the assessment processes of tertiary education. (p.16)

Davison (1998) also refers to this tension in the way the 'academy' might relate to RPL.

RPL could ... be a very concrete way of reaffirming Gramsci's belief that all people are intellectuals and not just those fortunate enough to have gained whatever rewards there are from university learning due, in part, to their class or cultural capital. Thomson (1994) suggests that RPL can hoist academics, specifically teacher educators, with their own petard. He claims it can force them to ask their students to consider: what counts as (worthwhile?) learning; under what conditions can this occur; who should this learning be for; what can be accepted to confirm that such learning has occurred. (pp.4–5)

But, according to Davison, RPL is a double-edged sword. It can, and does, encourage some academic staff to increase the specificity of academic requirements. This can help universities resist RPL by

incorporating RPL into existing conventional and traditional practices in ways that suit well established ends, often couched in terms of 'maintaining' standards. There all kinds of standards in addition to academic ones and the standards that are likely to be maintained by universities incorporating RPL would include: that university standard learning should occur in universities; this learning should be administered and overseen by someone tertiary prepared for this; written submissions in academic discourse demonstrating appropriate structure, syntax and academic capdoffing is the best way of demonstrating that university standard learning has occurred ... (1998, p.5)

Up against or with competency-based training

The most significant recent reform in Australian education and training has been the promulgation of competency-based training. In many ways, the major impetus for formalizing and extending RPL in Australia came from competency-based training. So, in this respect, RPL is with competency-based training. In other respects, however, competency-based training offers restraints to the further development of RPL. This is the implication in the subheading that RPL is 'up against ... competency-based training'.

The Commonwealth and all state and territory governments took a decision in 1990 that Australia's vocational education and training system would become 'competency-based'. At the heart of this decision was the notion that the essential competencies required by workers to carry out defined job functions could be identified, and that formal assessment processes would then be able to certify that an individual had demonstrated achievement of those competencies. Moreover, it was a core assumption that the means by which such competencies had been acquired was not relevant to the certification decision.

RPL was, in that light, an obvious development. It was seen as simply an assessment process for judging competence. It differed from on-course assessment only in the administrative sense that it did not also involve the provision of opportunities for, and the facilitation of, learning. However, it also differed from traditional forms of assessment. Competence was about the ability to 'do the job', and hence was not something to be assessed by pencil-and-paper exams. The competency-based training movement offered the opportunity to overthrow the tyranny of traditional assessment, and RPL was a significant sign of the shift being made.

In terms of developing the country's skills base, RPL was seen as a vital strategic element because it would facilitate recognition of the skills of workers in many industry sectors where, historically, few or no formal education or training systems had operated. Once competency standards for that sector had been developed, recognition against those standards could quickly follow.

It did not take long before a number of assumptions that underpinned competency-based training and RPL were questioned. It was soon recognized, for example, that, having defined the standard of competence to be achieved as 'that required for effective performance in the workplace' (National Training Board 1991), assessment could rarely be a simple one-off event. Rather, competence often needed to be demonstrated in a range of different settings and over time. In the context of the understanding of the notion of 'competence' and, hence, of competency-based assessment that emerged progressively during the early 1990s, assessment involved the collection of evidence to enable an informed judgement to be made (see, for example, Gonczi 1993; Hagar, Athanasou and Gonczi 1994). For instance, in the case of competencies involving interpersonal relationships, accumulating such evidence might need to occur over weeks, if not months.

A second issue to emerge also related to the nature of 'competence'. Initially, it had been assumed by many that competence was essentially a behavioural manifestation: that to prove competence required simply demonstrating that you could 'do the job'. Increasingly, however, it was recognized that competence also involved knowledge and the application of knowledge. Moreover, it was often either difficult or inefficient to assess knowledge in the context of normal work. This was an issue for both RPL and regular assessment, but was especially salient in the context of RPL, which had been seen to be a cost-effective alternative to traditional training arrangements.

Another, and still largely unresolved, issue relates to the currency of competence. This is an issue which has salience for all competency certification, but in the case of RPL it had particular significance. In essence, the issue involved is shelf-life. How long after being certified as competent in some specific area does that assessment of competence remain valid? Does a person necessarily remain competent at, say, conducting chemical titrations 20 years after being first certified as competent? In many cases of RPL practice, vocational educators had adopted pragmatic responses to the amount of time a full assessment of competence would require and relied, instead, on assessment based around portfolios which documented past work (or other) activities in which the applicant had demonstrated competence. For many, this was a dubious approach to take, so they sought to redefine the principle by talking instead of the recognition of current competence (RCC). This clarified the notion by emphasizing that recognition was only to be provided where the competence could be demonstrated now, rather than where it had been demonstrated in the past. RCC has, however, never been adopted as official policy, though some providers practise it.

The issues outlined above are technical. A deeper, perhaps philosophical, issue is the claim that the current single set of rules for constructing competency assessment standards is stifling the way

prior learning is conceived and assessed. Accreditation and regis-
tration rules state that competency assessment standards must be
written in a hierarchical, itemized and check-list fashion. If RPL is
tied to competency assessment, it forces RPL applicants and assessors to conceive of prior learning in such a way that it matches a
detailed check-list. In some cases, RPL applicants are being asked to
provide items of evidence for each assessment criterion or check-list
point. The theory is that competency standards, despite their significant detail and uniform structure, need not shape the way people
teach, learn and assess. The contrary argument is that the rules for
constructing standards as check-lists, in practice, are directly shaping
curriculum and assessment practices. A holistic assessment approach
suggests it is not necessary to assess all criteria, at least not in itemized
fashion. But the very shape of the standards in a check-list form begs
the question: If there is a list of criteria, should all of them be assessed?

And the queries continue. Why do assessment standards have to be
written in check-list form? Why can't they be written in narrative?
Why do they have to be written? Could they be constructed through
diagrams and pictures? Or could they be constructed through narrative prose which is documented on video or tape? The way standards
are constructed has implications for the way learning is conceived.
For some people who are used to books and lists, existing competency
standards may be fine. For people who may be quite 'learned' but are
not used to books and lists, the competency standards may appear as a
straitjacket. Take the case of Lenny, the RPL applicant discussed
earlier in the chapter. He found the process of matching his prior
learning to the subject descriptions and lists of objectives an arduous
and forced exercise because he did not conceive his learning in the
traditional way of the 'academy'.

Waldman (1993, p.83) suggests that competency assessment
'seems to sit comfortably alongside the empiricism and scientific
evidence so beloved of traditional education. Therefore it is likely that
the values which have underpinned higher education for so long have
barely shifted at all'. Stuart (1995) continues:

> In other words, AP(E)L is not challenging the traditional knowl-
> edge base as established within the academy. It is simply trying to
> find methods and structures to fit the alternative ways people have
> used to gain that knowledge into an acceptable accreditation
> framework for the establishments. This does not seem to be good
> news for people who have gained their knowledge outside the edu-

cation system, especially if that knowledge was gained within a different societal framework. (p.162)

Up against time and cost

A particular constraint for RPL has been that of cost. Providers have learnt that carefully designed assessment for RPL purposes is, in many cases, expensive, both in time and material requirements. Indeed, the view is often expressed that it is cheaper for someone to enrol normally in the course than for a provider to assess them for RPL.

A similar view has been expressed by many students. Assessment for RPL purposes often involves considerable commitment of time and critical reflection on the part of the applicant. Development of portfolios, for example, when being done in retrospect is a time-consuming activity. Students often choose to enrol in the full programme as an 'easier option' rather than apply for RPL. Moreover, there is evidence that this reluctance to seek RPL is not uniform across the population of aspiring applicants. Students who are less confident of their ability, or who come to formal study through less traditional pathways, appear to be less likely to seek recognition than those from more privileged backgrounds (Australian National Training Authority 1996).

Hence the ambivalent 'with or against' relationship which exists between RPL and the academic establishment; the system of competence-based training and the market itself extend to the pockets and minds of individuals themselves. This is a far cry from the three potential benefits proclaimed by the Australian Qualifications Framework Advisory Board in 1997 (as quoted at the beginning of this chapter). How far those principled expectations can be realized in the future, or come to be seen as another piece of unrealistic idealism, is at this stage impossible to predict.

References

Australian National Training Authority (1996) *Recognition of Prior Learning for Aboriginal and Torres Strait Islander Peoples 1995: Project Report.* Melbourne: ANTA, National Staff Development Committee.

Australian Qualifications Framework Advisory Board (1997). *Recognition of Prior Learning*, Carlton, Victoria: Australian Qualifications Framework Advisory Board.

Cohen, R., Flowers, R., McDonald, R. and Schaafsma, H. (1993) *Learning from Experience Counts.* Sydney: University of Technology.

Davison, T. (1998) 'The recognition of prior learning in Australian universities: The right reasons by the wrong consequences.' Conference Paper, Griffith University.

Eyres, V. (1997) *Recognition Practices in the Australian Secondary Schools Sector.* Carlton, Victoria: Australian Qualifications Framework Advisory Board.

Garrick, J. and Kirkpatrick, D. (1997) *Work Based Learning.* Sydney: Flexible Learning Action Group, University of Technology.

Golding, B., Marginson, S. and Pascoe, R. (1996) *Changing Context, Moving Skills: Generic Skills in the Context of Credit Transfer and the Recognition of Prior Learning.* Canberra: Australian Government Publishing Service.

Gonczi, A. (1993) 'Integrated approaches to competency based assessment.' Paper presented to VEETAC National Assessment Forum, Sydney.

Hagar, P., Athanasou, J. and Gonczi, A. (1994) *Assessment: Technical Manual.* Canberra: Australian Government Publishing Service and Department of Employment, Education and Training.

Haydon, A. (1997) *The Nature and Extent of Recognition of Prior Learning in Higher Education.* Carlton, Victoria: Australian Qualifications Framework Advisory Board.

Jones, M. and Martin, J. (1997) 'A new paradigm for recognition of prior learning.' In W. Fleet (ed) *Issues in Recognition of Prior Learning.* Melbourne: Victorian RPL Network.

Kenyon, R. (1997) *The Status of Recognition of Prior Learning in Vocational Education and Training.* Carlton, Victoria: Australian Qualifications Framework Advisory Board.

McDaniel, M. and Flowers, R. (1995) 'Adult education and indigenous Australians.' In G. Foley (ed) *Understanding Adult Education and Training.* Sydney: Allen & Unwin.

McDonald, R. (1995) *Recognition of Prior Learning: Report on Case Studies.* Sydney: Assessment Centre for Vocational Education.

McDonald, R. (1997) 'Research into RPL: Only three issues left.' In W. Fleet (ed) *Issues in Recognition of Prior Learning.* Melbourne: Victorian RPL Network.

National Training Board (1991) *National Competency Standards: Policy and Guidelines.* Canberra: National Training Board.

Stuart, M. (1995) '"If experience counts, then why am I bothering to come here?": AP(E)L and learning.' In M. Stuart and A. Thomson (eds) *Engaging with Difference: The 'Other' in Adult Education.* Leicester, UK: National Institute of Adult Continuing Education.

VEETAC (1992a) *National Framework for the Recognition of Training: A National Framework for a Competitive Australia.* Canberra: VEETAC Working Party On The Recognition Of Training.

VEETAC (1992b) *Nationally Recognised Training: Bringing it Together.* Canberra: VEETAC Working Party On The Recognition Of Training.

VEETAC (1993) *Arrangements for the Recognition of Prior Learning in Australia.* Canberra: Vocational Education, Employment and Training Advisory Committee.

Waldman, J. (1993) 'Gender and AP(E)L: Reinforcing social and sexual divisions?' In J. Storan (ed) *Getting to the Core of AP(E)L.* London, UK: Southern England Consortium Credit Accumulation and Transfer.

Yasukawa, K. and Griffin, J. (1998) Discussion paper arising from a literature survey of research in informal learning in the workplace. Sydney: Flexible Learning Action Group, University of Technology.

CHAPTER 9

Recognition of Prior Learning: The Promise and the Reality for New Zealanders

Phil Ker, Mary Melrose and Maureen Reid

Overview

The driving force behind recognition of prior learning (RPL), as we know it in New Zealand, came from the New Zealand Qualifications Authority (NZQA), which was established with the task of creating a more open and flexible qualifications framework – one which would be concerned with 'gate opening that creates more possibilities for students, while maintaining national standards' (NZ Govt 1989, 2.2.3).

NZQA worked from a specific legislative obligation to develop a national framework where 'there is a flexible system for the gaining of qualifications with the recognition of competence already achieved' (Education Amendment Act 1990). NZQA was proactive in encouraging widespread interest in RPL, identifying a range of benefits which could accrue to education and training in New Zealand. Individual learners were to benefit on a variety of levels: gaining a qualification in a shorter time at lower cost; having valid skills and knowledge recognized in their own right, or as building blocks for a qualification; and enhanced self-confidence and sense of self-worth. RPL would open doors to further study, new careers and new opportunities. Industry would benefit because workplace learning would be credited towards formal qualifications and training dollars would be more accurately targeted. Educators were to benefit from close links with industry and from the diversity of experiences which, inevitably, they would come across in their role as assessors of prior learning.

More importantly, NZ society would benefit from what was promising to be an important educational efficiency strategy. Scarce educational dollars would not be wasted on teaching people what they already knew; consequently, places on educational programmes would be opened up to those previously denied access. Equally important, RPL would be a significant educational equity strategy: creating opportunities for those who may be denied access to further education because they lacked formal educational prerequisites. In particular, RPL would offer real opportunity to Maori people, and to women, whose life experiences and associated learning have traditionally been undervalued.

Thus, the promise: improved access to education, a more efficient education system and much closer linkages between industry and educational providers. Alas, some seven years down the implementation track, RPL has failed at a national level to make a significant impact on any of these fronts. The history of RPL in New Zealand is one of vision without leadership, rhetoric without resources, and of local initiative without consistent support. Of course there are success stories, but these are confined, so far, to individual learners and a handful of institutions. Only a few polytechnics, colleges of education and industry training organizations have succeeded in embedding RPL processes into their everyday activities. Within the remainder of our educational providers, including universities, RPL activity is spasmodic, occurring often at the initiative of individual enthusiasts. NZ universities have absented themselves from the whole qualifications framework initiative. Usually, they have reacted to RPL as if it is politically and conceptually inextricably entangled with the framework, as NZQA was persistently promoting both together in the early 1990s.

The history of recognition of prior learning in New Zealand educational institutions

The polytechnics and the colleges of education have led New Zealand's tertiary sector in policy development and implementation of RPL. There are historical and philosophical reasons for this. Polytechnics in NZ primarily focus on vocational and work-oriented programmes. They endeavour to provide access to tertiary education for those who were early school leavers but may have had considerable work experience, to promote equal opportunity in education for previously disadvantaged groups and to strengthen links with industries, businesses, Maori trusts and other community groups. Staff of teacher training colleges are primarily interested in the theories and practices of teaching, learning and assessment, and are accepting of the principles of lifelong learning and equivalence of learning wherever it occurs.

It was always the intention of NZQA to establish a seamless qualifications system from school to university. However, the universities have resisted the establishment of the national framework of assessable units of learning, especially at the level of degree and postgraduate programmes. Further, the universities have consistently opposed the idea of formal articulation schemes because of a perceived threat to their autonomy. Each individual university has continued to stipulate the transfer of credit which is acceptable into its own programmes from degree programmes at other universities and, to a small extent, at polytechnics and colleges of education. For most universities, this is the main or only system of recognition of prior learning in operation, although some staff from Massey University, Victoria University and Waikato University have been active researchers and advocates in the field of RPL (Harre-Hindmarsh 1992; Methven 1992).

Evidence of the early interest in, and support of, RPL by polytechnics and colleges of education can be seen in the pattern of activity in the early 1990s in NZ. The first exploratory study in NZ of what was termed 'assessment of prior learning' was carried out at Palmerston North College of Education (Griffin 1990). Late in 1991, NZQA contracted Nelson Polytechnic to develop guidelines on how RPL policies might be introduced (McDougall and Gunn 1992). By the end of 1992, many polytechnics or departments within them were already drafting policies (Gunn 1992; Harre-Hindmarsh 1993). NZQA sponsored research in the early half of the 1990s at Christchurch College of Education (Sheehan 1992), the Open Polytechnic (Hornblow 1994) and Victoria University (Harre-Hindmarsh 1992). The NZ Council for Educational Research, in partnership with NZQA, set up on-line RPL databases for use by providers and carried out some research themselves (Benton 1991; 1995). Benton (1995) writes that institutions at the forefront of the RPL movement in NZ included Christchurch, Waikato and Nelson Polytechnics, Wanganui Regional Community Polytechnic, Palmerston North and Christchurch Colleges of Education and a number of private training establishments.

The early 1990s saw a flurry of NZQA-sponsored activity, which included training sessions in the Broadmeadows RPL system. The

Broadmeadows College of Technichal and Further Education (TAFE) consisted of three phases: the request, the assessment and the review (Davis 1992). In the request phase, the RPL facilitator advised the applicant about course requirements and how to present past experiences in relation to course outcomes. In the assessment phase, a panel assessed the application and interviewed the applicant. The panel decided either to grant recognition, deny recognition or require further assessment. The review phase was used to check the assessment methods, gather further information or to judge appeals.

In 1993, Broadmeadows trainers offered programmes in Auckland and Wellington, and polytechnic staff predominated as trainees. Early trials of RPL in polytechnics were based on the Broadmeadows model at Auckland Institute of Technology (AIT) and Christchurch Polytechnic (Sheehan 1993). Methven (1992) and Harre-Hindmarsh (1993) reported on activities which were occurring or planned in NZ educational programmes. As well as RPL for teacher training, there was provision for RPL for students of management (AIT), nursing and human or health sciences (AIT, Manawatu Polytechnic and Taranaki Polytechnic), community and social work (Waikato Polytechnic) and catering (Christchurch Polytechnic). As it transpired, the Broadmeadows model was shortlived, in the New Zealand context. Dissatisfaction emerged with the Broadmeadows model in terms of resource intensiveness and cost, and of the reliability of interviewing as a dominant assessment methodology (Ker 1993b).

NZQA sponsored a national conference on RPL in 1993, with some 150 participants, of which 61 were from polytechnics and colleges of education and only eight were from universities. Papers were, however, presented 'by a broad spectrum of representatives from polytechnics, colleges of education, universities, employees, industry, Maori, Pacific Island (*sic*), private training providers, government agencies and other groups' (NZQA 1993b, foreword). This conference represented the last significant public initiative by NZQA in support of RPL, although in 1995 an RPL Institute was established with NZQA involvement to run seminars to disseminate some of the results of research into RPL (Hornblow 1995).

In 1996, NZQA commissioned a three-year research project into the state of RPL in New Zealand. This research was to investigate the extent to which RPL for unit standards was taking place, and to identify and report examples of good practice, with a view to encouraging further activity (Reid *et al.* 1996a, 1996b, 1997). The research project was cut short at the end of 1997 after two years, following a strategic realignment of the role of NZQA to being a policy and quality monitoring agency only, thus bringing to an end NZQA's active involvement in RPL.

Early leaders in the implementation of RPL were the tertiary teacher training programmes at AIT (Melrose 1992) and Wellington Polytechnic (Wicks 1993). Not only were trainees (polytechnic staff and community educators) able to have their prior learning recognized, but also they were able to undertake training in the theory and practice of RPL facilitation and assessment. Indeed, the availability of credit-bearing RPL modules preceded the development by NZQA (in 1994) of its own unit standards for RPL facilitation and assessment.

It is important in tracing the history of RPL in New Zealand to recognize the changing emphasis placed by NZQA on RPL as the National Qualifications Framework (NQF) developed. Initially, RPL was promoted as a significant feature of the NQF in its own right (NZQA 1991), and educational providers were expected to demonstrate RPL capability as part of the accreditation process to offer nationally recognized qualifications (NZQA 1993a). This relatively high profile for RPL contributed to significant institutional activity in terms of policy development and RPL trials.

In 1995, NZQA shifted the emphasis from RPL as a stand-alone strategy to RPL as part of a broader conceptualization of assessment that is, assessment as a process involving diverse forms of evidence, of which evidence from prior learning was a part. Accompanying this shift was the beginning of the new terminology: assessment of prior learning. This change in emphasis was significant. It was interpreted by many decision makers within provider institutions that RPL was no longer a requirement, and it undoubtedly served to reduce the momentum of implementation (Reid, Melrose and Ker 1996).

RPL in the New Zealand workplace

A key component of the NQF was that unit standards would be assessed, not only by teachers within educational institutions but also by workplace assessors in the workplaces of New Zealand. Assessment of prior learning against unit standards was to be an important part of the drive to credentialize the existing workforce of NZ. Since NZ educationalists were traditionally experts in assessment and recently had become experts in RPL, and since workplace supervisors and industrial training organizations (ITOs) had little experience in formal assessment, partnerships developed between industry and educational organizations. Southland Polytechnic was one of the first to set up an assessment centre in conjunction with local industries (Methven 1992). In the mid-1990s, several polytechnics were accredited by NZQA to train workplace assessors, and these training courses continue to the present day. Some polytechnics have agreements with the relevant ITOs to carry out a form of collaborative assessment, where the employer and the polytechnic staff members both have an input into assessing unit standards in that industry. Typically, polytechnic staff assess theory and the employers assess practice. In other cases, a polytechnic department is contracted by the ITO to do all the assessment of particular unit standards (Reid *et al.* 1997).

A survey of 25 places known to carry out workplace assessment (Reid *et al.* 1997) established that almost all were assessing against NQF unit standards at the lower levels, with a few conducting assessments related to in-house programmes. Forty per cent of those responding indicated that they assessed prior learning (that is, competencies gained by employees prior to the training provided in the workplace), and a similar percentage provided support (such as RPL policy, facilitation, explanation, encouragement or further training for employees interested in RPL). However, activity levels were low. This finding reinforced observations by Capper (1996), who noted very little RPL in the workplace and that workplace trainers were struggling with how they might conduct RPL. Assessment of prior learning in the workplace tends to be linked to the developmental stage that each industry has reached in implementing NQF-based workplace training. It appears that for most industries the general implementation of workplace assessment is a significant challenge in its own right. Consequently, the practical implementation of RPL has been assigned a relatively low priority.

Current levels of RPL activity

The most recent information on RPL activity is provided by Reid and her colleagues (Reid *et al.* 1996a; 1996b; 1997). Of the 39 organizations which responded to the 1996 survey, 29 conducted some form of assessment of prior learning (all of the polytechnics and colleges of education and half of the private training establishments and ITOs). The educational fields within which assessment of prior learning for framework units was occurring at four or more organizations were: engineering and technology; agriculture, forestry and fisheries; business and financial services; and computing and information technology. In addition, assessment of prior learning against non-framework standards was occurring in: health; education; arts and crafts; business and financial services; and computing and information technology.

However, activity levels were low, limited to only a few fields of learning and generally at the lower levels of the qualifications framework. Interestingly, the majority of prior learning assessments were not against unit standards, but were in relation to provider qualifications. This reflects the fact that most assessment activity was undertaken by public sector education providers. There has been a relatively low uptake of unit standards by these providers, who, by and large, have preferred to maintain their own educational programmes for which they seek national accreditation. This may well reflect the relative importance of professional qualifications in the programme mix of public sector providers, and the fact that most unit standard development has occurred at lower levels of the NQF.

It remains to be seen how extensively unit standards will be incorporated into the programmes which polytechnics and colleges of education are offering, and therefore the extent to which assessment of prior learning will be against NQF unit standards. The uptake of unit standards will depend, to a degree, on the extent to which ITOs are able to control qualifications for their industry. In some cases, the ITO and relevant employers are demanding that providers teach to, and assess, the unit standards that make up national qualifications. This is the case with automotive engineering, the first industry to have unit standards approved on the NQF. For this industry, the polytechnics have formed a consortium and are in partnership with the industry training organization over delivery of a modified and flexible programme (Sorenson 1996).

The 1996 survey (Reid *et al.* 1996a) showed that the practice of assessment of prior learning was frequently fragmented within organizations, being confined to a few fields, programmes or teaching departments. Assessors were often practising in isolation within the organization, without knowledge of other assessors within their own organization and usually without contact with other assessors in their own subject area in other organizations. Over half of the organizations which were surveyed had some form of training for assessors of prior learning, but only eight required assessors to undertake the training before they conducted assessments.

There was a great diversity of practice concerning requirements to implement prior learning assessment. The initial implementation of

RPL policy and procedures in this sample of tertiary organizations in NZ seemed to depend, to a greater extent, on the enthusiasm of individuals, often at a programme or student-support level, and, to a lesser extent, on the support from senior staff for some RPL policy or system at the organizational level (Reid *et al*. 1996a; 1996b). Most of those sampled had a clear policy framework for RPL, but few required staff to be proactive in offering prior learning assessment; and few actively advertised or promoted prior learning assessment. Rather, the institutional approach seemed to be one of reacting to student requests when and if they occurred.

There was a considerable range in organizational attempts to monitor the quality of RPL. A hands-off approach, allowing those who were implementing prior assessment to carry it out and record it without any moderation, existed as one extreme. In the middle was an 'internal consultant' approach to quality, whereby those who were engaged in assessment sometimes made use of trained specialists as mentors. At another extreme, there was an internal accreditation process, where the teaching department demonstrated to other academics within the organization a basic capability and preparedness to offer RPL as a service (Reid, Melrose and Ker 1996).

The follow-up survey was conducted in 1997, with two-thirds of the respondents reporting significant changes in prior learning assessment over the previous year (Reid *et al*. 1997). Some reported an increase in the range of fields for which they were offering RPL. For most, the changes were to offer RPL for higher-level programmes (especially as degrees become more common in the polytechnics and colleges of education) or to increase the frequency at which RPL was occurring for students on current programmes. As expected, there was a growth in the amount of RPL being granted for unit standards. One ITO reported increased learning activity with respect to unit standards, and one polytechnic reported increased inquiries from ITOs for assistance with RPL. The influence of industry and ITOs, the enthusiasms of particular staff, management initiative (for example, in formulating or reviewing policy or appointing an RPL co-ordinator or committee) and sudden demand were listed as the most important factors influencing the overall modest, but steady, growth in RPL activity (Reid *et al*. 1997).

RPL and educational equity

In promoting RPL as an important part of its proposed framework, NZQA highlighted its potential for advancing the educational opportunities of those who traditionally had been disenfranchised or poorly served by New Zealand's tertiary education system – particularly women, Maori people, Pacific Island people and those people living with the effects of disabilities.

It is clear that early RPL enthusiasts, who organized a range of pilot programmes to develop RPL experience, were mindful, and often hopeful, of equity outcomes. RPL was envisaged as a positive mechanism for redressing the limited formal educational opportunities of disadvantaged groups, and of enabling such people to gain access to employment by shortening the time it took to get a qualification. Although not a panacea for socio-economic disadvantage, RPL was seen as a significant way in which people could be empowered and hence gain access to resources and jobs (Coleman *et al.* 1993).

RPL was seen by many as having potential to benefit Maori people in particular, by affirming their cultural learning context as well as their cultural skills (Benton 1995). There has been a notable uptake of RPL in some fields of study (for example, social services, education and training), where experienced Maori are needed as role models and educators for the new generation. As well, RPL has taken a secure foothold in affirming prior learning in qualifications which incorporate *Te Reo* (Maori language) and *Tikanga* (Maori culture). Active marketing of the opportunities for RPL within the Maori community and on *marae* (Maori meetings) by Maori staff is considered essential for the improvement of access to educational programmes. Group seminars and panel assessments are a popular method of encouraging Maori applicants through the process of RPL (Coleman *et al.* 1993; Reid *et al.* 1996b).

However, RPL was seen as more than just an equity strategy in favour of disadvantaged groups. It was also to be a means of removing some of the barriers to further education that contributed to New Zealand's relatively low rates of participation in tertiary education by the population at large (Ker 1993a). Unfortunately, the potential of RPL as a means of advancing educational equity in New Zealand has not been fulfilled in practice. It is difficult to pin down specific reasons for this, although it is suspected that it has much to do with the particular approaches to assessment that have been adopted in practice and with practicalities surrounding the resourcing and administering of RPL. Coleman *et al.* (1993) found in their pilot study that the process of transferring learning from a *marae* context to a social service fieldwork context was problematic; and students had difficulty in relating their life experiences to the prescribed competencies of the particular qualification. Ker reported that the business studies pilot in which he was involved consciously ruled out from the pilot group participation those who 'had not committed themselves to formal study at an institution, and who may have reservations about formal study' (Ker 1993b, p.2), on the grounds that the support necessary to do justice to these people was beyond the resources and capabilities of the project team.

The dominant approach to the assessment of prior learning in New Zealand has been one of requiring applicants to match clearly defined competence or learning outcomes and assessment criteria as detailed in course documentation. Assessment practice most commonly makes use of challenge testing and portfolios; there is limited resort to interviews and virtually no acceptance of attestation as a form of evidence. Thus, assessment of prior learning tends to follow classroom assessment practice (Reid, Melrose and Ker 1996).

Further, courses of learning in NZ polytechnics and colleges of education have tended to be tightly prescribed (a consequence of institutional interpretation of NZQA's course approval requirements), making it difficult for people with broad experience to find exact learning matches between the evidence of their learning and prescribed learning outcomes in courses. This difficulty is exacerbated where the assessment itself is focused on detailed assessment requirements, rather than on broader outcomes; that is, if assessment is disaggregated, rather than holistic. Common practices for describing courses and for assessing learning tend to erect barriers to education, which it was intended RPL would remove.

Officially, and as encouraged by NZQA, courses were to be described in more accessible ways and assessment was to be holistic. Even if this were to be the case, it is doubtful that educational equity would be any further advanced, because RPL practice does not receive the resourcing needed to support those most in need. Those approaching tertiary education for the first time, perhaps with only loosely formed ideas about where they would like their studies to take them, require significant support and guidance if they are to make a sound case for receiving academic credit for the learning they bring with them. Such support requires institutions to invest relatively heavily in an RPL facilitation service. The lack of investment in RPL infrastructure, and facilitation in particular, is a feature of RPL activity in New Zealand today (Reid *et al.* 1996a; 1996b, 1997). Thus, even if the potential which RPL might offer was widely known within NZ society (which it is not), institutions are simply not geared to provide adequate help to those who might come forward. Rather than being a service for those seeking to enter tertiary education, RPL is, in NZ, a service for those who are already there.

Conclusion

The implementation of RPL in New Zealand has had a relatively short history, beginning in the early 1990s with the initial development of the New Zealand qualifications framework. The period from late 1991 to 1994 was one of intense interest and experimentation, during which most polytechnics and colleges of education developed sound policies, with many of these institutions setting up pilots to test implementation procedures. Unfortunately, the early promise has not translated into a significant level of activity. In most cases, RPL processes failed to find fertile ground at an institutional level. Primarily, this was the result of a lack of resources (at both national and local levels); a lack of leadership (again, at both national and local levels); and a failure by many of those institutions which showed an early interest in RPL to put into place sound co-ordinating mechanisms and support services for both applicants and teachers.

NZQA accreditation requirements for national programmes and degrees require some RPL provision within the programme documentation, but there is no coherent national support or networking system for RPL policy development or implementation. While there was an early proliferation of training programmes, seminars and research projects funded wholly or partially by NZQA in the early 1990s, this source of financial support has now completely evaporated. NZQA's perceived stop-start policy implementation has been identified as a factor causing institutional equivocation in implementing prior learning assessment (Reid, Melrose and Ker 1996). In addition, there is growing staff concern over the effect of prior learning on funding (Reid *et al.* 1996a; 1996b, 1997). The Ministry of Education will not fund educational institutions for RPL facilitation or assessment processes and, if RPL is granted, the student effectively becomes enrolled in a shorter and smaller programme, with a potential loss of funding for the institution (if the student cannot be replaced for that component of the programme). Thus, decision makers within tertiary institutions often perceive RPL as having negative financial effects, rather than focusing on RPL's potential benefits.

However, there are some institutional success stories (Reid *et al.* 1997), which offer reason for hope that RPL may yet take hold, and the encouraging signs of a slow but steady growth in activity. Recent research into good practice in RPL (Reid *et al.* 1996a; 1996b, 1997) has identified a range of key factors (see Appendix for RPL Good Practice Guidelines) which contribute to those successes which prevail in New Zealand. First, successful implementation of prior learning assessment requires effective systems to be put in place and maintained. It is clear that the success is largely dependent on: the appointment and training of prior learning personnel (facilitators and assessors); adequate resourcing; and some degree of central co-ordination within the organization. Second, there is a clear link between the quality of facilitation and the efficiency and reliability of prior learning assessment. Where applicants have access to good-quality support, the evidence which is presented for assessment is almost always matched more carefully to learning outcomes and assessment criteria. Assessors are then likely to evaluate the evidence efficiently and can draw conclusions with greater reliability. Third, for assessment of prior learning to be implemented successfully and in a fair, transparent way, assessors must be willing to seek and to acknowledge an equivalence of learning for on-course students and prior learning applicants. Assessors must also be open to different approaches to assessment and to accept diverse sources of evidence which demonstrate that appropriate learning has taken place. Further, it appears that where RPL is flourishing there are some common contexts: relationships have been forged between ITOs and those providers who promote RPL; professions value qualification recognition and upgrading for their members; community and provider support exists for cultural and equity initiatives; and programmes are based on experiential learning processes which incorporate vocational practice situations.

What of the future? RPL has a foothold in educational practice in New Zealand. Its future will continue to depend on the initiatives of individual providers, and of individual enthusiasts working within provider organizations. NZQA is unlikely to provide any further significant impetus, given its current and likely future roles in standards setting and quality monitoring, rather than in implementation – unless, of course, NZQA includes in its quality requirements evidence that RPL is occurring and is appropriately resourced. ITOs, which could be a significant force for implementation of RPL, face an uncertain future in terms of their financial viability and must contend with the increasing contestability in the provision of education and training.

Further, New Zealand tertiary education is moving to another level of provider competitiveness, brought about by the recent government decision to fund all enrolments in tertiary courses. Without the constraint of capped enrolments, providers have every reason to try to increase the total tertiary market and to improve their market shares. RPL will offer, as it always has, the potential to open the doors to a tertiary education for a significant proportion of the New Zealand population who are currently not participants. Perhaps those providers who are proactive in RPL will gain competitive advantage over others.

References

Benton, N. (1991) *From Hegemony to Symphony*. Wellington: NZCER & NZQA.

Benton, N. (1995) *Recognition of Prior Learning: An Introduction*. Wellington: NZCER.

Capper, P. (1996) 'Assessing workplace skills for the National Qualifications Framework.' Paper presented at the Partnerships in the Assessment of Student Achievement Conference, Auckland, September.

Coleman, B., Hopkins, J., Matheson, R., Rivers, S. and Waaka, A. (1993) 'Recognition of prior learning in the social services: Personal, political and cultural issues.' Paper presented at the Recognition of Prior Learning and the National Qualifications Framework Conference, Wellington, April.

Davis, S. (1992) *Recognition of Prior Learning, Ford/TAFE Articulation Project*. Principal Report. Broadmeadows College of TAFE.

Education Amendment Act (1990)

Griffin, H. (1990) *Assessment of Prior Learning*. Report prepared for the Palmerston North College of Education, Te Kupenga O Te Matauranga. Palmerston North: Palmerston North College of Education.

Gunn, C. (1992) 'Recognising prior learning: What is it? What does it involve?' *NZ Journal of Adult Learning 20*, 2, 51–64.

Harre-Hindmarsh, J. (1992) *Recognition of Prior Learning: An Exploratory Study in a NZ University*. Wellington: NZQA & Victoria University of Wellington.

Harre-Hindmarsh, J. (1993) 'Recognition of prior learning in Aotearoa: Recent developments.' *Lifelong Learning in Aotearoa, 4*, 11–12.

Hornblow, D. (1994) *Recognition of Prior Learning: Making a Case at a Distance*. Wellington: The Open Polytechnic of NZ & NZQA.

Hornblow, D. (1995) *Recognition of Prior Learning*. Proceedings of the RPL Institute, Auckland–Wellington–Christchurch, August. Wellington: RPL Services.

Ker, P. (1993a) 'Implementing processes for the recognition of prior learning.' Paper presented at the Tertiary Education Conference, Wellington, April.

Ker, P. (1993b) 'Implementing procedures for RPL: Issues arising from a pilot programme at Auckland Institute of Technology.' Paper presented at the

Recognition of Prior Learning and the National Qualifications Framework Conference, Wellington, April.

McDougall, J. and Gunn, C. (1992) *Recognising Prior Learning: Guidelines in Policy Development*. Nelson: Nelson Polytechnic & NZQA.

Melrose, M. (1992) 'Developing a curriculum for teacher education and staff development at the tertiary level.' *Tutor 40*, The Journal for New Zealand Polytechnics, 11–17.

Methven, P. (1992) 'Recent developments in the accreditation of prior learning in New Zealand.' Paper presented at the AARE/NZARE Conference, Deakin University, November.

New Zealand Government (1989) 'Learning for life: Education and training beyond the age of fifteen. Policy Decisions.' Wellington: New Zealand Government.

NZQA (1991) *Designing the Framework*. Wellington: NZQA.

NZQA (1993a) *The Recognition of Prior Learning*. Wellington: NZQA.

NZQA (1993b) *Recognition of Prior Learning and the National Qualifications Framework*. Conference Papers, 21–23 April. Wellington: NZQA.

Reid, M., Horsburgh, M., Ker, P. and Melrose, M. (1996a) 'Assessment of prior learning research project.' Progress report to the New Zealand Qualifications Authority, Auckland Institute of Technology, June.

Reid, M., Horsburgh, M., Ker, P. and Melrose, M. (1996b) 'Assessment of prior learning research project, phase two: Semi-structured interviews.' Progress report to the New Zealand Qualifications Authority. Auckland Institute of Technology, November.

Reid, M., Ker, P., Melrose, M. and Horsburgh, M. (1997) Assessment of Prior Learning Research Project: Phase 3 Workplace Assessment and Assessment of Prior Learning Survey 1997, Draft Assessment of Prior Learning Guidelines: Progress report to NZQA. June. Auckland: Auckland Institute of Technology, June.

Reid, M., Melrose, M. and Ker, P. (1996) 'Assessment of prior learning in the New Zealand tertiary sector.' Paper presented at the Partnerships in Assessment of Student Achievement Conference, Auckland Institute of Technology, September.

Sheehan, D. (1992) *Recognition of Prior Learning Trial: Final Report*. Christchurch: Christchurch College of Education & NZQA.

Sheehan, D. (1993) 'Organisational culture and RPL.' Paper presented at the Recognition of Prior Learning and the National Qualifications Framework Conference, Wellington, April.

Sorenson, D. (1996) 'Initiatives in education and industry links in developing and implementing a new training system.' Paper presented at the Partnerships in the Assessment of Student Achievement Conference, Auckland Institute of Technology, September.

Wicks, A. (1993) 'Prior learning and the Diploma in Tertiary Teaching' *Tutor 40*, The Journal for New Zealand Polytechnics, 8–10.

CHAPTER 10

Learning Assessment in South Africa

Yunus Ballim, Rahmat Omar
and Alan Ralphs

Introduction

The context of transition to democracy in South Africa is as complex
and difficult as it is profound. It is now nine years since the release of
Nelson Mandela from 27 years in prison, and seven years since the
inauguration of a democratically elected government and the writing
of a new constitution. During this period, South Africans across the
board have been drawn into programmes of policy formulation,
legislation and *masakhane* (let us build together), aimed at removing
the legacy of apartheid and focusing the nation on the challenges of
reconstruction and development.

The story of prior learning assessment, more commonly referred to
in South Africa as the recognition of prior learning (RPL), forms a
part of this complex history and, more recently, of the strategic
initiatives aimed at promoting a new culture, curriculum and capacity
for lifelong learning. In this chapter, we will cover some of the
significant milestones in this story, with specific reference to: the
socio-economic realities and challenges; the history and development
of the National Qualifications Framework in SA; links with leading
international organizations; and the work of the Joint Education
Trust in promoting new research and development programmes at
the interface of higher education and workforce development.

Education and inequality: The socio-economic scene in South Africa

While the past few years have seen a significant move towards racial
integration and nation building, South African society is still largely
characterized by the unequal and fragmented social and economic

formations established during the apartheid years. This has a profound effect on national thinking and planning around issues of RPL and skills development and on achievable targets over the next few years.

Population poverty and unemployment

South Africa has a population of approximately 43 million, of which 88 per cent are black (previously disenfranchised: 77% African, 9% coloured and 2% Asian) and 12 per cent are white (Calitz 1996). The country has a gross domestic product of around US$75bn or US$1740 per capita (South African Institute of Race Relations 1997). However, black people are significantly overrepresented in the poorer sections, where 53 per cent of the population live in the poorest 40 per cent of households and spend less than US$70 per adult per month, while the poorest 20 per cent of households spend less than US$36 per adult per month (Department of Finance 1997).

Estimates of the level of unemployment in South Africa vary widely, but it is generally accepted that the rate of unemployment is in the region of 29 per cent of an economically active population of 14.3 million people (Central Statistical Services 1996). The phenomenon of mass unemployment amongst the youth of South Africa remains one of the most vexing problems facing our new democracy, with most authors citing figures in the region of two million in 1998 (Department of Education 1998).

But perhaps more important is the changing nature of employment opportunities and the spatial and sectoral distribution of unemployed adults and youth. These originate in the systemic and structural conditions of life under apartheid, where influx-control legislation and the Bantustan policy of separate development forced the majority of black people into patterns of rural–urban migration, with severe restrictions on land ownership, employment, education and residential rights outside of the so-called homelands.

Since the removal of the apartheid laws and restrictions, the country has seen a rapid growth in urban population densities, with a concomitant increase in demands for education and employment. These expectations have not been met, particularly in the formal sector of the economy which saw a loss of 440,000 jobs between 1988 and 1995, the largest proportion of these losses being in the lower-grade employment categories of mining and construction. Ironically, the position of those who previously had access to better education and training has improved dramatically: job opportunities are reported to have increased by 290,000 from 1994 to 1995 (South African Institute of Race Relations 1997), and it appears that most of these have been created in the higher employment categories, requiring workers with higher training and skill levels.

Education and training

A central pillar of the apartheid government's apparatus was the development of an inferior system of mass-based schooling which left a devastating legacy of millions of young people and adults whose basic education is hopelessly inadequate and incomplete. In 1995, 13 per cent of South Africans over the age of 20 had not had any formal education, while 30 per cent had less than six years of formal education (Central Statistical Services 1996). The corresponding figures for the white population group are 0.2 per cent and 0.8 per cent respectively. A further analysis of the figures shows that, in 1995, 55 per cent of black South Africans had a level of education which was not sufficient to qualify for formal access into artisan training programmes, which represents the lowest level of post-secondary school training for employment.

The inherited inequalities of the system of higher education are reflected throughout the network of some 21 universities, 15 technikons and 140 colleges in the country. The University Education Act of 1959 established the basis of separate and inferior facilities for black South Africans, so that by 1993 the participation rates for Africans in higher education was 6.3 per cent, in contrast to the 54.4 per cent of whites and 62 per cent for Indians (NCHE – National Commission for Higher Education 1996). Even more significant are the racial and gender inequalities which prevail across the disciplines. Figures cited in the NCHE Report show that 'in 1991 fewer than 35 per cent of the students enrolled for professional degrees in fields such as business, computer science, agriculture and engineering were black and more than 70 per cent of the students registered for natural sciences were white' (p.10).

Currently, there is no single higher education qualification framework. Instead, what exists are separate, disarticulated qualification structures serving universities and technikons. These are characterized by closed (impermeable), rigid boundaries, allowing for very little articulation between sectors or with the rest of the education and training system. The result is minimum transfer and mobility of students horizontally and vertically within the system.

One of the striking features of education and training provision in South Africa has been the emergence and growth in the 1980s of a large number of non-governmental organizations (NGOs), providing education and training opportunities to thousands of out-of-school youths and illiterate adults, and to teachers, workers, community organizers and other individuals not served by the apartheid government. This was the time when experiential learning programmes, inspired by the work of noted education theorists such as Paulo Freire, Carr and Kemmis, and others, became a prominent feature of the student, labour and community-based organizations involved in a protracted war of position against the apartheid state (Alexander 1989). Substantive amounts of sympathetic local and foreign funding fuelled the development of new programmes and modes of course delivery, particularly in the fields of adult education, teacher in-service training and early childhood 'educare'. While these organizations played an important role, their growth remained largely uncoordinated and unregulated – their programmes were rarely recognized and accredited, either by mainstream education and training institutions or between NGOs themselves.

There are clearly two imperatives which drive the need for innovative approaches to adult and experiential learning in South Africa. The first is the large gap between the increasing skills expectations of the job market and the levels of education and training of a large proportion of the population. Given the political and economic path which the country has taken, RPL represents a vital piece in the strategy to accelerate opportunities for working adults and the unemployed to acquire the knowledge and skills for their effective participation in socio-economic development. The second, and equally important, imperative is the need to address the racial imbalance in opportunities for employment. Much of the accelerated skills development needs to be targeted at the black sector of the population, not only to address the disadvantage caused by past political policies, but also because of the recognition that the skills demands of the new development vision for the country cannot be satisfied by the white sector of the population alone. In order to meet these imperatives, the new government has had to create a policy environment within which change and innovation can be successfully implemented within the institutions of learning and between them and the institutions of civil society and the economy.

New policy frameworks for adult learning and workforce development

The purpose of policy and legislative development since 1994 has been driven by the greater goals of reconstruction and development, a central pillar of which is the development of our human resources (African National Congress 1994).

> The challenge we face at the dawning of a democratic society is to create an education and training system that ensures people are able to realise their full potential in our society as a basis and a prerequisite for the successful achievement of all other goals in this reconstruction and development programme. (p.59)

To meet this challenge, the new government has chosen a course of transformation, including the development of a National Qualifications Framework (NQF), which arguably constitutes the most comprehensive and complex component of curriculum transformation in the education and training system since 1948. The origins of the NQF can be traced to two high-profile projects which were launched in 1992 and 1993 and which have substantially shaped numerous policy and legislative developments, including the White Papers of 1995 and 1997, the Skills Development Bill of 1997, the Higher Education Act of 1997, the South African Qualifications Authority (SAQA) Act of 1997 and the Further Education and Training Bill of 1998.

The National Training Strategy Initiative (NTSI) was first convened in 1993 under the auspices of the National Training Board, and produced its main discussion document in April 1994 (National Training Board 1994). The significance of this initiative lies not only in its timing and substance but also in the effective participation of representatives of organized business, labour unions and the technikon principals on the core team and various working committees. This gave legitimacy to the process and to its proposals for change which, in many respects, complemented those of a separate policy initiative, established by the African National Congress (ANC), that culminated in the production of the Implementation Plan for Education and Training (IPET) in May 1994.

The NTSI document (p.6) sets out the vision for a new approach to education and training in terms of the following: 'A human resources development system in which there is an integrated approach to education and training and which meets the economic and social needs of the country and the development needs of the individual.' It goes further in articulating the core principles upon which such a system is to be built and assessed. These include the principles of integration, relevance, coherence and flexibility, standards, access, legitimacy, articulation, progression, portability, recognition of prior learning, and guidance of learners. With reference to RPL, the NTSI document offers the following:

> Education and training should through assessment, give credit to prior learning through formal, non-formal and informal learning and/or experience. Of particular import in South Africa where for reasons of history, learners have been denied access to one or other of the formal, non-formal and informal learning systems, and have had to learn in some other way, for example by experience or by correspondence in another country. This principle accepts that no person entering the learning situation is without learning and aims to measure and give credit for that prior learning. (p.11)

The IPET document derives its focus from the policy objectives of the ANC and the principles which are to underpin the future national learning system. First in the order of principles is 'the right of the individual to access lifelong learning'; this is followed by seven others, including the recognition of prior learning. The document sets out detailed proposals for the establishment of a national statutory body, the South African Qualifications Authority (SAQA), 'to oversee the effective implementation of the framework including the achievement of its central purposes' (African National Congress 1994, p.6).

With this as background, it was hardly surprising that the first Draft White Paper on Education and Training, presented by the Minister of Education in 1995, articulated the government's commitment to the development of a national qualifications framework as a central component of the strategy to secure the effective realignment of the programmes and institutions of learning, to redress inherited inequalities, to ensure meaningful ownership and participation in the economy, and to accelerate the transition towards a more united and democratic society.

> Successful modern economies and societies require the elimination of artificial hierarchies, in social organization, in the organization and management of work, and in the way in which learning is organized and certified. They require citizens with a strong foundation of general education, the desire and ability to continue to learn, to adapt to and develop new knowledge, skills and technologies, to move flexibly between occupations, to take

responsibility for personal performance, to set and achieve high standards, and to work co-operatively. (White Paper, 1 Feb 1995)

Whereas the White Papers of 1995 and 1997 formalize the direction and priorities of the new government, the context within which change strategies have been implemented has remained extremely complex and volatile. Attempts by the state to restructure national and provincial departments, to redeploy teachers and to introduce new curricula, materials and staff development programmes have all come up against frustrating internal constraints related to finance, regulatory procedure and sheer capacity to plan and manage change on this scale. Yet despite these obstacles there is progress – very often manifest in pilot projects commissioned by business or labour unions, or both, or crafted in partnership agreements between NGOs and government departments.

The rest of this chapter offers a summary of some of these projects, specifically those which have focused on efforts to explore, research and develop appropriate models for RPL within the context of higher education and workforce development internationally and in South Africa.

Some initial experiences of RPL piloting
RPL and workforce development

The first introduction of RPL activities in South Africa can be attributed to the initiatives of the Congress of South African Trade Unions (COSATU) in the 1980s, whereby agreements with business around the provision of adult basic education and workforce development were negotiated. In the context of the 1990s (political transformation; entry to the global economy and the associated trade and market liberalization), COSATU fought for the rights of workers to have increased access to higher education opportunities (and hence improved employment and promotional opportunities) in the face of increasing retrenchments and capital-intensive investment.

In addition to these economic imperatives, the socio-political task of RPL has been seen by COSATU as reconstructive and developmental, thus bridging the gap between those groups which had traditionally had access to institutions of higher education (in particular, middle-class whites) and working-class Africans who had been systematically denied access. Part of the appeal of RPL for COSATU was that it would also allow for the recognition of the knowledge which workers had acquired through experience at work and in organized union activity, and could thus be linked to the improvement of workers' wages, grading and working conditions (Lugg *et al.* 1997).

Realizing these hopes and aspirations has unfortunately proved to be more difficult than expected. This is evident in a number of bruising experiences that adult workers have had to face in some leading pilot projects initiated in the mid-1990s, which are distinctive in their ability to discount workers knowledge and ways of knowing whilst privileging *status quo* standards and assessment techniques.

In 1995, the Building Industries Training Board (BITB) and FAS International Consulting Ltd ran a pilot project on RPL under the auspices of the National Training Board (NTB). The purpose was to contribute to the development of a functioning RPL system (for the building industry in South Africa) for persons with claimed prior learning experience in the occupations of carpenter and bricklayer. The implementation plan, which was overseen by a steering committee representative of key stakeholders (including the Department of Labour, NTB, BITB, FAS Consulting, trade unions, independent experts), focused on three main activity areas:

- the development of an RPL framework
- the training and certification of key RPL practitioners
- implementation of RPL process and certification of skilled workers.

An executive summary of the project (BITB 1995) records the fact that 315 workers were originally screened, most of whom had never previously undertaken institutional training or been informed of the national standards relating to the skill tests. Of these, 259 completed the advisory stage; only 182 were assessed, and, of these, only 38 were admitted to a qualifying trade test. Ironically, the report argues that this represents an 'effective RPL process', somehow missing the point that not only were 42 per cent of the original workers excluded from the assessment altogether but in the end only 132 gained some certification of skill, whilst less than 20 per cent of those assessed managed to secure full trade certification.

The report, which is framed in an uncritical account of the assumptions which underpin the formulation of 'standards' for the building industry in South Africa, acknowledges that 'in practice most candidates failed by being unable to achieve the standards within the time allowed' and that 'misinterpretation of the process occurred where it was not possible to have in place advisers and assessors representative of the multi-ethnic mix of the client group' (BITB 1995, p.9).

Another demonstration of the contested nature of RPL practice is highlighted by the research project documenting the experiences of workers in the mining and motor industries (Lugg *et al.* 1997). The research, which was commissioned by the National Union of Mine-workers and the National Union of Metalworkers of South Africa (NUMSA), was a retrospective study of two RPL processes in which the unions took part. In the case of NUMSA, the automotive industry assessed workers against Australian unit standards which bore little resemblance to South African realities. In the case of the mining industry, the RPL process advantaged those workers who had more advanced levels of numeracy and literacy. Also, the assessment process itself was problematic, in that many workers had no advance warning about either the timing or the method, and were thus completely unprepared for what it was that they were supposed to be doing.

The research has identified the most problematic aspect of these two RPL projects as being tied to the fact that management and unions entered into the process with different agendas. In the case of the automotive industry, management wanted a skills audit, whereas the union saw the exercise as part of a move toward improved job grading and wages for workers. In the mining industry, management saw RPL as facilitating career-pathing and work reorganization, while the union saw it as part of a strategy to increase access to further training. In both cases, once the process was completed, no reconciliation of the opposing views was possible. Workers saw little benefits in either improved wages or a significant increase in access to further training. In fact, workers believed that the process as they experienced it was deliberately designed to act as an exclusionary mechanism.

What has become clear is that RPL cannot be separated from broader epistemological, political and ethical issues. Questions such as: Whose knowledge is important? Who benefits from RPL, and who is disadvantaged and how? Who are the gatekeepers and on whose authority? Whose standards and outcomes are used, and how are these arrived at? How are assessment methods selected, and what kinds of inputs do adult learners have into the use of those methods and the assessment process itself? All those questions point to the fact that constructions of knowledge – what is worth knowing and (then) how knowledge is assessed – reflect particular power relations in society (Buchler and Ralphs 1998; Michelson 1997).

RPL and higher education

Adult access to higher education in South Africa has its roots policy formulated after the Second World War, whereby provisions in the Universities Act facilitated the admission into degree studies of war veterans. These provisions, known colloquially as the *'oupa matriek'* (grandfather matriculation), applied to anyone over the age of 45 years, irrespective of the level of their previous qualifications. Provisions for 'mature age exemption' were also introduced for those whose path from school or work to university had been interrupted by their participation in the war. Applicants between 30 and 44 years old could be admitted for degree studies, provided that they had completed four approved matriculation subjects. The definition of 'mature age' has progressively been reduced from 30 years to 25 years, and currently is pegged at 23 years.

Current practice in the recognition of prior learning is largely restricted by its primary focus on admissions and certification. The Universities Act of 1959 established the Committee of University Principals as a statutory body responsible for, amongst other things, the regulations pertaining to university entrance and certification. By and large, the universities still determine admissions on school-based qualifications. To assist further with selection and admission, prospective students can be requested to present themselves for interviews, to complete special 'academic aptitude' tests (which generally test language competence, subject expertise and reasoning skills), to complete a biographical questionnaire and to submit a CV. Faculties can specify additional criteria, and intake can be restricted.

The Centre for the Evaluation of Educational Qualifications (CEEQ) at the Human Sciences Research Council (HSRC) evaluates qualifications from foreign and local accredited institutions. The CEEQ has been mainly concerned with rendering a service in relation to formal accredited qualifications, but is also consulted by employers, educational institutions, prospective students and qualification holders with regard to the formal educational level at which a particular non-formal qualification is, or should be, recognized.

More recently, the HSRC has funded some interesting RPL research in association with two higher education institutions in the Western Cape. The project for adult educators at the University of Cape Town (UCT) was set up to pilot the development of RPL models for the admission of learners (those without the 'traditional' matriculation plus 3-year qualification) to the advanced diploma for adult educators at UCT. In reflecting on what was a difficult and not very successful exercise, the departmental staff involved came to realize that they were trying to fit learners into the academic modes of knowing which were prevalent in the department and its curriculum – a practice which Jones and Martin (1997, p.16) refer to as 'Procrustean RPL': 'According to Procrustes, a ruler in Greek mythology, everyone could fit into his bed regardless of their size and shape. If anyone was too short, he placed them on a rack and stretched them. If they were too long, he would chop off their feet.'

In retrospect, the issue of whether the staff were in fact attempting to 'unlock' prior learning or attempting to test 'academic readiness' within the department's predetermined curriculum became an important. For those involved, this dilemma pointed to the need for conceptual clarity, particularly regarding the social purposes of RPL, which are not always what they seem to be (Harris *et al.* 1998).

In the field of health care, South Africa currently has a complex regulatory framework which acts as an obstacle to many nurses wishing to improve their professional status and qualifications. A research project was initiated at the Peninsula Technikon to test the feasibility of using RPL to access a 'bridging diploma' for nurses who either do not have community nursing as a discipline or who do not have matriculation. Successful completion of this diploma would access opportunities to post-basic training which would otherwise have been denied to these nurses.

The empirical research focus of this particular project was on the process of drafting criteria (meshing expectations of what community health nurses should be able to do, know, etc., with the realities of what community health nurses bring into the diploma) and designing context-appropriate evaluation methods with the participation of a wide range of stakeholders. Issues which emerged include: the tension around drafting criteria which reflect 'the changing nature of professional and clinical practice'; who participates in such a process and how wide-ranging the level of representation of stakeholders is; and the fact that a clear methodology is required so that 'implicit and varied understandings' of issues such as competencies can be made explicit and shared understandings can develop (Harris *et al.* 1998).

Exploring international experience

During the latter part of 1994, two groups of South Africans undertook study tours to the USA and the UK with a view to interacting with model programmes and practices in adult experiential learning which were likely to support the objectives of the NQF. Both tours were organized by the Chicago-based Council for Adult and Experiential Learning (CAEL) and funded by the Ford Foundation. The first of the study groups also visited projects in the UK, where they were hosted by the Learning from Experience Trust. Participants in the tours (33 in total) were drawn from community, education, the engineering profession, government, industry and trade union structures or organizations. They were all in some way involved in education and training issues in South Africa. In exposing the groups to adult and experiential learning programmes and thinking in these countries, the objectives of the study tours were to:

- expose South Africans to working RPL programmes in the USA and the UK, and thereby assist in the development of local programmes which would be in line with the new government's thinking on the need for accelerated skills development

- develop an understanding of issues such as financing of tertiary-level education and training for adults, skills standards and frameworks and relationships between the government, labour, business and education sectors and how these issues could be addressed in the South African context

- consider the possibilities for collaboration with US- and UK-based organizations in the development of a national RPL programme in South Africa

- establish an interacting cohort of people in South Africa who would be positioned to engage actively in the promotion and development of these issues in the country.

As expected, the experiences, concerns and issues raised by individual participants on the study tours varied widely, depending on the activities they interacted with and their own organizational interests. Nevertheless, a number of common points were raised, particularly with regard to policy and implementation strategies. There was general agreement that:

- South Africa has much to gain from a more detailed study and interaction with many of the projects visited, provided that the differences in political objectives and the social and economic conditions in these countries are appreciated.

- Before any significant initiatives are undertaken, there is a need for an audit of current RPL practice in South Africa, uneven as it may be, in order to identify the depth and extent of such activities as well as possible projects which could be stimulated and further developed.

- There is a need for assessor training to equip South African practitioners with the knowledge and skills to assess prior experiential learning, and to assist adults in the preparation for such assessment activities.

- It was necessary for a series of pilot projects to be initiated in South Africa; these would be used to deepen local understanding and experience with RPL while, at the same time testing the issues and identifying the likely problem areas in the implementation of the NQF.

While a number of proposals for possible pilot projects were suggested, the groups agreed that these projects must:

- be aimed at promoting partnerships across the stakeholder sectors in the country

- take account of the level of development of the NQF

- co-operate with each other

- contribute to capacity building within institutions to promote high-quality learning

- demonstrate long-term sustainability.

The Workers' Higher Education Project

The Workers' Higher Education Project (WHEP) is a new venture launched by the Joint Education Trust (JET) and sponsored by the Ford and Kellogg Foundations. Its aims are to contribute to the development of new policy and practices within South Africa to expand access to higher education for working adults who have been disadvantaged by apartheid. The project was established at JET in 1996 by Rahmat Omar, who is also a member of the SAQA Board. More specifically, the objectives of the WHEP are stated as follows:

- to support organizations and institutions which seek to pilot projects (in the fields of engineering, management, rural development and agriculture, and teacher development) that will contribute towards the accelerated development and implementation of adult learning programmes based on the principles established in the National Qualifications Framework

- to support the development of assessment standards and the capacity to access learning acquired through work or life experience for academic credit

- to support change in the higher education sector by promoting research and dialogue between various approaches to the provision of lifelong learning and the developments of the NQF

- to develop the capacity of South African institutions, labour and corporate organizations to implement new projects and strategies for adult learning and RPL.

To this end, a number of pilot projects and advocacy activities have been launched through the WHEP since 1996. These include the following:

- an audit of secondary- and tertiary-level institutions piloting new frameworks for articulation, transfer and recognition of prior learning in the fields of engineering and accounting

- RPL research and development activities designed to enhance access and recognition for underqualified, but experienced, teachers and school managers to diploma and degree-level courses at the University of Witzwatersrand and neighbouring teacher training colleges in Gauteng province

- RPL and curriculum development for new training courses at seven higher education institutions, including three technikons and four universities – These projects, which focus on supervisory management training, rural resource management and primary health care, involve collaborative ventures with industry, labour and the academic faculty of the participating institutions

- curriculum design and materials development for the distance education Regional Access Programmes for unemployed youth and working adults with the eight institutions which form part of the Eastern Seaboard Association of Tertiary Institutions

- negotiations with large corporations and parastatals (large utility supply corporations, partly owned by the state) for two workforce development projects through which the education and training needs of workers are investigated

- advisory programmes and services, and a corporate-level strategy for engaging secondary- and tertiary-level institutions to secure provision of accredited courses

- the formulation and advocacy of policy for adult learning and RPL relation to the work of SAQA, the National Commission for Higher Education, the Further Education and Training Task Team and the Skills Development Bill

- the planning and provision of training courses in RPL, curriculum and workforce development, advising for academics, trade unions and industry-based trainers in association with CAEL.

It is still too early to comment on the impact of the WHEP initiatives, although it has substantially opened the door to higher education institutions wanting to engage with the challenges and opportunities offered by the NQF. With this comes the awareness that RPL is but one piece of a greater puzzle which includes a more flexible approach to curriculum development, programme design and delivery, advising systems for adults wanting to return to learning, learner-centred planning and support systems, and assessor training for faculty whose primary point of reference is the youngster straight from school and not the experienced lifelong-learning adult.

Conclusion

The development of RPL practice and experience in South African higher education institutions has a long way to go. Pilot projects such as those mentioned will provide important lessons about the viability and feasibility of integrating RPL programmes and services on a larger scale, at all levels of provision within the NQF. This must be complemented by a more substantial and systematic programme of research and training aimed at improving the capacity of the institutions to deliver high-quality curricula and RPL services relevant to the needs of lifelong learners; and to provide a basis of information which can facilitate the evaluation of the claims made by proponents of RPL on the potential and actual benefits of RPL to learners, lecturers, institutions and other constituencies such as labour, employers and government.

A commitment to the development of learning opportunities for working and unemployed adults in South Africa is one which cannot be sustained without the vision, leadership and resources of organized business, labour and the higher education institutions. The challenge is to develop new ways of ensuring that those whose knowledge and experience was discounted and dishonoured in the past never again suffer the same indignity.

References

African National Congress (1994) *Implementation Plan For Education and Training.* Johannesburg: ANC.

Alexander, N. (1989) 'Liberation pedagogy in the South African context.' In C. Criticos (ed) *Experiential Learning in Formal and Non-Formal Education.* University of Natal.

Building Industries Training Board (1995) Unpublished report. Johannesburg.

Buchler, M. and Ralphs, A. (1998) 'The NQF and recognition of prior learning.' *Joint Education Trust Bulletin, 8.*

Calitz, J. (1996) *Population of South Africa: Updated Estimates, Scenarios and Projections.* Report No.109, Midrand: Development Bank of Southern Africa.

Central Statistical Services (1996) *October Household Survey 1995.* Statistical Release PO317, 27. Pretoria: Central Statistical Services.

Department of Education (1998) Green paper on further education and training: Preparing for the twenty first century through education, training and work. Pretoria: Department of Education.

Department of Finance (1997) *Budget Review.* Pretoria: Department of Finance, South African Government.

Harris, J., Moses, E., McMillan, J. and Small, J. (1998) 'A tale of two studies: UCT and Peninsula Technikon.' Unpublished research report submitted to the Human Sciences Research Council, Pretoria.

Jones, M. and Martin, J. (1997) 'A new paradigm for recognition of prior learning (RPL).' In W. Fleet (ed) *Issues in Recognition of Prior Learning.* Melbourne: Victorian RPL Network.

Lugg, R., Mabitla, A., Louw, G. and Angelis, D. (1997) 'Workers' experiences of RPL in South Africa: Some implications for redress, equity and transformation.' Unpublished draft.

Michelson, E. (1997) 'Multicultural approaches to portfolio development.' In A. D. Rose and M.A. Leaky (eds) *New Directions for Adult and Continuing Education.* San Francisco: Jossey Bass Publishers.

National Training Board (1994) Discussion on document on national training strategy initiative. Pretoria: Department of Education.

South African Institute of Race Relations (1997) *South African Survey: 1996/1997.* Johannesburg: SAIRR.

CHAPTER 11

2000 Plus?

Norman Evans

1974–2000; over 25 years and nine countries. That is the story told of
the spread across the world of AP(E)L – the assessment of prior and
experiential learning. It offers nine different accounts of the benefits
AP(E)L can bring to individuals, institutions and their faculties,
employers and national economies, and the different ways in which it
has been introduced and supported, if not promoted, in those different countries, and some of the outstanding problems which remain
before its potential can be fully exploited. But that is not the whole
story. Those accounts, of course, are offered by committed and
enthusiastic supporters of what AP(E)L stands for. Some make plain,
however, that there are serious intellectual, epistemological issues
involved, and it is far from being the case that academics generally
subscribe to what AP(E)L stands for; objections abound.

Running through each chapter, implicitly or explicitly, there are a
number of common denominators. There is the culture of a particular
country, its constitution, form of government and how its post-secondary education is organized as a system. As emphasized frequently,
the timing of any intiative about AP(E)L is perhaps the most critical
factor. Unless it fits into prevailing circumstances like a hand in a
glove, nothing will happen. Then motivation, which is almost a subset
of timing. Unless there is something in it for all the various actors,
again nothing will happen. Here there can be problems. Not all the
actors want the same thing. Then, somewhere, there needs to be a
champion in a key position with hands on the levers, ready and willing
to pull them. Only then can there be any sense of an intentional
strategy for development.

What and where next is a teasing question now – how may, even
could and perhaps should, AP(E)L contribute to future developments in higher education, which can then reach into issues of
employability in the context of the global economy. The world has

become a different place in the years since 1974. And in that different world, AP(E)L itself has moved on from adding a service available for adult learners. It has shown how to help enhance the employability of the workforce. It points to some of the radical changes which universities and colleges need to make if they are to become sufficiently responsive to the changing needs and characteristics of students and so to society. AP(E)L has helped, and is helping, to focus attention on the particulars of the responsiveness necessary to serve all students in the 'age of knowledge', telecommunications and lifelong learning. It has helped to highlight how ethnic diversity can enrich education and culture. At the same time, it has helped to draw attention to complex questions of equity which arise when a country's economic development leaves significant numbers of its workforce behind in stagnation. And that looks worse in the context of the global economy. Notions of empowerment can become part of complicated socio-political controversies about the perceived powerlessness of individuals confronted by the awesome might of multinational companies.

It is no part of the argument to claim that AP(E)L offers comprehensive answers to these issues. It is to claim that in some ways, having opened a door to expanding the services of adult learners, it has lighted on issues which go far beyond its immediate purpose, but where it may be able to make a useful contribution.

It is worth remembering that before 1974 there was nothing new, in any country, about admitting to higher education some individuals who had acquired knowledge and skill informally, outside the education system. That was standard practice in many higher education institutions, and was a prime argument used by many traditional universities for doing nothing more about it. Apart from in the USA, however, in no sense was what was done systematic. In the USA since 1943, Antioch College had tested all entering students for the knowledge they brought with them in the humanities and arts, social science, natural sciences, mathematics and writing. From 1972 onwards, Empire State College, Regents College and Thomas Edison College developed their own assessment systems. It was only since 1974, when the Cooperative Assessment of Experiential Learning project got to work, that generally applicable techniques have been devised and refined, and refined again, for the systematic assessment of informally acquired learning. Then some 40 institutions in the USA were identified as using some form of assessment of prior learning. So again, apart from the USA, there was no serious effort to think of procedures for the admission of older non-traditional students as a deliberate service to adults.

Now, in any one of the countries represented in this book, such systems are there to be found; systems and procedures not only to assess informally acquired learning but to do so within increasingly stringent demands for the transparent assurance of standards and quality and for accountability. And to a varying extent, such systems and procedures are true for much of post-secondary education, not merely higher education.

It is not too difficult to cite the reasons for these developments. They are most complex in the USA, where there was a movement of non-traditional higher education. History, the constitution and an economy and culture which has produced many richly endowed charitable foundations help to explain how that movement evolved. In the post-war period, when younger people were being offered expanding opportunities in post-secondary education, humanitarian concerns for the social, educational and economic well-being of huge numbers of older people in the country, including ex-service personnel, led to a highly developed range of institutions dedicated to adult learners. In no other country has there been anything comparable. It provided a vehicle for AP(E)L which was not available elsewhere. It also presents a large, almost bizarre, paradox.

To a greater or lesser extent in other countries, it was government or government agencies which provided the vehicle for development of AP(E)L services. Of course, in each country there were enthusiastic individuals cajoling, encouraging and, often, influencing what governments actually did. It did mean, and continues to mean, that outside the USA something like a system for AP(E)L could be created, sometimes nationally, sometimes provincially. But having created the academic basis for AP(E)L, the USA has created no federal governmental means of promoting developments nationwide. Some federal agencies, in particular the Department of Labour and the Fund for the Improvement of Post Secondary Education, and some state governments support developments. But predominantly, however, the application of AP(E)L has been extended by a few employers and some forward-looking trade unions that have understood its potential benefits, and through the efforts of non-government, not-for-profit bodies like CAEL.

Even so, AP(E)L would not have developed unless there were forces at play in society which suggested that it could be useful. So, are there common denominators which emerge in trying to understand these AP(E)L developments worldwide? And what, if anything, can they suggest about the role of AP(E)L in the future?

AP(E)L and its economy

There are two groups of factors: the global economy and equity. The first is essentially about productivity, competition, skills, skill shortages and how to correct them. The second is about labour market factors – employment and unemployment levels, pay and conditions, labour mobility and the changing distribution of occupations across the entire working population and the effect all that has on society generally. These two ways of looking at national policy overlap – the economic and the sociological. They even interlock, and one interlocking mechanism is employability. It is not inconceivable that the concept of employability can inform policies for lifelong learning, to give substance to the rather vacuous rhetoric which is used to trumpet the idea. It is difficult to see how AP(E)L will not be part of that substance.

That rhetoric about lifelong learning is now beamed at large companies, small and medium-sized companies, production industries, service industries, even public services, as they are all now forced to compete successfully in both national and international markets or face financial disaster. But rhetoric is not the same as having a policy, and policies concerning lifelong learning are hard to find. Economic factors notwithstanding, a policy for lifelong learning that is worthy of its name needs to accommodate and incorporate all the incidental learning which characterizes life for vast numbers of people. Conceiving lifelong learning as part of formal education alone, with qualifications attached, does disservice to the concept.

This is made worse because, in this new world of instant communication across the globe, politicians and their governments have diminishing influence on the international economy, but they are blamed for whatever painful experiences are rained down on their constituents. This puts governments in an unenviable position as they come under public pressure to do more about unemployment, redundancy, retraining, job creation and social security benefits. Hence, it can be reasonably deduced that behind much of the support for AP(E)L lie worries about national economies.

This is not the occasion to explore Keynesian and anti-Keynesian economic theories. But it is the occasion to say that whilst it may not feature much in public policy debates, beneath all the other arguments lie the social consequences of the ever-widening gap between the rich and comfortably well off and the poor.

AP(E)L and equity

It is in that context that questions of equity become acute. And that has a great deal to do with the emphasis being placed on lifelong learning and the employability of individuals. Lifelong learning for governments can easily become a mantra for individuals taking steps to sustain their employability. There is no need to rehearse the contribution which AP(E)L can make to both: equity and employability. The tricky issue is how to put that contribution into action. The corporate sector shows what can be done, especially in the USA; and no doubt, as time passes, more will follow suit, as increasingly the corporate sector goes global itself. But although governments seem replete with initiatives designed to promote both lifelong learning and employability, the rhetoric collides with problems of funding from the public purse and institutional structures. Tax money will no longer foot all the bills which have to be met. Many existing structures are unsuitable for meeting the new requirements. The post-secondary institutions and their funding regimes were created to do a different job. The claim here is that AP(E)L should be a catalyst to help them adapt to the 21st century.

Of course, questions of equity receive differing attentions in the countries represented in this book. The 'movement' in the USA and organizations like CAEL put those questions at the heart of their activities. In Canada, the efforts of the First Nations Technical Institute, the Canadian Association for Prior Learning Assessment and the Canadian Labour Force Development Board have seen to it that equity is a priority question for PLAR schemes there. In the UK, the government's current insistence that widening access as an aspect of lifelong learning is something which universities must take as a policy requirement serves to underline equity as a national priority, backed as it is by financial inducements. Demography forced Ireland to cope with the huge increase in school leavers entering HEIs, while struggling to accommodate the needs of adult learners. For South Africa, equity is at the top of the list of anticipated benefits from their developments in PLA. The Maori in New Zealand insisted that, for them, using PLA towards a more equitable post-secondary education system was central to their interest in PLA developments. In France, equity of provision marches with the interest in financial savings. In Australia, concern for equity was one prime reason for interest in

AP(E)L. And the emphasis and postioning of empowerment arguments not only differs between countries, but changes within countries as part of wider social changes. So how the combined concerns about employability and equity get played out in the future in those countries, only time will tell. In any case, AP(E)L is only one potential influence among many for promoting greater equity in societies.

AP(E)L, students and institutions

How equity influences developments in any one country will depend to some, perhaps, a limited extent on the way HEIs adapt themselves to their ever-changing environment, especially to changes in the student body and to the funding regimes which support them. Begin with students. Ask the question 'who is a student in the 21st century?' and it is like shaking a child's kaleidoscope bottle where coloured pieces fly around and settle finally into different, unpredictable patterns, dispositions and relationships. All the indications are that, early in the 21st century, the distinction between full-time and part-time student will be blurred increasingly. As costs rise, and student indebtedness with them, more students will 'work their way through college', following mixed periods of study and earning in an infinite variety of patterns, each arranged to fit individual needs. Incidentally, there is little evidence in any of the countries that rising tuition fees are deterring applications. In some, applications are even increasing. But more and more, students will rate convenience of study more highly than their predecessors. Brought up with PCs and computer games as part of the home furniture, many, if not most, will assume that the range of activities on the internet is a normal element in learning and teaching technologies. They will resist attending courses to learn what they know already. They will relish opportunities for learning while earning – work-based learning on negotiated learning agreements. If they are to pay more, they will be more demanding. It all amounts to the probability that the customary 3 or 4 years of full-time consecutive study will move towards an oscillating shuttle between learning and earning over an unknowable number of years. And they will be looking for credentials. AP(E)L will be an important facility for their educational programming.

It will not be so for all students, or for all institutions. But for a significant proportion in the mass higher education system which now obtains in the countries covered in this book, this looks like being the case. And it will be worked out at a time when governments are on the lookout for ways of shifting the burden of financial support from tax payers' money to individuals' cash accounts. Individuals are being expected to pay more. Government funds contribute less, proportionally. It is a dramatically significant change in the societal position of post-secondary education.

What kind of institutions look like being best able to serve those kinds of students? All the usual clichés click in. Tutors as facilitators and learning managers. Institutions as learning resources. Services on the internet, interactive video and conference calls. Employment contracts which facilitate round-the-clock and calendar-long services. But behind that lurks the nagging question: If student pieces get shaken up in the bottle to form new configurations, what new patterns does a shake of the institutional bottle produce?

Whatever else there may be to say, except for the well-established research institutions with worldwide reputations, efficiency and effectiveness of learning will be a hallmark of successful surviving universities and colleges. Not that research institutions will be immune from efficiency and effectiveness tests. But for the others seeking to sustain enrolments, student perceptions of the correlation between tuition fees and dues and 'value for money' learning will be a telling factor – convenience learning. The overall environment will matter too. This does not merely mean well-kept grounds and buildings. It looks to a supportive framework for learning where 'high tech' and the personal supplement one another. How to achieve all that is contentious, controversial and difficult.

It is a reasonable assumption that institutions which succeed in sustaining healthy enrolments with a reputation for good value for money will be those which invest shrewdly. They need to invest specifically in ways to enhance the quantity and quality of learning which students can achieve for any finite sum of money; efficiency and effectiveness of learning. They need to invest in people so that they have time to absorb pedagogical approaches to tackle enhancing learning effectiveness, to monitor efforts to do so, and create a database of successful strategies open to all academics and other staff in the institution. That implies, too, carefully considered investments in telecommunication systems which relate directly to the overall goal of making maximum use of student and faculty time as effective learning time.

AP(E)L and the curriculum

Then there is the curriculum itself. Here the relevance of AP(E)L is direct. As an example, take the concept of a negotiated, even student-generated, curriculum and apply it to the environment. Quite what influence environmental factors will exert on higher education in the future is impossible to know. It is a reasonable guess, though, that more students will want to know more about the environment at local, national and international levels. In some ways, therefore, the environment could offer an institution an opportunity for curriculum development which supported its overall strategy for enhancing learning and teaching.

This is because several things coalesce for environmental study. There is a huge amount of information put out daily in the press and on radio and television. This is fuelled by the most astonishing range of research projects all over the world, whether Arctic or Antarctic, tropical, anthropological or archaeological, in marine or animal biology, or concerning all the baffling interstices between the brain, nervous systems and behaviour; never mind controversies over pollution, genetically modified foods and global warming. The result is that while it is difficult for teachers to keep abreast of the latest revelations in their particular discipline, many of the increasing proportion of adult students in the system not only know a lot about environmental issues but pay considerable attention to reports and discussions. They have a direct bearing on their domestic lives, especially as parents. This is where a student-generated curriculum could relate to the strategies for seeking institutional success in the future.

There is nothing new in the idea of a student-generated curriculum. In medieval times, there were no prescribed curricula and examinations as we understand them. Students travelled throughout Europe to itinerant scholars or to one of the few universities and engaged in a debate which resulted in what nowadays would be called 'negotiated curriculum'. The premise for this arrangement was that some students knew what it was they wished to learn more about and sought out the scholars who would enable them to learn it. Some went to the universities of Padua or Louvain or gathered in the homes of people like Sir Thomas More, where scholarship and professional responsibilities went hand in hand. But some went to printing shops spread around Europe, where scholars and craftsmen were often indistinguishable from translators at work on recently found Greek documents. In some ways, we are returning to similar circumstances, only on a vastly enlarged scale. For printing shops read cyber cafés.

It is generally accepted now that, in addition to formal education provision, learning goes on at work, in leisure, and through the media. Through telecommunications, people have access to knowledge and data on every conceivable topic, at times of their own choosing. Necessarily, that means that the increasing proportion of older students know more than they used to know about more things. And since they live in an increasingly turbulent world where life and livelihood are fraught with uncertainties about financial, domestic and social problems, many have very shrewd perceptions of what additional learning will serve them best. Hence the relevance of a student-generated curriculum.

This is not saying that in formal education anything goes, that students ought to be free to choose what they learn and how they learn it. It is saying that taking seriously what adults bring with them, using AP(E)L, can establish both the foundations for further learning and the suitability of whatever it is that a student seeks to learn next. If the topic meets the requirements for higher education study, then negotiation between tutor and student can produce a draft negotiated learning programme of study; content, methodology, criteria and evidence of learning and assessment procedures can be written down and agreed formally. It used to be the case that such a negotiated course could only run with, say, 8–12 students. Now, telecommunication technology means, in theory, that a single student could follow such a course. In many ways, though, details like that are irrelevant. The point is that an institution which wants to be successful in the future needs to take far more careful account of what students say they want to learn than they have done in the past, and it needs to ensure that they have the means of doing so without compromising its an institution's inacademic integrity. Perhaps successful institutions of the future will increasingly resemble aspects of their predecessors centuries ago.

Two other connections with the curriculum follow: the concept of partnership and the reality of ethnic diversity. Partnership for higher education now, too often, means nothing much more than arrangements which, at worst, spread costs or, at best, make money. For the curriculum, however, the idea of partnership is analogous to taking account of students' views on what they want to learn next. Community and voluntary organizations all have their own agendas for future learning. So do for-profit commercial enterprises and the not-for-profit public service organizations. Success for many higher education institutions in the future is bound to depend partially on the extent to which they can apply their drive for efficiency and effectiveness in learning for the economic benefit of such partner organizations, in helping them in their own ways to keep up to date and so ensure their survival, if not prosperity.

Thus, partnerships can have a direct influence on the curriculum. Negotiations for partnerships involve, necessarily, keeping institutional courses and programmes up to date. And that means, wherever possible, incorporating employers' views of what they want employees to learn in the requirements for standards and assessment in academic study. In this way, the institution's curriculum can be enriched at the same time as providing an enhanced service to the partner organization. These sorts of arrangements are an element in the prescription for successful institutions of the future, if for no other reason than enrolment. Without sufficient numbers of enrolled learners, institutions will be in trouble. Whether those numbers are made up of regular full-time or part-time attenders on campus, or through distance learning, on-line provision or through partner organizations is irrelevant. Provided learning programmes are up to standard, how they are studied is increasingly of secondary importance. And, as with negotiated programmes with students, it is obvious that with such partner organizations AP(E)L is of central significance – what is the baseline for their employees' further learning, the length of time and cost of study and all the other potential benefits?

Ethnic diversity is a curriculum in itself. In some ways, a diverse faculty and student body can draw attention to changes which can benefit an institution, even making it easier to see them. Elements of a negotiated student-generated curriculum could help promote such developments. Some call it celebration.

The context for higher education

If these are some of the characteristics of institutions which will attempt to serve students under new regimes, it is the national and international context in which higher education finds itself that makes this all so complicated. Pressure comes from all sides. There are epistemological arguments raging in relation to quality, standards, accountability and transparency. Insistence on the centrality of a knowledge-based economy for prosperity connects with the globalization of activities which span almost the entire range of human endeavour. Education is expected to feed this with a flow of employees for a high-skill economy, without there being agreement of what a high-skill economy actually means. Like companies, universities and colleges are urged to become learning organizations, with more and more attention being paid to professional staff development. The employability of students raises a myriad of questions about experience and how to make the best use of it. And underlying it all comes insistence on efficiency and effectiveness, with expectations of greater productivity and financial stings in the tail.

That is not all. There is a different side to this. The voices of some political theorists are being raised to query the validity of globalization as the inevitable route reaching into the future, with a corresponding reduction in the role of the nation state. If the price of dependence on global activities for financial prosperity is increasing insecurity for growing numbers of individuals, however employable they may be, and the social disturbance that can cause, then it would not be surprising if government intervention reasserted itself on behalf of the electorate. Should that occur, then it would affect the context in which higher education functioned. The international connections which have been fostered so energetically could be paralleled by more home-grown preoccupations affecting the curriculum and, indeed, student perceptions about their own futures.

Others take a different critical line. They castigate the polarization of the debate about globalization as between right wing pro and left wing anti. The globalization of economics is important, they say, but so is the globalization of culture, the rule of law, the environment and democratic politics. Worldwide there are indications of all those factors at work. And they all have profound implications for postsecondary education wherever it is provided. Alarmed at what can be interpreted as disintegrating forces in society some claim to detect a shift from the 1960s me, me, me insistence on the right of the individual towards an acceptance that individuals have their being essentially in communities. This line of argument poses questions about civic responsibility to the curriculum.

It is in that maelstrom of influences that new learning opportunities are bound to multiply, and with them questions about how best to deploy them to benefit students. However, whatever new learning opportunities may be devised, and however strong the pressure to use the needs for employability to turn higher education into a work preparation arena, three things are clear. At their peril, universities and colleges must never abandon their central purposes. First, the pursuit of truth: developing and understanding a body of knowledge; critical analysis to differentiate the real from the nebulous or false; the social context of their studies. And that implies an academic independence which safeguards that pursuit of truth from government or commercial interference. Second, and allied to that, opportunities for a personal relationship between teacher and taught must be preserved. Without time and space for the magic of the personal chemistry to develop between the two, something irreplaceable will be lost. And last, access. It is the most intractable of all, because of its complicated mixture of nature and nurture, financial and social context. But post-secondary education, and higher education in particular, will be seen to have failed unless their services make a distinctive contribution to creating a more equitable society. Access must take equity explicitly as its guiding principle.

How any one institution will juggle those requirements to adjust to its changing relationship with society is impossible to know. What we do know is that institutions such as Oxford, Cambridge, Imperial College and University College in the UK, Harvard and Yale in the USA, Victoria in New Zealand, Sydney in Australia, and other outstanding institutions, will be substantially the same whatever internal shifts may take place. Their precious excellence must be preserved. But within the range of institutions with diverse missions serving mass higher education, there will be other versions of excellence. And it is a fair guess that as a catalyst, AP(E)L will make its contribution to those excellences.

AP(E)L, companies, competition and change

AP(E)L could have another particular significance. As for much of the story, the USA offers clues. There is a competitive struggle going on between regular universities and colleges, both state and private, and fully accredited, private for-profit institutions such as the University of Phoenix, which is part of the Apollo Group quoted on the New York stock exchange. These for-profit institutions are not to be confused with the so-called corporate universities like McDonalds. These 1000 or so institutions, which have appropriated the name university, are really in-house human resource departments. They exist partly because they can have superior resources, and partly because they find it more effective for the company's purposes to develop their own employees instead of sending them away on courses which are likely to be more general. No time away off-site. Learning when it is convenient for the employer. Costs contained internally. And in a global economy, this type of company provision could go worldwide. Geography is immaterial. Convenience shopping, convenience foods and cooking are all the rage. This is convenience learning. And it is not dependent on formal education institutions.

AP(E)L can feature in a different way within some companies. Learning on the job has proved highly effective, where what is to be learned is planned and intentional. But to make it successful, coaching has to be a vital element in the pedagogy of learning and teaching in work-based learning. And it has to begin with AP(E)L. Without a dipstick reading of what employees have learned already, the foundations for further learning and development are missing. Intentional learning as an assignment makes sense when the starting point is clear. This is another way of talking about convenience learning.

It all amounts to a warning to formal higher education throughout the world. For some of it, and there is no means of knowing how much, its task is to invent its own versions of convenience learning. As it does, AP(E)L is bound to feature. How far they will be able to compete successfully with corporate institutions, which these days have far greater resources to devote to education and personal development than universities and colleges themselves, is a conundrum they have to face. If corporate institutions can do all that for their own employees, there would appear to be no reason why they should not advertise their courses to attract paying members of the general public. In the USA, some are already doing so. Microsoft sells training programmes to the public. Others there seek formal accreditation for courses from regional accrediting bodies. These possibilities suggest to some that some higher education institutions will simply disappear, forced out by that sort of competition. That view is based on the belief that, as potential students have better understanding of the quality of provision which technology is making available, they will vote with their feet and bank balances.

Against that, universities and colleges can assert convincingly that they are more than just places where learning materials can be studied and credits accumulated. To capitalize on what that means they need to produce schemes of convenience learning which remain faithful to the three principles: the pursuit of truth; the preservation of opportunities for personal chemistry between tutor and taught; and the widest possible access – all within the social attributes which from the first have been one of their essential characteristics. And convenience learning means institutions being boldly inventive as they seek ways of making learning available. Going hard for collaboration with industry and commerce is one line to take, provided higher education can demonstrate it can satisfy requirements. Tailor-made courses incorporating AP(E)L, with on-site classes at hours suitable for the company, might head off some further initiatives for corporate universities. Off-campus learning opportunities, again incorporating AP(E)L, could meet the needs of many students of the future, as they juggle the competing elements in their complicated lives. And there the rather blinkered approach to distance learning needs to take the blinkers off.

At it's simplest, distance learning means providing learning materials, ideally with some local personal tutorial support (or if not personal, then as personal as telecommunication can make it), for studying away from the campus. The internet has brought distance learning to some sort of maturity. A British Hotel and Restaurant Master's programme includes, as well as AP(E)L, the option of taking a couple of courses provided by a university in Wisconsin for those who want to learn about some of the legal issues governing those activities in the USA. University College of the University of Maryland has 18 undergraduate degree programmes already available on-line. Scores of examples make the same point. It is easy to see how that simple means of expanding the curriculum could extend over vast ranges of study.

However, there needs to be a health warning. Claims for programmes being interactive need close scrutiny. Transactional, yes. Interactive, rarely. This is more than semantics. It concerns the very nature of learning and the opportunities offered by telecommunications. Interactive implies people meeting physically in one place. Transactional describes procedures which enable exchanges to take place between individuals or within groups without meeting one another, and very impressive some of the results of this can be. But that is not interactive. Institutions need to be clear about what category of learning services they are providing. And if they are to capitalize on their traditional strengths, somehow they need to be able to demonstrate how they can deploy personal tutorial connections with students to convert transactional programmes into interactive programmes.

This becomes all the more important for another reason. There is talk these days of 'mega universities', and it is not talking about just size. It conjures up visions of an academic institution in partnership with a worldwide telecommunications provider creating a virtual university. Where, then, does that put what we now refer to as universities and colleges? The very idea is a reminder that institutions will have to convince sufficient numbers of potential students that what they have to offer is different from, more beneficial than, and more desirable than, other opportunities for studying.

But the institutional intranet can be just as important. If a student sitting in the library or own room can ring up materials for the physics or theology course being studied, then probably he or she has more time for reflection and to think about what is there to be learned. Student study groups can take on a different meaning and dynamic. Tutors could find themselves with time to help students as individuals rather than in large hordes in lecture theatres. And everyone might find it all more enjoyable. Technology and personal chemistry could feed off one another.

If all that seems a pie-in-the-sky vision for higher education, any cold-eyed assessment sets out extremely high stakes. Institutional arrangements wax and wane. Change is inevitable. There can be no guarantee that what we have continues to be what we will have. That means for some of it, survival is on the agenda. The argument running through this book is that AP(E)L offers one particular way of promoting learning and its assessment which some institutions may choose to consider as they seek a prosperous future. In doing so they will contribute to national economy, the employability and well being of individuals in their communities. And that is not just for the activity itself but because one of the most remarkable characteristics of AP(E)L is that it can raise just about every question in the academics' and institutions' professional books. Conceptually, its power as a catalyst for development and change is extraordinary.

Just as in 1974, no one could have predicted the extent to which AP(E)L has moved around the world in 25 years, or the uses to which is has been put, no one can say where it will have reached in 2025 or over what arenas it will have been applied. It seems inconceivable that the momentum will stop, however much it may falter. In the next quarter of a century, where, if at all, will AP(E)L feature in, say, China, Indonesia, India, eastern Europe? So the end of the international story is an assertion. AP(E)L has a future as a vital ingredient of post-secondary education, there for the making in the context of the global economy which now exists. Philosophically and pedagogically, AP(E)L is based upon the respect of persons – both for belief and practice. Questions of social justice and equity will not go away. Nor will issues of human dignity and employability. AP(E)L will go on worrying at both.

The Contributors

Dr Yunus Ballim, Associate Professor, Construction Materials, Department of Civil Engineering, University of Witzwatersrand, Johannesburg, South Africa.

Deborah Blower, PLAR Facilitator, Red River College of Applied Arts, Science and Technology, Winnipeg, Manitoba, Canada.

Norman Evans, Visiting Professor, Goldsmiths' College, University of London; formerly Founding Director, and now Trustee, the Learning from Experience Trust, England.

Michel Feutrie, Director, Formation Continue, Université des Sciences et Technologies de Lille, France.

Rick Flowers, Director, Centre for Popular Education, University of Technology, Sydney, Australia.

Geof Hawke, Director, Centre for Vocational Education Research, University of Technology, Sydney, Australia.

Morris Keeton, Senior Scholar, Institute for Research on Adults in Higher Education, University College, University of Maryland; formerly Founding President, Council for Adult and Experiential Learning, USA.

Phil Ker, Student Services Manager, Auckland Institute of Technology, New Zealand.

Denis McGrath, Registrar, National Council for Educational Awards, Republic of Ireland.

Dr Mary Melrose, Principal Lecturer for Staff and Educational Development, Auckland Institute of Technology, New Zealand.

Rahmat Omar, Project Co-ordinator, South African Institute for Distance Education; member of the South African Qualifications Authority.

Alan Ralphs, Division Manager for Lifelong Learning, Joint Education Trust, Johannesburg, South Africa.

Fiona Reeve, Department of Learning and Education Development, Glasgow Caledonian University, Scotland.

Maureen Reid, Manager, Career Centre, Auckland Institute of Technology, New Zealand.

Norman Sharp, Head of Quality Assurance Agency, Scottish Office, Scotland.

Ruth Whittaker, Department of Learning and Education Development, Glasgow Caledonian University, Scotland.

Subject Index

Name Index